AS-Level
Geography

This book is packed with thorough notes and detailed case studies
covering everything you need to know for Edexcel AS-Level Geography
(including all the optional topics for Unit 2).

It's also got plenty of stuff to help you prepare for the exams.
There are warm-up and exam-style practice questions for every topic,
plus an Exam Skills section full of tips for maximising your marks.

And of course, we've done our best to make the whole thing vaguely entertaining for you.

Complete Revision and Practice
Exam Board: Edexcel

Published by CGP

Editors:
Ellen Bowness, Katie Braid, Charlotte Burrows, Adam Moorhouse, Karen Wells, Dawn Wright.

Contributors:
Margaret Collinson, Kevin Cooper, Karen Holdich, Robert Morris,
Helen Nurton, Sophie Watkins.

Proofreaders:
Joe Brazier, Rosie Gillham

ISBN: 978 1 84762 136 8

With thanks to Laura Jakubowski for the copyright research.

Clipart from Corel®
Printed by Elanders Ltd, Newcastle upon Tyne.

Based on the classic CGP style created by Richard Parsons.

Contents

Unit 1: Topic 1 — World at Risk

Global Hazards 2
Hazard Distribution 4
Disaster Hotspot Case Study — California 6
Disaster Hotspot Case Study — The Philippines 8
Evidence for Climate Change 10
Causes of Climate Change 12
Impacts of Climate Change 14
Climate Change — Case Studies 16
Coping With Climate Change 18
Global Hazards — The Future 20

Unit 1: Topic 2 — Going Global

Introduction to Globalisation 22
Global Groupings 24
Trans-National Corporations 26
Global Winners and Losers 28
Consequences of Globalisation 30
Migration and Globalisation 32
Population Basics 33
Changes in the UK Population Since 1900 36
Impacts of an Ageing Population 38
Migration into Europe 40
Intra-EU Migration 42
Rural-Urban Migration 44
Megacities 46
Urban Sustainability 48

Unit 2: Topic 1 — Extreme Weather

Extreme Weather Events 50
Extreme Weather — Fieldwork and Research 54
The Impact of Extreme Weather 56
The Impact of Extreme Weather — Case Studies 58
Increasing Risk from Extreme Weather 62
Increasing Flood Risk — Fieldwork and Research 64
Managing Extreme Weather 67
Drought and Water Management 70

Unit 2: Topic 2 — Crowded Coasts

Coastal Population Growth 72
Coastal Development and Conflict 74
Coastal Processes 78
Coasts Under Threat — Erosion and Flooding 80
Coastal Flooding — Case Study 82
Coastal Erosion — Case Study 84
Coastal Management 86
Coastal Management — Case Studies 88

Unit 2: Topic 3 — Unequal Spaces

Introduction to Inequalities 90
Causes and Effects of Urban Inequalities 92
Strategies to Reduce Urban Inequalities 94
Urban Inequalities — Case Study 96
Causes and Effects of Rural Inequalities 98
Strategies to Reduce Rural Inequalities 100
Rural Inequalities — Case Study 102

Unit 2: Topic 4 — Rebranding Places

Introduction to Rebranding Places 104
Urban Rebranding Strategies 106
Urban Rebranding — Case Study 108
Rural Rebranding Strategies 110
Rural Rebranding — Case Studies 112
Evaluating Rebranding Strategies 114

Exam Skills

Exam Structure 116
Answering Questions 117
Answering Case Study Questions 118
Answering Fieldwork & Research Questions 119
Answering Resource Interpretation Questions 120
Investigative Skills 123
Graph and Map Skills 124
Statistical Skills 127

Answers 129
Acknowledgements 139
Index 140

Global Hazards

A bit of mayhem and disaster always makes geography more interesting... Hazards are nasty things, as you might be able to guess. They come in all shapes and sizes and some of them are getting more frequent. I'm scared.

There are **Different Types** of **Hazard**

1) A **hazard** is something that's a **potential threat** to **human life** or **property**.

2) **Natural hazards** are caused by **natural processes**, e.g. a lava flow from a volcanic eruption.

3) Natural hazards can be divided into **two** types:

> **Hydro-meteorological hazards** (caused by **climatic** processes) — these include **droughts**, **floods**, **tropical cyclones** and **storms**.

> **Geophysical hazards** (caused by **land** processes) — these include **earthquakes**, **volcanic eruptions** and **landslides**.

You need to know these terms:

1) **Disaster** — when a hazard **actually seriously affects** humans.

2) **Risk** — the **likelihood** that humans will be seriously affected by a hazard.

3) **Vulnerability** — how **susceptible** a **population** is to the damage caused by a hazard.

A tropical cyclone is a hazard, but when it hits land and seriously affects people and property it's a disaster, e.g. Katrina (2005).

The **Disaster Risk Equation** Gives the **Risk** of a **Disaster Occurring**

The risk of a hazard **causing** a disaster can be shown using the **disaster risk equation**.

The risk of disaster **increases** as:

1) The **frequency** or **severity** of **hazards** increase (e.g. more and worse flooding).

2) People's **vulnerability increases** (e.g. higher population densities in areas vulnerable to flooding, like flood plains).

$$\text{Risk (R)} = \frac{\text{Hazards (H)} \times \text{Vulnerability (V)}}{\text{Capacity to cope (C)}}$$

3) People's **capacity to cope** is **decreased** — capacity to cope is the ability to deal with the **consequences** of a hazard, e.g. people in remote areas are further from help than people in central areas, so have a lower capacity to cope.

The disaster risk equation can be used to explain why **similar hazards** can cause disasters of **different degrees**.

> **Example**
>
> 1) Similar sized earthquakes occurred in **Kashmir, Pakistan** (2005) and **Izmit, Turkey** (1999).
>
> 2) Although the hazard was **similar** (both were earthquakes), the disasters they caused were **different** — Kashmir suffered **more loss of life** with over 75 000 deaths compared to around 18 000 in Izmit.
>
> 3) The **disaster risk equation** can help to explain **why**:
>
> - The people of Kashmir had a **lower capacity to cope** — it's a remote, mountainous location, which makes **access difficult**. Access was made even worse by **landslides** that buried roads into the region.
>
> - The population of Kashmir is **vulnerable** — the people are **poor** and buildings are often **badly constructed**. When some of these buildings collapsed after the earthquake, people were buried.

Global Warming is Arguably the *Greatest Current Global Hazard*

1) **Global warming** describes the **recent increase in average global temperature**.

2) It's a type of **climate change** (a significant change in the weather of a region over a period of at least several decades).

3) It also **causes** other types of climate change (see page 14 for more).

4) There's a **scientific consensus** that global warming is due to **human activity** (see p. 13).

5) Global warming is a **context hazard** — it's **global** in scale (affects all parts of the environment) and has the potential to **trigger other hazards** or make them **worse**.

6) Global warming is also a **chronic** (long-term) hazard — it's a **constant threat** and can't be solved **quickly** or **easily**.

7) Hazards such as global warming highlight **issues of injustice** — it isn't necessarily the people **causing** the problem who are **most affected**, e.g. richer countries often contribute **most** of the pollutants that are thought to cause global warming, but poorer countries often **suffer more** from the effects.

8) Any **solution** to global warming will be **complex** because the **causes** and **effects** are complex and not fully understood. It's a global problem requiring **international cooperation** between **governments**, **businesses** and **individuals** (see p. 19).

There's loads more on climate change on pages 10-19.

Global Hazards

Hydro-meteorological Hazards are Becoming More Frequent

1) The number of **hydro-meteorological** hazards has been **increasing** in recent years.

2) But the number of **geophysical** hazards **hasn't changed** much.

3) It's thought that the **increase** in the number of hydro-meteorological hazards is due to the **increasing** effects of **global warming** — which is thought to be largely due to **human activity** (see page 13).

4) The number of **disasters** is **increasing**. ⟹ ⟹
This is because of a combination of **factors**:

Human factors

- Rapid **population growth** and **urbanisation** — this increases the **number of people** who are **vulnerable** to hazards, especially in poor countries.

- **Increasing world poverty** — poor people are more **vulnerable** to hazards.

- **Exploitation** of **resources** — e.g. **deforestation** and **loss of wetlands** can lead to an **increased risk** of **flooding** and **landslides**.

Physical factors

- **Global warming** — it's thought to be increasing the number of **hazards**, e.g. floods and severe storms, which increases the number of **disasters**.

- **El Niño** events (oceanic current and temperature fluctuations) — these **change global weather** in an **unpredictable way**, which makes hydro-meteorological hazards more **unpredictable**.

5) Another reason why it may seem that the number of disasters has increased is because of **greater media coverage** — **more** disasters are **reported** than in the past, so it seems as if more are **actually happening**.

Deaths are Decreasing but Economic Losses are Increasing

1) The **number of deaths** caused by disasters has been **decreasing** because of improvements in **risk management strategies**:

- **Prediction** — improved technology means **some** hazards can be predicted, e.g. the **path** of **tropical cyclones** can be predicted to some extent. Advance warning means people can be **evacuated** and **property secured**.

- **Prevention** — natural hazards can't be stopped, but they can be **prevented from becoming disasters**, e.g. by using sandbags to **protect** against the effects of flooding.

- **Preparedness** — **educating people** on what to do in case of a disaster helps to **reduce** the number of deaths, e.g. **Japan** has a 'disaster preparedness day' each year when **practice earthquake evacuation drills** are carried out.

2) There's been a **levelling off** in the trend of decreasing deaths recently because the **increasing number** of **vulnerable people** in poorer countries means **more people** are being affected by disasters, leading to more deaths.

3) **Global economic losses** due to disasters are **increasing rapidly** though.

- **Actual financial cost** is the amount of money lost — this is **greatest** in **richer countries**.

- **Relative financial cost** is the amount of money lost relative to how much the people have to start with — this is greatest in **poorer countries**. **Less** actual money is lost, but the **effects** of the loss are **greater**.

> Disasters can lead to further, indirect economic losses, e.g. if a country gets a lot of money from tourism, this could be affected by a disaster, which could affect the economy.

Practice Questions

Q1 Explain the difference between a hazard and a disaster.

Q2 Name one type of hazard that's increasing in frequency and give a possible explanation.

Exam Question

Q1 Describe and explain how the number of deaths and the amount of economic loss caused by disasters is changing. [15 marks]

Reality TV shows — a global hazard...

So, seeing your dad trying to be groovy on the dance floor is only a hazard as long as you keep clear of him. It causes a disaster when he tries to make you join in and waves at your friends — teenagers are particularly vulnerable to this.

Hazard Distribution

*Don't know about you, but I want to know where all these hazards are happening, so I can be somewhere else.
Having said that, Britain's hardly a disaster hotspot, unless you attend a trainspotter's fashion show of course...*

Geophysical Hazards Usually Occur Near Plate Boundaries

1) The Earth's **crust** is made up of huge plates called **tectonic plates** that sit on top of the **mantle**.

2) Plates are made of **two types** of crust:
   - The **thicker** (but **less dense**) crust is called **continental crust** — it's mostly **above** sea level.
   - The **thinner** (but **more dense**) crust is called **oceanic crust** — it's mostly **below** sea level.

3) The plates **move** because of **convection currents** in the **mantle** — the currents are caused by **temperature differences** within the mantle.

4) **Volcanoes** and **earthquakes** most commonly occur at the **boundaries** where the plates **meet**.

5) There are **three types** of plate boundary — **constructive**, **destructive** and **conservative**.

Volcanoes and Earthquakes Occur at Constructive Boundaries

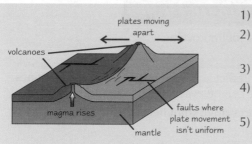

1) A **constructive boundary** occurs where two plates are moving **apart**.

2) The mantle is under **pressure** from the plates above. When they move apart, the pressure is **released** at the **boundary**.

3) The release of pressure causes the mantle to **melt**, producing **magma**.

4) The magma is **less dense** than the plate above, so it **rises** and can **erupt** to form a **volcano**.

5) For example, the **Eurasion plate** and **North American plate** are moving apart at the **mid-Atlantic ridge**. **Iceland** has been formed where magma has **risen** through the gap to form **volcanoes**.

6) The plates don't move apart in a **uniform way** — some parts move faster than others. This causes **pressure to build up**. When the pressure becomes **too much** the plate **cracks**, making a **fault line** and causing an **earthquake**. **Further earthquakes** may also occur along the fault line once it's been created.

A fault line is where a plate has cracked under pressure.

Volcanoes and Earthquakes Also Occur at Destructive Boundaries

A **destructive boundary** occurs where two plates are moving **towards each other**.

1) Where **continental crust** and **oceanic crust** are moving towards each other, the **more dense oceanic** crust is **forced under** the **less dense continental** crust (it's **subducted**).

2) The oceanic crust is **heated** by **friction** and **contact** with the upper mantle, which melts it into **magma**.

3) The magma is **less dense** than the continental crust above and will **rise** back to the surface to form **volcanoes**.

4) For example, the **Pacific plate** (oceanic crust) is subducting beneath the **Eurasian plate** (continental crust) at the **Japan trench**. The **Japanese island arc** has been formed where magma has **risen** through the crust to form **volcanoes**.

5) The same process occurs where **two plates** of **oceanic crust** are moving towards each other — the **denser** of the two will be subducted, e.g. this has formed the volcanic islands of **Indonesia**.

6) As one plate moves under the other they can **get stuck**. This causes **pressure to build up**. When the pressure becomes **too much** the plates **jerk** past each other, causing an **earthquake**.

7) Where two plates of **continental crust** are moving towards each other, **neither** is subducted so there aren't any volcanoes — but the pressure that builds up between them can cause **earthquakes**, e.g. the **Kashmir** earthquake (2005).

Hazard Distribution

Earthquakes Also Occur at Conservative Boundaries

A **conservative boundary** occurs where two plates are **moving past** each other.

1) The two plates get **locked together** in places and **pressure builds up**. As with destructive boundaries, this causes the plates to **jerk** past each other (or to **crack** forming **fault lines**) releasing the **energy** as an **earthquake**.

2) For example, the **Pacific plate** is moving past the **North American plate**. Many earthquakes occur along this boundary and at its fault lines, e.g. the **San Andreas fault** runs through **California**.

Conservative boundaries, laughed Winthorpe — they keep out the riff-raff, what!

Some Volcanoes Occur Away from Plate Boundaries

Volcanoes can occur **far away** from any **plate boundaries**, e.g. in **Hawaii**. These volcanoes are thought to be caused by **magma rising** from a **large chamber** beneath the crust. Areas like Hawaii are called **volcanic hotspots**.

Tropical Cyclones Occur over Warm Water

Tropical cyclones are huge **storms** with **strong winds** and **torrential rain**.

1) Tropical cyclones develop **above sea water** that's **26.5 °C or higher**. As warm, moist air **rises** and **condenses**, it releases energy which **increases wind speed**.

2) Tropical cyclones **lose strength** when they move **over land** because the **energy supply** from the warm water is **cut off**.

3) Most cyclones occur **between 5° and 30° north** and **south** of the **equator** — more than 30° away from the equator, the water **isn't warm enough** for cyclones to occur.

4) Cyclones spin because of the **Coriolis effect** (the force that deflects the path of winds due to the Earth's rotation).

5) Cyclones don't occur **0-5° either side** of the equator because the Coriolis effect there **isn't strong enough** to make them spin.

6) The Coriolis effect is also why they move **away from** the **equator**.

7) They move **westwards** due to the **east-west winds** in the **tropics**. For example, the **trade winds** move tropical cyclones westwards **across the Atlantic Ocean** towards the **Caribbean Sea**.

8) Tropical cyclones are also known as **hurricanes** (when they occur in the **Atlantic Ocean** or **Caribbean Sea**) and **typhoons** (when they occur in the **Pacific Ocean**).

Global warming could lead to an increase in the strength of tropical cyclones because of increasing sea temperatures.

Atlantic Ocean

Pacific ocean

Bay of Bengal

Tropic of Cancer (23° north)

Equator

Caribbean Sea

Indian Ocean

Tropic of Capricorn (23° south)

path of tropical cyclone

sea surface temperature 26.5 °C or higher

Practice Questions

Q1 Describe where tropical cyclones develop.

Q2 Explain why tropical cyclones don't develop within 5° of the equator.

Exam Questions

Q1 Explain why earthquakes occur at plate boundaries. [3 marks]

Q2 Describe and explain the global distribution of volcanoes. [10 marks]

Did you hear the one about the plate that went mad? It cracked...

So, the Earth's just like a big jigsaw puzzle, except with not many pieces. I love all this stuff about tectonics — I always found it really interesting, but then, I also have a lifesize cardboard cut-out of Han Solo in my room, so judge for yourself...

Disaster Hotspot Case Study — California

Maybe I was doing California a disservice when I said a trainspotter's fashion show was a disaster hotspot. California's the real deal — it's positively brimming with natural ways to be distinctly uncomfortable.

California *is a* Disaster Hotspot

Disaster hotspots are **vulnerable places** at risk from **two or more hazards**.

The state of **California** in the **USA** has many **highly populated** towns and cities at **risk** from a **variety of hazards**. The map below shows **examples** and **locations** of **past hazards** that have caused **disasters**.

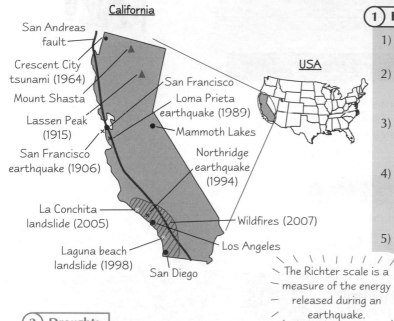

California

- San Andreas fault
- Crescent City tsunami (1964)
- Mount Shasta
- Lassen Peak (1915)
- San Francisco earthquake (1906)
- La Conchita landslide (2005)
- Laguna beach landslide (1998)
- San Diego
- San Francisco
- Loma Prieta earthquake (1989)
- Mammoth Lakes
- Northridge earthquake (1994)
- Wildfires (2007)
- Los Angeles

USA

The Richter scale is a measure of the energy released during an earthquake.

Some hazards can increase the likelihood of other hazards occurring, e.g. droughts make wildfires more likely.

1 Earthquakes

1) The **San Andreas fault** runs the length of California — it's a **conservative** plate boundary (see p. 5).
2) **Earthquakes** occur when **pressure** between the plates **builds up** and then is **suddenly released** as they jerk past each other.
3) California has **two or three** earthquakes **each year** that are powerful enough to damage structures (5.5+ on the **Richter scale**).
4) Studies of the **frequency** and **magnitude** of **past earthquakes** show that there's a **good chance** of an earthquake of magnitude 7.0+ hitting the San Francisco Bay area **before 2025**.
5) Past disasters include the **San Francisco earthquake of 1906** (thought to have measured 7.8), which along with subsequent fires, **destroyed** much of the city.

2 Droughts

1) Drought in California can be caused by **anticyclones** (**long-lasting** periods of **high air pressure** with **sinking, dry air**). Dry, sinking air means **no rain**.
2) Drought can also be caused by **La Niña** events (periods when the **surface water** in the **eastern Pacific Ocean** is **cooler**). This means **less evaporation**, so there's **less precipitation**.
3) Another cause of drought is **increased wind** blowing westward from the **desert areas** that are east of California, e.g. from Arizona. The dry air has **no moisture** to cause **precipitation**.
4) The most devastating effect of drought in California is **wildfires** — dry vegetation is extremely flammable, so fires **spread quickly** over **wide areas**.
5) The wildfires in **southern California** in October 2007 **killed 22 people** and destroyed **1300 homes**.

3 Tsunamis

1) A **tsunami** is a series of **large waves** that can **flood coastal areas**.
2) They can be **caused by earthquakes** on the sea bed, or **landslides** into the sea.
3) Earthquakes under the **Pacific Ocean** could cause a tsunami along the California coastline.
4) An earthquake off the coast of **Alaska** in 1964 caused a tsunami to strike the coast of northern California, **killing 12 people** in **Crescent City**.

Volcanoes in California — they'll be back.

4 Landslides

1) **Landslides** occur on **unstable steep land**. Land can be made unstable by **coastal erosion** or **extreme weather** (rainstorms). Landslides can also be **triggered** by **earthquakes**.
2) The risk of landslide disasters in California is high because of **building on and around steep slopes**, as well as building on **coastal land** overlooking the ocean, e.g. **La Conchita**.

5 Volcanoes

1) There hasn't been a **volcanic eruption** in California since **1915** (**Lassen Peak**).
2) But there are volcanoes **being monitored** for **potential eruptions**, e.g. **Lassen Peak, Mount Shasta** and the volcanoes around **Mammoth Lakes**.

Disaster Hotspot Case Study — California

California is *Wealthy* but *Parts* of the *Population* are *Vulnerable*

Even **wealthy parts** of **wealthy nations** have populations that are **vulnerable** to the risks from hazards:

1) More than **70%** of California's population live **within 50 km** of a **fault line** (see p. 4).
2) There's a lot of building on **unstable land** — this can lead to **soil liquefaction** during earthquakes (where the ground can become more like a **liquid**), which damages buildings and **increases** the **risk of landslides**. This was a major problem during the **Loma Prieta** earthquake in 1989.
3) There are many buildings along the **coast** that are vulnerable to **tsunamis**.
4) California is a **wealthy state**, but there are very **poor areas within it** — around **20%** of the residents in **Los Angeles** live **below** the official **poverty line**. These people have the **lowest capacity to cope** when affected by a hazard (see p. 2).
5) California has a **massive economy**, so there are likely to be **huge economic losses** when a disaster occurs.

You Need to *Research Hazard Risk* in *Your Local Area*

Looking at **disaster hotspots** shows that some places are at **more risk** than others. California's obviously a bit of a nasty spot for hazards, but you need to think about places **closer to home** — in the exam they might ask you about **real** (where hazards do occur) or **potential** (where they could occur) **hazard risk** in your **local area**. You need to be able to talk about:

1) Any **past events** that might have happened in the area you live, e.g. rivers that have **flooded**.
2) Any **likely future events** that could happen, e.g. landslides caused by **coastal erosion**.
3) The **impact** of these events on **people**, **property** and the **environment**.

It's important to think about how the risk of hazards in your area may be **changing** because of things like **global warming**. If global warming causes more **extreme weather**, or **rising sea levels**, it'll affect the **potential risk** in your area.

You can research **hazard patterns** and **risk potential** in different ways:

1) Use **Ordnance Survey® (OS®) maps** to find **where** potential hazards could happen, e.g. to find the location of **rivers** and the **populations at risk** if they flood.
2) Use OS maps to look for **vulnerable populations** near to **potential hazards** — where it's more likely a **hazard** could cause a **disaster**, e.g. housing estates on a river flood plain.
3) Use **Geographical Information Systems (GIS)** — **computer programs** that are used by geographers to look at hazard patterns and risk potential on a **local** scale. They usually look at different bits of **locational information** together (like different maps overlaid on top of each other). For example, a map of the **tectonic plate boundaries** could be overlaid with a map showing **river flood plains** — this would show where the two hazards **coincide**.

Practice Questions

Q1 Define the term disaster hotspot.

Q2 Describe one way you could research hazard risk potential in your local area.

Exam Question

Q1 Using specific examples, explain why California is considered to be a disaster hotspot. [15 marks]

Landslides — not as much fun as they sound...

California's a great place and everything, but crikey, I can think of more sensible places to build a load of massive cities — it's got the lot — volcanoes, earthquakes, massive waves (in a bad way surfers), landslides, droughts, dragons, alien invasions... Maybe I got carried away a little, but my point stands. There have already been some disasters and it's likely there'll be more.

Disaster Hotspot Case Study — The Philippines

If you thought California was a bad spot for people who like their surroundings to not try to kill them, then wait till you get a load of the Philippines...

The Philippines *is a* Disaster Hotspot

The Philippines is a group of islands in **south-east Asia** with a **vulnerable population** at **risk** from a **variety of hazards**. The map below shows **examples** and **locations** of **past hazards** that have caused **disasters**.

1) Volcanoes

1) The Philippines is near to a **destructive plate boundary** (see p. 4), where the **Philippine plate** is being **subducted** beneath the **Eurasian plate**.

2) The islands were formed by a combination of **folding** at the boundary and **volcanoes** formed from magma that has **risen** to the surface from the mantle below.

3) **Mount Pinatubo** is a volcano that erupted in 1991. Many people were **evacuated**, **buildings collapsed**, **crops** were **destroyed** and **agricultural land** was **ruined** by falling ash.

2) Earthquakes

1) The **Philippine plate** and the **Eurasian plate** can become **locked together** as one moves under the other. This causes **pressure** to **build up**. When the pressure is too much the plates **jerk** past each other, causing an **earthquake**.

2) Earthquakes also occur at **fault lines** in the area, where the plate has **cracked** under pressure.

3) Earthquakes occur **daily**, but most **can't be felt** (they're low on the **Richter scale**).

4) An earthquake of **magnitude 7.8** occurred on **Luzon island** in 1990, killing over **1500 people**.

> Multiple hazards in one area can increase the likelihood of other hazards occurring, e.g. falling ash from a volcanic eruption can combine with typhoons to cause mudflows (lahars).

3) Landslides

1) The Philippines get a **lot of rain**. If a lot of rain falls in a **short space of time** in areas with **steep slopes**, **landslides** can occur.

2) Landslides can also be **triggered** by **earthquakes**.

3) A landslide occurred on **Leyte island** in 2006 after it had been raining heavily for **10 days**. A whole village was **buried** (including a school), **killing hundreds**.

Some people love a good lahar at the end of a hard day.

4) Typhoons

1) The Philippines have around **10 typhoons** (tropical cyclones, see p. 5) **every year**.

2) They **develop** in the Pacific Ocean and move **westwards** over the islands.

3) **Typhoon Xangsane** swept across **Manila** and the surrounding **densely populated area** in the North in 2006. High winds and torrential rain **destroyed homes** and caused **flooding**, **landslides** and the **loss** of power and water.

5) Tsunamis

1) **Earthquakes** in any of the oceans surrounding the Philippines could cause a **tsunami** (see p. 6).

2) In 1976 an earthquake of **magnitude 7.9** caused a tsunami that hit the coastline around the **Moro Gulf** on the southern island of Mindanao. **Thousands were killed** and several cities were **devastated**.

Disaster Hotspot Case Study — The Philippines

6) Droughts

1) Some parts of the Philippines have a distinct **wet** and **dry** season, e.g. **Manila** (and the surrounding densely populated area) is **dry** between **November** and **April**, and wet between **May** and **October**.

2) **Drought** can occur when the wet season hasn't brought **enough rain** to last the dry season, or the dry season is particularly **harsh**.

3) There was a **drought** on **Luzon island** in **2005**. The reduction in rainfall decreased water flow in rivers, which affected **power production** from **hydroelectric** power plants. This affected the **power supply** to the **entire region**. Without power for an **extended period**, **economic** and **social** activity were severely **reduced**.

7) Flooding

1) During the wet season, **floods** can be caused by **typhoons** and **heavy rain**.

2) Flooding affects many areas, even some that are also affected by **drought**.

3) **Major floods** occurred in the **lowland areas** around **Manila** in the 1970s and in recent years. **Crops** were **devastated** in this major rice growing region.

The **Population** of the Philippines is **Vulnerable**

The Philippines isn't a really poor country (some bits of it are very wealthy), but much of its population remains **vulnerable** to the effects of a hazard, or has a **low capacity to cope**.

1) When a hazard strikes a **densely populated area**, there's a **greater risk** it will become a **disaster**, e.g. the island of **Luzon** and the area around **Manila** are more at risk because they have a **high population density**.

2) **Population pressures** have led to **deforestation** of upland areas for agriculture. This **increases** the risk of **landslides** in populated areas.

3) The Philippines has a **fast growing economy**, but there are still many people **below the poverty line** who will be most severely affected by a disaster.

4) Some **fast growing settlements** have been built near to **hazardous areas**, e.g. **Angeles** was built near to **Mount Pinatubo**. It wasn't thought of as a threat because it hadn't erupted for a **long time** (since 1380).

5) Many people live in **unstable locations**, e.g. the **Aeta tribe** were living on the slopes of **Mount Pinatubo** when it erupted in 1991.

Practice Questions

Q1 Name four hazards from which the Philippines are at risk.

Q2 Give two reasons why the people of the Philippines are vulnerable to disasters.

Exam Question

Q1 a) Mark on the map of the Philippines (right) the location of any plate boundaries and fault lines, as well as one example of an earthquake disaster and one example of a volcanic disaster. [4 marks]

b) Using specific examples, compare and contrast the Philippines with California as a disaster hotspot. [15 marks]

I like my cup of typh-oooooon milky with three sugars...

As my geography teacher used to say, case studies are here to 'put the meat on the bones'. Hmm, regardless of how odd that may sound, the point is that it's all very well learning the theory, but with geography it's really important that you know details of real-world examples (case studies) — that's how you'll get top marks in your exam.

Evidence for Climate Change

Climate change is the big cheese, the head honcho and the top dog when it comes to hazards at the moment.
Global warming's a big part of how the climate's changing right now, but it's not the first time the climate's changed...

Climate *is* Constantly Changing

Climate change is any **significant** change in the **weather** of a region over a period of at least **several decades**, e.g. increasing average **temperature** or **rainfall**, or a change in the usual **wind direction**.

The climate **constantly changes** over **long**, **medium** and **short** time scales, it **always has**, and it **always will**.

Long-term climate change

1) Taking **temperature** as an indicator of climate, there have been **huge changes** over Earth's history — temperatures have been much **higher** at some points in the **past** than they are **today**.

2) Looking at more detailed data for the **last 400 000** years, you can see a more detailed **fluctuation**.

3) Climate shifted between **cold glacial periods** that lasted around 100 000 years and **warmer interglacial periods** that lasted around 10 000 years. We're in an **interglacial period now**.

Temperature change in the Antarctic over the last 400 000 years

Temperature change in Greenland over the last 20 000 years

Scientists use the past temperature from one place, e.g. Greenland, as an indication of global temperature at that time.

Medium-term climate change

1) The last glacial period **ended** around **18 000 years ago**.

2) The **warming** of the climate after this was **fast** at times, but it wasn't **constant** — about 13 000 years ago the climate **switched back** to cooler conditions for about 1000 years.

3) Around 5000 years ago, temperatures were **1-2 °C higher** than today.

Short-term climate change

1) **Global warming** is the term used for the **rapidly increasing global temperature** over the **last century** — there's been a **sharp rise** in temperature when you look at the last **1000 years**.

2) The **overall pattern** over the last century shows a general **increase** in **temperature**, but the pattern hasn't been **constant**.

3) Global temperatures **rose steadily** from the **early 20th century** until the **1940s** (although they fluctuated annually), then **dropped** back down. Scientists thought there would be another **glacial period**, but temperatures have **risen rapidly** again **since** the 1970s (this is **global warming**).

Modelled temperature change over the last 1000 years

Temperature change over the last 150 years

You need to think about **global warming changes** in the context of all the **other climatic changes** that have occurred.

It's important to remember that climate change **isn't fully understood** — but the **changes in temperature** (and the **speed** at which they're occurring) over the last century are **worrying** because they're **thought to be unprecedented** (never seen before).

Evidence for Climate Change

There's Evidence for Long, Medium and Short-Term Climate Change

Long-term change

① Ice cores

1) Scientists drill deep into **ice sheets** (**huge masses** of ice) to extract **cores of ice**. Ice sheets are made up of **layers** of ice — **one** layer is formed **every year**. So the ice at the bottom of the core is really, really old.

2) They can analyse the **gases** trapped when the ice formed to tell what the **temperature** was each year. Then they can figure out how temperature has **changed over time**.

3) E.g. a core has been extracted from the **Antarctic ice sheet** to a depth of **3000 m** and has been used to show temperature for the last **400 000 years** (see long-term climate change graph on previous page).

② Pollen analysis

1) **Pollen** from plants is often **preserved** in **sediment**.

2) The preserved pollen can be **identified** and **dated** to show when it was **released**.

3) Scientists know the **conditions** that plants live in now. When they find preserved pollen from similar plants, it indicates that **conditions** were **similar** when that pollen was **produced**.

③ Sea level change

1) **Sea level** is affected by things like the volume of water **stored as ice**.

2) Past sea levels are shown by **raised beaches** (formed when sea levels were **higher**). Raised beaches can be **dated**. They can indicate that **less water** was stored as **ice** (i.e. it was **warmer**).

Medium-term change

① Historical records

Historical records can **indirectly** indicate **different conditions** in the past. E.g. **agricultural reports** (such as harvest times) show changing conditions throughout **human history**.

② Tree rings

1) A new **tree ring** is formed each year as a tree grows. If conditions that year were good, the tree ring produced will be **thick**.

2) Scientists can take **cores** and count the rings to find the **age** of a tree. They then look at the **thickness** of each ring to see what the climate was like **each year**.

3) Tree rings can reliably **show** and **date** climate conditions up to **10 000 years ago**.

③ Retreating glaciers

1) Scientists can tell **how big** a glacier was and how far it **extended** by looking at the position of **rocks deposited** by it. These rocks can be **dated** to show when they were deposited.

2) The **distance** of the rocks from the current glacier **indicates climate change**. E.g. if the front of the glacier is now miles away from the rocks it indicates that **temperatures** have **increased** over that period of time.

Short-term change

① Weather records

1) Details of **weather conditions** have been consistently **collected since 1861**.

2) These can be used to show detailed **climate changes** over the short time period they've been collected.

② Polar ice melt

1) Current research into the behaviour of **polar ice** shows a **reduction** in the amount of ice at both poles.

2) Changes in the **extent of polar ice** shows changes in the climatic factors affecting them, e.g. **increased melting** shows **increased temperatures**.

③ Ecosystem changes

Changes in temperature affect the availability of **food** and **shelter**. This affects what **species** live in an area. So scientists can use **changes** in how species are **distributed** to indicate changes in the **climate**.

Practice Questions

Q1 Suggest two ways of investigating medium-term climate change.
Q2 Suggest two ways of investigating short-term climate change.

Exam Question

Q1 Outline the sources of evidence for long-term climate change. [10 marks]

Ice cores tells us that ice was mostly mint flavoured 100 000 years ago...

Another thing my geography teacher used to say was 'Does that make some sort of sense?' I'd say 'Yes, it makes perfect nonsense.' Hopefully, this is all OK — the climate's always been changing, but global warming's an unusually large and rapid change.

Causes of Climate Change

So here's the answer to what's causing all this climate change — aliens. I wish. Actually, it's a little more complicated...

The **Causes** of **Climate Change** May be **Natural** and **Human**

Some changes in climate are caused by changes in how the **Sun's energy** is **received**, **trapped** and **distributed** around the Earth, e.g. when **more energy** is received, the Earth will get **hotter**. When **less energy** is received, the Earth will get **cooler**.

However, some changes in climate are caused by **human activity** (see next page).

Earth's Climate Changes **Naturally** Without **Human Influence**

1 Variations in the Earth's orbit

The way the Earth **moves around** the Sun **affects** the way the Earth **receives energy** from the Sun. Earth's movement around the Sun **gradually changes** in **three ways**, which in turn affect **global climate**.

1) **Stretch**
   - The path of the Earth's orbit around the Sun **changes** from an almost perfect **circle** to an **ellipse** and back again about every **96 000** years.
   - This changes the **distance** from the Sun to the Earth, and so the **amount of energy** the Earth receives from the Sun (at different times of the year).
   - Earth's orbit is **elliptical** right now — it's **closest** to the Sun in **January** and furthest away in **July**.

2) **Tilt**
   - The Earth is **tilted** at an angle as it orbits the Sun, called its **axis** (currently 23.5°).
   - This changes between about 21.8° and 24.4° over a cycle of about **41 000** years.
   - The change in **tilt** changes the **amount of energy** that different **latitudes** receive, **changing global climate**.
   - When the tilt is **greater** (24.4°) areas that receive **lots of energy**, such as **the tropics**, will be **larger**. Other climate regions, such as the **temperate zones** beyond the tropics, will be **smaller**.

3) **Wobble**
   - The axis of the Earth also **wobbles** like a spinning top on a cycle of about **22 000** years.
   - Because Earth is closest to the Sun in January, winter in the northern hemisphere is **mild** and summer is **cool**.
   - The wobble of the axis means this **gradually changes** — the **seasons** will eventually **swap over**.
   - When this happens, the Earth will still be closest to the Sun in **January**, but this will now be **summer** in the **northern hemisphere**. The Earth will still be furthest away from the Sun in **July**, but this will now be **winter** in the **northern hemisphere**.
   - So in the northern hemisphere, winter would then be **colder** because it would be at the time when the Earth is **further** from the Sun, and summer would be **hotter**, because it's at the time when the Earth is **closer** to the Sun.

Remember — all three orbital changes are going on at the same time, affecting each other.

2 Variations in solar output

1) The Sun's output of **energy** isn't **constant**.
2) **Sunspots** are darker areas on the Sun that **increase** solar energy output.
3) They're thought to **increase** and **decrease** in number in an **11 year cycle** — though there's variation within this cycle.
4) E.g. a period of **cooling** in the late 17th century called the **little ice age** is thought to have coincided with a period when sunspot activity was very **low**.

3 Meteor impacts

1) The impact of a **meteor** (up to 10 m across) or an **asteroid** (larger than 10 m across) forms a large crater and can throw up huge amounts of **material** into the **atmosphere**.
2) This can result in a lot of **sunlight** (energy) being **blocked** out for **months** or even **years**, changing the climate.
3) E.g. the mass extinction of the **dinosaurs** is widely thought to have been caused by the **climate change** brought about by a massive **asteroid impact**.

Causes of Climate Change

4) **Volcanic eruptions**

1) Major **volcanic eruptions** also eject large quantities of **material** into the **atmosphere**.

2) This can also block out **sunlight** (**energy**), which changes the climate.

3) E.g. the eruption of **Mount Tambora** in **Indonesia** in **1815** is thought to have **lowered global temperature** by about **0.5 °C**.

Human Activity is Causing the *Recent Change* in *Climate*

The recent **rise** in **global temperature** (**global warming**) and the **rate** of this increase is **unheard of** in **historical terms**. There's a **scientific consensus** that this temperature rise is **caused** by human activity (it can't be **explained** by **natural causes**, which usually happen **more slowly**).

Climate is affected **most** by **two human activities**:

1. Enhanced greenhouse gas emissions

- **Greenhouse gases** include CO_2, **methane**, **ozone** and **water vapour**.
- The **greenhouse effect** is where greenhouse gases absorb **outgoing energy**, so less is **lost** to space. It's **essential** for keeping the planet **warm**.
- But **too much** greenhouse gas in the atmosphere means **too much** energy is trapped and the planet **warms up**.
- CO_2 is **released** into the atmosphere when **fossil fuels** like coal, oil, natural gas and petrol are **burnt**, e.g. in power stations or in cars.
- Since the industrial revolution in the mid-19th century levels of **atmospheric CO_2** have **increased** from **280 ppm** (parts per million) to **380 ppm**. The level had been **broadly stable** for the previous 10 000 years.
- The **increase** in CO_2 has caused the **increase** in **temperature** (**global warming**) over the same period because of the **enhanced greenhouse effect**.

> Ozone is a greenhouse gas in the lower atmosphere. Don't get it confused with the ozone layer higher in the atmosphere (which filters out harmful UV). Human activity has caused a reduction in the ozone layer in some places, e.g. above the Antarctic.

2. Destruction of natural CO_2 sinks

- CO_2 **sinks** store CO_2, keeping it out of the atmosphere — so it's **not contributing** to the greenhouse effect.
- The biggest sinks are the **oceans** — CO_2 **dissolves** in sea water and gets moved to the deep ocean by natural currents.
- Another big sink is **plants** — plants **take in CO_2** and convert it into **organic matter** using photosynthesis. It's also stored in the soil as **dead organic matter**.
- CO_2 is **released** into the atmosphere when trees are **burnt** by forest fires or to make way for agriculture.
- It was thought that a lot of **greenhouse gas emissions** from humans could be **stored** in CO_2 sinks. It's now thought they **won't** be able to **keep pace** with **increasing** emissions, so more CO_2 will go directly into the **atmosphere**.

Practice Questions

Q1 Name two natural events that can affect climate change.

Q2 Explain how one variation in the Earth's orbit can affect climate.

Exam Question

Q1 Describe and explain how human activity is affecting climate change. [15 marks]

Destruction of sinks — no more washing up for me then...

So, the unusually large and rapid change I was talking about has rather a lot to do with us. It isn't just that the planet's as fickle as a fridge that thinks it's an oven — I'm hot, no, I'm cold, hang on, I'm roasting, no, I'm freezing, I'm burning, I'm melting...

Impacts of Climate Change

Oooo, now we're getting into the juicy bits — what's going to happen to us and the planet and how we can predict it.
Come on, I'll give you a pound if you can guess how accurate our predictions are.

Global Warming is Causing Ice to Melt...

1) The melting of **ice on land** (e.g. the Greenland and Antarctic ice sheets)
means that water **stored** as ice returns to the oceans.

2) This **increases** the **volume of water** in the oceans and causes the **SEA LEVEL** to **RISE**.
This kind of sea level change (caused by an increase in water volume) is called **eustatic** sea level change.

3) If **all the remaining ice sheets** melted it would cause global sea level to rise by between **60 and 80 metres**.

4) Increased global temperatures also means that the oceans get **warmer** and **expand**.
This **thermal expansion** also **increases** the **volume** of the water, causing sea level to rise **further**.

5) This could raise sea levels by between **8** and **80 cm** for each increase in global temperature of **1 °C**.

Don't forget — global warming is a type of climate change.

Predictions of how much sea level will rise in the future are **uncertain** and **differ a lot** (see next page). An international group of scientists, called the **Intergovernmental Panel on Climate Change** (**IPCC**), look at the **risks** of climate change — they think sea levels could rise by between **18 and 59 cm** by the end of the century.

Only melting ice on land affects eustatic rising. If sea ice, such as Arctic ice, melts it just replaces its own volume in the water.

Any rise in sea levels will have a **global impact**, but it will be **greater** in some places than others. For example:

Larry the lamppost looked fondly on his last sunset before the sea swallowed him forever.

Bangladesh

1) **80%** of the land area in Bangladesh is **low-lying**. Any rise in sea level will **submerge large areas**.

2) This would affect lots of people as Bangladesh has a **very high population density** (around 1000 people per km²).

3) The situation would be made worse as it's a **poor country** — the population are **vulnerable**, with a low **capacity to cope**.

The Maldives

1) The Maldives are an extremely **low-lying** set of islands in the **Indian Ocean**. A rise in sea level of 0.5 m would submerge most of the **country**.

2) Although the population isn't poor, the economy is **dependent** on **tourism**, which would be threatened by a rise in sea level.

...And Permafrost to Thaw

1) Permafrost is **ground** that has been **permanently frozen** for two years or more.
It covers around 20% of the Earth's land surface.

2) Areas of permafrost are **natural sinks** of CO_2 (see p. 13). It's stored as organic material in the soil.
Thawing of permafrost **releases** some of this, contributing further to global warming.

3) Thawing of permafrost causes the **collapse** of **buildings** and **pipelines** built on it. It may also bring **economic benefits** to **humans** though, e.g. it's easier to look for and extract **natural resources** (like fossil fuels) in areas of **unfrozen ground**.

Global Warming is Also Causing Other Changes in Climate

Changes in global temperature affect **global weather patterns**. For example, global warming is thought to be causing:

1) An **increase** in the **frequency** of **extreme weather events**, e.g. increasing ocean temperatures may mean an increased risk of **tropical cyclones** over a wider area.

2) A **change** in the **distribution of climatic regions**, e.g. **colder polar** regions may **shrink** and **warmer tropical regions** may **advance** to higher latitudes.

   • This affects **ecology** (the distribution and abundance of organisms). Species will have to **migrate** to remain in a suitable climate and, if they can't migrate, they may become **extinct**.

   • It also affects **agriculture** — e.g. some areas become unsuitable for **cultivation** as **climatic factors** such as **temperature** and the **timing of the seasons** alter.

   • Regional climate changes may bring **benefits** to some **human activities**, e.g. **economic benefits** of **tourism** where the climate has become warmer.

Impacts of Climate Change

Emissions Scenarios are Used to Predict Impacts of Global Warming

There's a scientific consensus that human factors, such as CO_2 **emissions**, are **causing** global warming. Scientists try to **predict** how **emissions** will **change** in the future, so they can try to predict the **change in climate** and its **impacts**:

1) The **IPCC** has produced a number of **emissions scenarios**, which are **predictions** of how human CO_2 emissions will **change** up until 2100.

2) Scenarios include:
   - Emissions **not increasing** much more (scenario 5, minimum emissions).
   - Emissions continuing to **grow** as they are now ('**business as usual**').
   - Emissions **increasing** by a lot (scenario 1, maximum emissions).
   - Emissions being controlled by **sustainable management** strategies.

3) They can put all these different scenarios into **global climate models** (computer models of how the climate works), to see how the climate could **change** with each scenario, e.g. how much global temperature will **rise**.

4) Then these can be used to show how the **different climate changes** can cause **different impacts**, e.g. different levels of **sea level change**.

[Graph: CO₂ concentration (ppm) vs Year, showing Scenario 1: maximum emissions and Scenario 5: minimum emissions, with curves labelled 1-5]

Scenario	Sea level rise between 2000 and 2100
2	0.23 - 0.51 m
3	0.21 - 0.48 m
4	0.18 - 0.38 m

It's **difficult to predict** the impacts of changes in the climate because there's so much **uncertainty**:

1) We don't actually know how emissions will **change**, i.e. which emission scenario is most **accurate**.

2) We don't know how much of the emissions will be **absorbed** by things like **natural CO_2 sinks** (see p. 13).

3) We don't know what exact **climate changes** each emission scenario will **cause**.

4) The extent of climate change due to **natural causes** (without human influence) **isn't known**.

5) We don't know what attempts there will be to **manage the impacts** of climate change, or how **successful** they'll be.

Combined Impacts May Lead to a Tipping Point

Climate change could reach a **tipping point** — where a slight rise in temperature would cause **catastrophic** and **irreversible** changes to the environment, creating a much **more hazardous** world.

This may happen because of **positive feedback loops** — where a **change** in the climate is **speeded up** by the impacts it's **already caused**. For example:

> Global warming causes melting of Arctic sea ice. As sea ice melts it leaves darker sea water in its place. Sea water has a lower albedo (the amount a surface reflects the sun's radiation) than ice, so more radiation is absorbed by the water. This warms the water, which causes more ice to melt, and so on...

The boys on board the good ship Titanic II knew all about tipping points.

The **combined effect** of positive feedback on several of the impacts of global warming, e.g. ice melt and the destruction of CO_2 sinks, may lead to a **tipping point**.

Practice Questions

Q1 Explain how global warming causes eustatic rise in sea level.

Q2 Other than eustatic sea level rise, name two other potential impacts of global warming.

Exam Question

Q1 With reference to IPCC emissions scenarios, explain why the impacts of global warming are difficult to predict.

[15 marks]

I.P. in the C. — and the sea level rises...

Did I say a pound? I meant a pound of potatoes. Predicting climate change and its impacts isn't an exact science — maybe nothing will change and the future's just rosy, or maybe the whole world's going to blow up/melt down/sink. Take your pick.

Climate Change — Case Studies

Aaaah we're back in case study land — a chance for you to make some real-life sense of my theoretical jibber-jabber. Global warming's affecting the whole planet, but some places are really getting it in the neck.

The **Arctic** is a **Vulnerable Environment**

The **Arctic** is the area around the **North Pole**. It includes the northern parts of Asia, North America and Europe. **Global warming** is affecting the Arctic **directly**:

1) The **area** of **Arctic sea ice** (frozen sea water) has been **shrinking** at an increasing rate — some scientists think there won't be any sea ice in the summer by **2030**.

2) The **Greenland ice sheet** is **melting** — most scientists think the rate of melting has **increased** in recent years.

3) The **permafrost** (see p. 14) **boundary** is moving **north** and the area covered by permafrost is **shrinking**.

4) The **treeline** (the point beyond which trees can't grow) is moving **north** and the area where trees can't grow is **shrinking**.

These effects are having **indirect impacts** on the **environment** and **ecology** (the **distribution** and **abundance** of organisms) of the Arctic.

Minimum extent of sea ice   Permafrost boundary
— 1979-2000 average   — present
— 2007   — year 2100   ······· treeline

Global Warming Will Have a Variety of Impacts on the Arctic

Environmental impacts

1) Melting of ice sheets like the **Greenland ice sheet** will mean an injection of **fresh water** into the sea. This will cause changes in the **density** of the water and could **disrupt ocean currents** like the **north Atlantic drift**.

2) Thawing of permafrost **releases** more CO_2 and methane — permafrost's a **natural sink** (see p. 13).

Ecological impacts

1) Changing **climatic regions** (see p. 14) means the **habitats** (where species live) of some species are being **reduced** or **lost**. E.g. polar bears use areas of **sea ice** to hunt for food. As this is lost polar bears may become **endangered** in the wild.

2) Some parts of the Arctic have very **sensitive ecosystems** — there are **few species**, so the loss of one may have **devastating** impacts on other species that rely on them.

3) In other parts of the Arctic, like the ocean, the **number** and **diversity** of **species** (e.g. fish) may **increase** as **sea ice coverage** is **reduced** and **temperatures increase**.

Socio-economic impacts

1) Shrinking sea ice could open up **new shipping routes** in the summer.

2) **New natural resources** may be exploited, e.g. less sea ice increases the area available for **fishing**.

3) It's also thought there are **undiscovered oil** and **gas** reserves in the Arctic — unfrozen ground would make them easier to **find** and **extract**.

4) Access to new resources may lead to **conflict** over which countries **own them** though.

5) **Warmer** soils and climate may **increase** the **opportunity** for **agriculture** or **forestry**.

6) **Thawing of permafrost** can result in **collapsed buildings** and **broken pipelines** where ground has become **less stable**.

It's an **unfair world** — it isn't necessarily the people **causing** climate change who are **most affected**. As with the Arctic, the greatest **environmental and ecological** damage often happens **away** from those causing the problems.

Arctic Warming Has Consequences for the Rest of the World

Interlinked systems — if you change one system, all the others change too.

The **impacts** of global warming on the Arctic will affect the rest of the **planet** too.

1) **Melting ice sheets** will add to **rising global sea levels**.

2) **Ocean currents** in the Arctic are affected by **salinity changes** (freshwater from melting ice sheets changes the **density** of sea water), which affects **global ocean currents** because they operate as an **interlinked system**.

3) Changing **temperatures, sea ice** and **landscapes** affect **air currents** in the Arctic. This also affects **global weather patterns** because the atmosphere also operates as an **interlinked system**.

Climate Change — Case Studies

Africa's Population is Vulnerable to the Impacts of Global Warming

Africa has a range of **different climates** from dry deserts to tropical rainforests.
Global warming is having **different** impacts in **different** areas.

1) Areas that are **already dry** (arid and semi-arid environments) are getting **drier**.

2) **Wetter areas** (tropical and sub-tropical environments) are getting **wetter**.

3) The whole continent is getting **warmer** — around **0.5 °C warmer** in the last century.

Because Africa's population is **vulnerable** (poor countries and people) the **economic impacts**
of global warming in Africa are **complex** and the **relative financial costs** are massive:

1) Poor people have a **reduced capacity to cope**, e.g. **subsistence farmers**, who only grow enough to meet the needs of their family and have **no income**, will be at risk of starvation if **climate change** affects their crops.

2) Poorer countries are less able to **prepare for** and **respond to** the impacts of climate changes.

3) **Political turmoil** can mean the appropriate responses **aren't made**, making the impacts of climate change worse.

Here are some **examples** of impacts:

Global warming is causing **desertification** — the process by which **fertile** land becomes **unusable** for agriculture. It's a major problem in the **Sahel region** (the belt between the Sahara desert and the fertile area to the south). This causes a **decrease** in **agricultural production**, which leads to more **poverty, unemployment, malnourishment** and **starvation**.

Global warming has caused a **reduced growing period** over much of the continent. This **decreases agricultural production**. In the Sahel region agriculture forms around 70% of the **employment**, so any reduction leads to increased **unemployment, poverty, malnourishment** and **starvation**.

Global warming means **tropical areas** are experiencing **longer growing periods**, and may **financially benefit** from better agricultural conditions.

Global warming may have improved **conditions** in some areas of Africa for **mosquitoes** that spread **malaria** — a disease which kills over a million people each year. The **costs** of health care and the **reduction in productivity** (combined with reduced interest in **tourism and investment**) mean the economies are put under **strain** and prevented from **growing**.

Global warming is causing a more **erratic climate**. E.g. **Mozambique** suffered **drought** and **widespread crop failure** in **1995**, then **flooding** in **2000**, which displaced lots of people. Homes and infrastructure are **destroyed** in areas where people are unable to **rebuild** and **recover**.

.... Sahel region
change in length of growing period (days)
● 1-50 fewer   ○ 1-50 more
● 50-113 fewer   ● 50-100 more

It's an **unfair world** — the poorest people of Africa have contributed **little** to the causes of global warming and yet suffer the **most**. The **economic losses** that would be **minor** in well developed countries can have more **disastrous consequences** in poorer countries, resulting in **loss of life**.

Practice Questions

Q1 Describe one environmental, one ecological and one socio-economic impact of global warming on the Arctic.

Q2 Describe one environmental change caused by global warming in Africa.

Q3 Describe one way in which global warming changes in Africa could affect the economy.

Exam Question

Q1 Explain the environmental and ecological impacts of global warming in a named area of the world. [10 marks]

What's white, furry and has a hole in the middle — a polo bear...

Hmm, I'm thinking the world's a little bit unfair, and it's a little bit more than 'ref that was never a penalty' unfair. It's always the most vulnerable people and places that suffer the most, and more often than not, they didn't cause the hoo-ha in the first place. Try to learn as much as you can, and even, shock horror, do some extra research on these case studies — it'll help in the exam.

Coping With Climate Change

So, what to do about global warming and all its impacts? It's a toughie for sure — there are loads of great ideas, but the problem is trying to get all those world leaders to agree on what's best. And they normally get on so well...

There are **Different Strategies** for **Coping** with **Climate Change**

Approaches to coping with the climate changes caused by **global warming** can be divided into **two categories:**

1) **Mitigation strategies** involve taking action to **reduce how much** climate change **occurs**, e.g. **reducing emissions** may help to **slow** the temperature increase, so **less ice** may melt and the sea level would **rise less**.

2) **Adaptation strategies** involve taking action to **reduce** the **impacts** that the changes are having, e.g. sea levels are rising so **defences** could be built to **protect** vulnerable settlements.

Here are some examples:

Mitigation strategies

Carbon tax — taxing companies or people who produce CO_2. Increasing costs discourages overconsumption of energy.

Changing the energy mix — changing the mix of sources of energy, i.e. lowering the proportion of energy made from fossil fuels and increasing energy from sources that produce less greenhouse emissions, e.g. nuclear power.

Modified agricultural practices — cut methane generation from farm animals, e.g. by developing new types of feed.

Emission-cutting technologies — carbon capture and storage involves storing the CO_2 produced (e.g. by power plants) using methods like injecting it into geological formations, e.g. coal seams.

Energy conservation — using less energy, e.g. switching off home appliances when they're not being used.

Waste strategies — increasing the amount of waste that's recycled, which should directly cut methane emissions from landfill sites.

Tree planting — planting new trees creates new carbon sinks so more CO_2 will be stored as organic matter.

Carbon offsetting — individuals and companies can calculate the amount of CO_2 their activities are producing, then offset them by paying for activities that take up an equal amount of CO_2 (like tree planting).

Adaptation strategies

Lifestyle adaptations — people adapt the way they live to suit the new conditions, e.g. planting new crops that will flourish in the new climatic conditions.

Improved risk assessment — looking at the likelihood that people or property will be damaged by climate change impacts, and evaluating the need for insurance policies.

Flood adaptations — building physical defences such as flood barriers to reduce the impacts of flooding, and having better flood warning systems.

Water resource management — using freshwater resources more efficiently to cope with drought conditions, e.g. installing water meters in homes to discourage people from using a lot of water.

Community awareness — educating local communities on the potential impacts of climate change. Emergency action plans can be tailored for specific communities.

1) Some of these strategies need to be applied on a **global scale** (e.g. changing the energy mix, introducing emission-cutting technologies) while others can be done at a **local scale** (e.g. community awareness, waste strategies).

2) **International agreements** (see next page) are another example of **global** strategies to tackle climate change.

3) Many of the strategies have only a **small impact** on their **own**, e.g. energy conservation in homes, but when all the strategies are **combined** the impacts can make **long-term** differences.

Strategies Have **Limitations** and **Side Effects**

Some strategies have **limitations** which reduce their effectiveness, while others have **side effects** that impact on other things:

1) **Limitation** — e.g. building physical flood defences works whilst flooding remains **below** a certain point. If sea levels continue to **rise** defences like the **Thames barrier** won't be **high enough** to cope with the higher flood waters.

2) **Side effect** — e.g. changing the energy mix would **reduce emissions**, but using more **nuclear power** would produce more **nuclear waste**. It's a long time before the waste becomes **safe**, so it's **expensive** and **dangerous** to dispose of.

Coping With Climate Change

Agreeing on How to Cope with Climate Change is Complex

Strategies to cope with climate change need to be **developed**, **managed** and **carried out**. This is done at **different levels** by **various groups**. There are **key players**, each with a **different role** that can sometimes be conflicting:

1) **Governments** — develop strategies on an **international**, **national** and **local** scale.

2) **Businesses** — can be responsible for **contributing** to climate change, or can help to **slow it down**. They may **lobby** governments to **reduce restrictions** and allow them to continue producing greenhouse gases, or they may help by investing in **new technologies** to **combat** climate change.

3) **Non-governmental organisations (NGOs)** — can have many roles and views depending on what they're set up to do and who their members are, e.g. **Greenpeace** is an environmental pressure group that tries to **persuade governments** to recognise and take action **against** climate change.

4) **Communities** and **individuals** — strategies developed on a larger scale are carried out at a **local level**, e.g. a government may decide to encourage recycling, but the recycling is actually done by **individuals**.

There are different **views** and **levels** of **influence** between and within the key players, e.g. not all governments **agree** on the right thing to do, and some key players may have **more power** than others to influence decisions.

Developing agreements on the nature of climate change and how to respond is very **complex**. Here's an example:

The Kyoto Protocol

1) The Kyoto Protocol was an **international agreement** between more than **180 countries** to **monitor** and **cut** greenhouse gas emissions by **2012**.

2) The agreement divided the countries into two groups — **developed** and **developing**.

3) **Developed countries** agreed to **cut emissions** (overall by 5%).

4) **Developing countries** didn't have to cut emissions, but needed to **monitor** and **report** their emissions.

5) The agreement set up a **market** to trade in **carbon 'credits'** — all countries and businesses were given a **limit** on the **emissions** they could produce. If they produced less, they could **sell** the **extra carbon credits** — if they produced more, they needed to buy more credits. They could also gain credits by helping to **reduce emissions** in developing countries — so developed countries **invested** in developing countries to help them develop in a **sustainable way**.

6) **Four countries** with the **highest emissions** (the **USA**, **Australia**, **China** and **India**) **didn't sign up** for the original agreement in 1997. The **USA** and **Australia** felt signing would affect their **economies** and that the developing countries should have targets **as well**. **China** and **India** thought it would slow their **rate of growth**.

7) Most joined the agreement in the end but there was still lots of **criticism** — some people felt the targets weren't **high enough** and others thought there was no point if the highest polluters **weren't included** (the **USA** didn't **fully** join).

The Kyoto Protocol was due to expire at the end of 2012, but many countries agreed to extend it to 2020.

Individuals Can 'Act Local, Think Global'

A carbon footprint is the amount of greenhouse gases a person produces, i.e. how much they might be contributing to global warming.

International agreements help at the largest scale, but changes need to be coordinated at **all levels**. Most people think the approach should be to 'act local, think global' — individuals can make **small changes** that will help the global problem, e.g. reduce their **carbon footprint**.

Some people think that if everyone took steps to **decrease** their carbon footprint, it would make a **big difference**. Others believe that individual impacts **aren't significant**.

It's likely that changes to emissions will be **incremental** rather than gradual (change occurring in **steps**, rather than **constantly**), as large-scale initiatives and changes to attitudes cause **sudden changes**.

Practice Questions

Q1 Explain the difference between mitigation and adaptation strategies.
Q2 Name three adaptation strategies for coping with climate change.

Exam Question

Q1 Using a named example, explain why global agreements on coping with climate change are complex. [15 marks]

The Kyoto photocall — these politicians are so vain...

After lots of talking, plenty of arguing and several lost dummies, international agreement on coping with climate change still isn't there. Hmm, maybe if you learn all the strategies I've written out then you can come up with a better solution than they can.

Global Hazards — The Future

And finally, let's end the section on an upbeat, optimistic note. Oh, hang on a minute, turns out the world is getting more hazardous and the impacts of the hazards are getting in the way of our efforts to manage them. Sorry, I tried.

The **World** is Becoming **Increasingly Hazardous**

Global **risk** and **uncertainty** are **increasing** as many hazards increase in magnitude and frequency (see p. 3). This threatens **major disruption** to **people** and the **environment**.

One problem associated with increasing risk and uncertainty is **water shortages**, which lead to reduced **food security** (the **availability** and **access** to food).

Here's an example of how increasing **global warming** is causing **water shortages** and **reduced food security**:

Global hazards? Poppycock!

1)   Global warming causes changes in **precipitation** and **temperature patterns**.

2)   In some areas, this results in **drier** conditions, which leads to **water shortages** and a **decreased ability** to grow food.

3)   Many **poorer** parts of the world are affected in this way, e.g. **sub-Saharan Africa**.

4)   **Poorer areas** have less money to find **technological solutions** such as dams, or to **import** sufficient food supplies.

5)   **Dehydration** and **famine** (widespread shortage of food) can occur in areas where global warming has affected a **vulnerable environment** with a **vulnerable population**.

I didn't believe the world was a hazardous place — look what happened to me.

Global warming affects the **supply** of **water** and **food**, and many developing countries have **rapidly increasing** populations — so the **vulnerability** of the population is increased and the **risk** of a **disaster** is much higher (see p. 2).

The Impacts of **Climate Change** May Lead to **Conflict**

The problems of water shortages and food security have caused **political disputes** between countries and can even lead to **armed conflict**. Conflicts can **escalate** as risk and uncertainty **increase** because of hazards like global warming:

1)   **Egypt** relies heavily on the river **Nile** for its **water supply**.

2)   The two main **tributaries** that feed the Nile flow through **Ethiopia** and **Sudan**.

3)   Egypt built a dam called the **Aswan High Dam**, which created a large lake to **store water** (Lake Nasser).

4)   Droughts in the 1980s led to **famine** in **Ethiopia** and **Sudan**, but **Egypt wasn't affected** because enough water was **stored** in Lake Nasser.

5)   If global warming continues to cause **shortages** of water and Ethiopia or Sudan **increase** their water use, Egypt's supply might be **reduced**.

6)   Egypt has stated that it's ready to **use force** to protect its **access** to the waters of the **Nile**.

Conflict can occur **within** countries and **between** countries where any type of resource **isn't enough** to support the population — and this will only **get worse** as climate change affects the **supply of resources**.

Other **Global Problems** Make **Managing Hazards More Difficult**

Conflict, **famine**, **poverty** and **climate change** make managing global hazards more **difficult**.

1)   These problems **increase** the **vulnerability** of the population — they may become **poorer** and **less healthy**, and the **infrastructure** to provide help may become **inadequate**.

2)   **Risk** is **increased** where the population is vulnerable — a **hazard** may become a **disaster** (see p. 2).

3)   A country suffering **other problems** like famine won't have the **resources to manage** the impacts of any other global hazards such as global warming. The **priority** will be to feed the nation, rather than **reduce** greenhouse gas emissions or stop deforestation.

4)   A **downward cycle** can occur where the hazards cause problems that eventually increase the risk of more hazards (**positive feedback**, see p. 15).

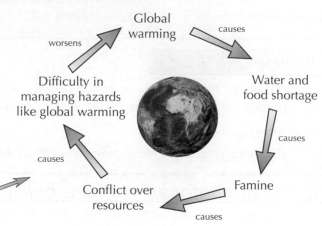

Global Hazards — The Future

Global Warming may be the Greatest Hazard to Life and Property

Global warming is considered to be one of the **biggest challenges** the world has faced:

1) Global problems like **famine**, **poverty** and **conflict** cause massive **loss of life**, but global warming has the potential to cause **much more loss of life** and **damage to property**.
2) It can be the **cause** of many other global problems and hazards (e.g. **famine**, **poverty** and **conflict**), and can **worsen** their effects — it's a **context hazard** (see p. 2).
3) It's a long-term hazard and the impacts may be **permanent** and **irreversible**.
4) Global warming affects the **entire planet** whereas other problems tend to occur in more **localised regions**.

There are lots of **strategies** that have been **proposed** and are **currently being used** to **cope** with the impacts of global warming:

1) **Increasing energy efficiency** — making the energy we produce **do more**.
2) **Energy conservation** — using **less** energy.
3) **Decreasing carbon emissions** — directly **slowing** the rate of global warming.
4) **Increasing alternative energy use** — using energy sources that produce less **greenhouse gases**.
5) **Reafforestation** — replanting trees to **increase** CO_2 uptake from the atmosphere.

See p. 18 for more on strategies to cope with climate change.

It's thought that global warming will be the **most difficult** and **costly** to manage of all global problems.

1) The **Stern Review** (2006) looked at the **economics** of climate change.
2) It concluded that an investment of **1%** of the world's **GDP** (Gross Domestic Product, the **total value** of production over a given period) would be needed to prevent the **worst effects** of global warming.
3) If this investment isn't made, GDP could be reduced by up to **20%** in the future.

You need to understand all these strategies and assess which are the most **cost-effective** for the **benefits** they'll bring — **cost-benefit analysis**. Achieving a balance requires **innovative solutions** (ideas that haven't been tried before) so governments perform this kind of analysis when deciding what approaches to take.

It's likely the most cost-effective and beneficial solutions in the long-term will be those that are **sustainable** (can be used **indefinitely** without **harming** the environment or **depleting resources**), e.g. **renewable energy sources** like solar power. But strategies are **most effective** when they're carried out by **everyone**, so the problem needs to be **recognised by everyone**.

Solutions to Hazards Should Focus on Risk and Vulnerability

The solutions to a hazardous world, whether they're on a **local** or **global** scale, need to focus on **assessing** and **altering** the **risk** the hazard poses (the **likelihood** the hazard will impact on humans) and the **vulnerability** of the population (how **susceptible** the population is to the impacts of a hazard).

The **United Nations** (**UN**) set up a programme in 1992 called **Agenda 21** which outlines action to be taken at **global** and **local** levels to help **sustainable development**. The first section looks at **vulnerability** and is about combating **poverty**, **changing consumption** and promoting **better health**. The second section looks at **reducing risk** by changing **emissions**, working against **deforestation** and protecting **environments**. Together they should help reduce **risk** and **vulnerability**.

Practice Questions

Q1 How does global warming lead to water shortages?
Q2 Outline two strategies used to cope with global warming.

Exam Question

Q1 Explain how global warming could increase water shortages, famine and conflict. [10 marks]

Stern Review — nothing to do with parents' evening...

I wish politicians talking about risk meant they were playing world domination board games. Alas, the board is in fact the real world, and the risk is the likelihood that something nasty's going to happen to us. Global warming's a big part of it all, and if there's going to be a solution it needs to focus on what and where the risk is and how vulnerable people are.

Introduction to Globalisation

Globalisation — the process that's bringing the world closer together. I know that sounds like an advert for some sickeningly soppy film, but the world really is coming together and it's happening faster than it used to. Read on...

Globalisation is How Countries Become More Closely Integrated

Globalisation's important because it's a big part of **how** and **why** the world's **changing** to become one **big global community**:

1) Every country has its own **political** and **economic systems** as well as its own **culture**.

2) **Globalisation** is the process of all the world's systems and cultures becoming more **integrated** — it's the **whole world** coming together like a **single community** with **similar, shared** systems and cultures.

3) Globalisation changes how people think of **distance** and **time**. People can **interact easily** with other people anywhere in the world, no matter how **far apart** they are — it feels like the world's **shrinking**.

4) For example, in a **globalised world** Great Britain could **potentially** have as much **political, economic** and **cultural interaction** with countries on the **other side** of the world, like **New Zealand**, as it can with its immediate neighbours, like **France**.

Bless my soul! She's in Peru but I can hear her through this box.

If everyone stayed in their own country and **didn't interact** in any way with other countries there would be **no globalisation**. If everyone **interacted freely** and countries were **fully integrated** so the global community acted like a **single society**, there would be **total globalisation**. The real world is somewhere **in between**. But as countries and people **interact more**, globalisation is **increasing**.

You can look at globalisation as a process that changes the **connections** between **people** and **environments** across the globe:

1) The connections between places are **lengthening** — **new links** are being formed between places that are **far apart**, e.g. you can fly to pretty much **any country** and companies operate in **multiple countries**.

2) The connections between places are becoming **deeper** — **more** people's lives are increasingly involved with far-away places, **not** just the richest people. E.g. **anyone** can buy products imported from **all over the world** in their **local supermarket**, and you can **easily reach** anyone in the world by **phone** or the **internet**.

Globalisation's a really important concept, but people have **different ideas** about what it means. Some people only think about **economic globalisation** (e.g. **trading goods** with people all over the world). Other people are only concerned with **cultural globalisation** (e.g. the adoption of **Western lifestyles** by many countries).
Remember, globalisation is about **all** these things — global **political, economic** and **cultural** integration.

Globalisation has Been Happening for Thousands of Years

Although globalisation might seem like a **recent concept**, in one form or another it's been going on for a **long time**:

1) **Exploration** and **war** have led to **interactions** between different populations for **thousands of years**. This has resulted in the **trading** and **sharing** of different **cultures, politics** and **beliefs**. For example, the **Roman Empire** spread across (and controlled) large areas of the world around **2000** years ago. They brought a new political system, **new technology** and a different culture, some of which **remained** long after they left.

We've come to conquer... Ahem, I mean share our culture.

2) **Goods** have been traded around the globe for a **long time**, though the **global economic system** we know today is a fairly **recent development**. The recent system started when **large companies** began to operate in **several countries**, e.g. in the 17th century the **East India Company** traded a lot with British colonies throughout **east Asia**.

3) Globalisation **accelerated** in the **19th century** because of **increasing trade** between **European empires**. Acceleration continued in the **20th century** because of increasing trade with the **USA**. Global trade was **slowed** by the First and Second **World Wars** because they **severely damaged** European economies, slowing globalisation.

4) Globalisation has really **accelerated** since the 1980s. Huge **global brands** and **corporations** have **easy access** to most countries and are known **all over the world**, helping to create a sense of **global community**.

Introduction to Globalisation

Globalisation *is* Accelerating

Globalisation is occurring at an **increasing rate** due to four **key factors**:

1) Trans-National Corporations (TNCs)

GDP (Gross Domestic Product) is a measure of a country's income.

1) TNCs are companies that **produce**, **sell** or are **located** in **two or more** countries, e.g. **Sony** manufacture **electronic products** in **China** and **Japan**, and **sell** many of them in **Europe** and the **USA**.
2) Some TNCs generate **more money** than the GDP of some nations, e.g. oil companies like **Shell**.
3) TNCs bring lots of **investment** into countries, spread **new technologies** and can promote particular **cultures**, e.g. **McDonald's** bring **Western-style** fast food to other countries.
4) **Potential investment**, the **creation of jobs** and access to **new technology** means TNCs can have **political influence**.
5) TNCs have **grown** in **size** and **number** in the last 50 years, and are **continuing** to move into **more countries**.
6) They're thought to be one of the **main driving forces** behind globalisation because of the economic, political and cultural **interactions** that occur **between** the countries where they operate.

TNCs are covered in more detail on pages 26-27.

2) New markets

1) The increasing prosperity of developing countries opens up new markets for companies, e.g. Western companies can sell more to countries like China and India, which have large populations and increasing wealth.
2) Global share trading involves buying and selling shares at stock exchanges. Exchanges in less developed countries are getting bigger and attracting more investment, e.g. Mumbai (India) and Shanghai (China).
3) The availability of new markets and stock exchanges encourages more global trade, which accelerates globalisation.

3) Improved communications

1) Communications can mean **transport mechanisms**, e.g. aeroplanes and high-speed rail, or **information exchanges**, e.g. the internet and e-mail.
2) Transport mechanisms have been **improving** since the mid-20th century. More people have **easier access** to **new products** and to places that are **further away**, making people **better connected**.
3) Electronic information exchanges allow **instant communication** for **individuals** and **businesses** to any part of the world.
4) Better communications make the world seem **smaller** — distance becomes much **less important**, allowing **businesses** and **individuals** to interact with **anyone**, **anywhere** (the world is **shrinking**).

4) International organisations

1) International organisations bring **people**, **money** and **information together** — helping to accelerate globalisation.
2) The **World Bank** offers **money** to poorer nations to help them **develop**. It provides **loans** to fund **development projects**, e.g. building schools and better roads. **Improved infrastructure** means poorer countries are more likely to attract **international investment**, helping to create **connections** between **rich** and **poor** countries.
3) The **International Monetary Fund (IMF)** is an organisation that **regulates** the global financial system and lends money to make countries more **financially stable**. Countries with **failing economies** find it hard to **trade** or **attract investment**. IMF loans **increase** economic stability, helping these countries to participate in **global trade**.
4) The **World Trade Organisation (WTO)** regulates the **rules of trade** between countries. It's designed to **reduce barriers** to trade between countries, e.g. setting up agreements where **tariffs (taxes)** on trade are **reduced** or **removed**. This increases **trade** between countries, which increases **interaction** and **globalisation**.

Practice Questions

Q1 Describe globalisation.
Q2 Name one international organisation involved in accelerating globalisation.

Exam Question

Q1 Describe and explain why globalisation has been accelerating. [15 marks]

Lengthening connections — I just use an extension cable...

Aaaaw, globalisation's making the world into one big happy family, and the fatherly forces of TNCs, big new markets, improved communications and international organisations are making sure the global family gets more quality time together.

Global Groupings

As globalisation increases and the world becomes more connected, it's useful to group countries together in certain ways. Global groupings are important because they show how money and power are shared out (and who's best buds with who).

Countries can be put into Economic and Political Groupings

Countries can be put into **broad economic** and **political groups** because **wealth** and **power** aren't shared out **equally** around the world. These groups **change** over time as the **wealth** and **power** of countries **change**. For example, most countries used to be classified as either **More** or **Less Economically Developed** (**MEDCs** and **LEDCs**). It's now thought that this system is too **simplistic** — there are too many **stages** of **economic development** to put all countries into only **two categories**. You need to learn these **three** groupings:

LDCs

1) **Least Developed Countries** (**LDCs**) are a group of around **50** countries that are defined by **very low incomes**, **poor health**, **low education**, **economic instability** and their **heavy debt** to richer countries, e.g. **Mozambique**.

2) Their economies are usually based on **agriculture**, so crop failures can lead to economic **disaster**.

3) Countries are **moved out** of the LDC group when conditions **improve**, e.g. **Botswana**.

NICs

1) **Newly Industrialised Countries** (**NICs**) aren't yet classified as **developed** countries (like the **UK**), but aren't thought of as **LDCs** (like **Bangladesh**) either.

2) Their economies are usually **growing** very fast, and there has often been a **recent move** from a mostly **agricultural** economy to one involving **manufacturing** and **exporting**.

3) The term was originally used for the **Asian 'Tiger'** economies of **Singapore**, **Hong Kong**, **South Korea** and **Taiwan**, although some people now argue they're **fully developed** and so shouldn't be referred to as NICs any more.

4) There's **no official** list of NICs, though **China** and **India** are **currently** thought of as NICs.

Ex-Soviet states — Middle-income countries

1) **Russia** and some of the surrounding countries in **central Asia** and **eastern Europe** used to make up **one large state** called the **Soviet Union**. A lot of **independent countries** have been created since the Soviet Union **collapsed** in 1991 — these are mostly now classed as **middle-income countries**, e.g. **Estonia**.

2) **Middle-income countries** have **growing economies**, but the growth isn't as **rapid** as the **NICs** and their development hasn't reached the **same level**, e.g. **Ukraine**.

3) Recent **growth** in some ex-Soviet states is due to the exploitation of **natural resources**, e.g. oil and gas in **Kazakhstan**.

4) The **privatisation of industries** (**state controlled** in Soviet times to **privately controlled** now) has led to economic **recovery** and **growth** in many ex-Soviet states, e.g. **Belarus**.

Countries can be Members of Voluntary Groups

The G8 is one of the world's most powerful and wealthy groups — it's made up of Canada, France, Germany, Italy, Japan, Russia, USA and the UK.

Some countries form voluntary groups to gain **mutual economic benefits**:

OPEC

1) The **Organisation of Petroleum Exporting Countries** (**OPEC**) is a group of **13** major **oil-producing** countries, e.g. **Venezuela**, **Iran**, **Angola** and **Indonesia**. OPEC countries control around **two-thirds** of global oil reserves.

2) Because they're a **large group** in control of a large amount of oil, they can make sure they get a **fair price** from oil-consuming countries (e.g. the **UK**).

3) Some members have **left** since OPEC was founded because they wanted to produce **more oil** than the agreed **OPEC quotas** allowed, e.g. **Gabon**. Other countries have also been invited to **join**, e.g. **Bolivia** and **Sudan**.

OECD

1) The **Organisation for Economic Cooperation and Development** (**OECD**) is a group of around **30** of the **richest** and **most powerful** countries. The top eight are called the **G8**.

2) They meet to **discuss** and provide possible **solutions** to **economic**, **environmental** and **social issues**.

3) Members of the OECD are always **changing** too, e.g. potential **new members** include **Brazil**, **China** and **India**.

Global Groupings

Countries can Group Together for Mutual Advantage

Trade blocs

Trade blocs are groups of countries that make **agreements** to **reduce barriers** to trade, e.g. by removing **tariffs** (**taxes** on imported goods). Blocs **increase** trade between members, and members can work together as a **larger organisation** to trade with non-members. **Benefits** of membership of a trade bloc are linked to **two** important concepts:

1) **Economies of scale** — the **advantages** companies gain because of **increased sales**. There's a **larger market** for all companies within the trade bloc because it's **easier to trade** with all the other member countries. This **increases sales**. More sales means **more products** need to be made, so companies can buy the **raw materials** for their products in **greater numbers**, **saving money**. Buying raw materials in **bulk** means each product **costs less** to make, so companies can make **more profit**.

2) **Comparative advantage** — countries can **concentrate** on developing **specific industries**. Being in a trade bloc means it's **easier to trade** for all the **different** goods and services a country needs, because trade is **less restricted**. So countries can **specialise** in producing the things they're **good** at making and trade for the things they're **not good** at making. Production will **increase** in each member country because they're concentrating on **what they do best**, so production will **increase** in the trade bloc **overall**.

> **Trade bloc example — NAFTA**
>
> 1) The **North American Free Trade Agreement** is an example of a trade bloc. It's called NAFTA because it's an agreement between the countries of North America — **USA**, **Canada** and **Mexico**.
>
> 2) It's made **trade** between the members **easier** by removing things like **import taxes** on some goods.
>
> 3) Trade between all three countries has **increased** but there are **other impacts**, e.g. **job losses** in the **USA** because the manufacture of some goods has been moved to **Mexico**, where labour is **cheaper**.

There are Inequalities in Wealth and Power Between Countries

These groupings of countries highlight the **inequalities** in **wealth** and **power** around the world. **Most** of the wealth and power is in the hands of a **few countries**, e.g. the **G8** have over **60%** of the **gross world product** (the **total income** of the world), and control most of the **military power**, even though they're **only eight** countries.

These groupings also show how wealth and power can **change**. For example, **Russia** didn't officially join the **G7** (to form the **G8**) until 1997 because of the power issues of the **cold war** (a period of **political struggle** between the **USA** and the **Soviet Union**) and **economic problems** in Russia after the **collapse** of the Soviet Union.

Because **wealthy countries** often form groups **together**, they become more **closely integrated**. This means they're more likely to get **even wealthier** and **develop solutions** to their own economic, environmental and social **problems** at a **faster rate**. This can lead to a **widening of the gap** between **poorer** and **wealthier** countries.

The annual meeting of the Jovial Organisation of Kipper Eaters (JOKE) was unexpectedly busy.

Practice Questions

Q1 Suggest one reason why some middle-income countries are growing in wealth.

Q2 Name the voluntary group that includes about 30 of the richest and most powerful countries in the world.

Q3 Name one example of a trade bloc and list the countries it involves.

Exam Questions

Q1 Compare and contrast LDCs with NICs. [4 marks]

Q2 Describe comparative advantage and state how countries in a trade bloc can benefit from it. [2 marks]

NICs — I thought they were a basketball team...

So there are global groupings that countries belong to because of how rich and powerful they are. Then there are global groupings countries agree to be in because it'll help them out, like OPEC and the OECD. It all sounds like the playground to me — there are the geeks and the jocks... I've gone all American — well that's globalisation for you.

Trans-National Corporations

Trans-National Corporations (TNCs) are worldwide companies that are bringing countries together by spreading themselves, and their cash, all over the world. Unfortunately, they don't seem to have spread any cash into my bank account.

TNCs are the Agents of Global Change

TNCs **accelerate globalisation** by **linking together** groups of countries through the **production and sale of goods**. In large **assembly industries**, the parts are often **made** in one country, **assembled** in a second country, then **sold** in a third. For example, **BAE Systems** make defence vehicles like **submarines**. They use components from **all over the world**, assemble the vehicles in large factories like the ones in **Barrow** (UK), then sell the vehicles to **other countries** such as the **USA**. TNCs **create links** between different countries in several ways:

> *Remember — TNCs are companies that produce, sell or are located in two or more countries (see p. 23).*

1) **Mergers** — a merger is where **two companies** (usually of **similar size**) agree to become one **bigger** company, e.g. the two oil and gas companies **BP** and **Amoco** merged in 1998. This helps **links** form **between** the countries where the two companies operate.

2) **Acquisitions** — an acquisition is where one company **buys** another (usually **smaller**) company, e.g. the **US** car company **Ford** bought the **Swedish** company **Volvo Cars** in 1999.

3) **Using Sub-contractors** — TNCs can use **foreign** companies to **manufacture products** without actually **owning** the businesses, e.g. **NIKE** products aren't always made in factories NIKE **own**. This **links** the countries of the TNC and the sub-contracted company **together**.

4) **Foreign Direct Investment** (**FDI**) — this is any **investment** that gives a TNC a **long-term interest** in a country **outside** the one they're from. It can involve mergers, acquisitions and using sub-contractors, e.g. if **HSBC acquire** a bank in **Indonesia**, they're investing money in Indonesia (that's FDI).

Hi, I'm into murders and executions... I mean mergers and acquisitions... ahem.

A major **criticism** of TNCs is that much of the profit they make from foreign operations doesn't **remain** in the foreign countries — some of it **goes back** to the country of origin. E.g. some of the money made by **Volvo Cars** will be invested back in the **USA**, not **Sweden**.

TNCs can accelerate globalisation by bringing the **culture** from their **country of origin** to many **different countries**. The countries become **linked** by **common patterns of consumption**, e.g. companies like **McDonald's** sell **similar products** in **every country** they operate in. People in different countries are **linked together** because they can **buy** similar products.

Trade Blocs can Help or Hinder TNCs

Trade blocs can reduce or remove **import taxes** between countries in the bloc (see previous page). TNCs operating **within** a trade bloc benefit from these **reduced taxes**, but TNCs that operate across countries that are **in and out** of the trade bloc will have to pay **normal** import taxes. This affects where TNCs **locate** their operations, for example:

1) **Nissan** manufacture cars in **Sunderland** (UK) rather than in their country of **origin** (**Japan**) because it means they don't have to pay **tariffs** to import the cars into the **EU** (**European Union**, a trade bloc in Europe).

2) TNCs from the **USA** gain benefits from the **NAFTA** trade bloc (see previous page). They can produce goods in **Mexico**, but still sell them in the USA and pay less or no **import tax**. This means they can **cut costs** and **increase profit** because labour is **cheaper** in Mexico and they can still sell at the same prices in the **USA**.

Wal-Mart® is a Retail TNC from a Wealthy Country

Wal-Mart is a chain of discount **department stores** (**ASDA** is part of Wal-Mart). It's one of the **largest** TNCs in the world and the largest **retail** TNC (many of the top TNCs are **oil companies**). It's a case study, so here's your background information:

1) Wal-Mart began when **Sam Walton** opened the first discount store in **Arkansas, USA**.

2) More **stores** opened across Arkansas, then across the USA, and more recently across the **globe** via the **acquisition** of other retail companies. E.g. **Seiyu** in Japan, **ASDA** in the UK and **Bompreço** in Brazil.

3) Some Wal-Mart stores continue to trade under their **own name**, e.g. ASDA. Others have been **re-branded** as Wal-Mart, e.g. some stores in **Canada**.

4) Some acquisitions **weren't successful**, e.g. Wal-Mart was forced to sell its stores in **Germany** after **struggling** to **compete** with existing discount retailers there (like Lidl).

5) Wal-Mart is starting to **expand** into **NICs** like India, which have huge **new markets**. For example, Wal-Mart and an **Indian** company called **Bharti Enterprises** are opening new retail outlets **together** in the **style** of Wal-Mart stores.

Trans-National Corporations

Wal-Mart® Helps to Accelerate Globalisation

Like other TNCs, Wal-Mart helps to **accelerate globalisation** — it **links** countries together through the flow of **money**, **people**, **trade** and **information**. It also brings the **culture** of its country of origin (**USA**) to other countries.

In the USA, Wal-Mart gives customers all they need in **one building** at **low cost**. They've **successfully** introduced this in other countries, e.g. ASDA now stocks more non-food items. This hasn't been **successful** in all countries. They're trying a **different approach** in **India** where people like to shop in **traditional markets** rather than supermarkets.

Although Wal-Mart is a global brand it's retained a **local approach** by buying **local companies**. Its stores **aren't** all exactly the **same**, though many of the **products** are, e.g. **George** clothing supplies ASDA in the UK and Wal-Mart in the USA. Selling the **same products** globally helps to create **common patterns of consumption** between different countries.

Wal-Mart Divides Labour Across Different Countries

The **spatial division of labour** is basically splitting up the work of a company so that **each part** is carried out in a **different** location. Companies do this so each part is carried out in the most **cost-effective** place. For example, goods are manufactured where there's **cheap labour** (e.g. developing countries), but **research and development** is carried out where there's a **highly educated**, **skilled** workforce (e.g. more developed countries).

Wal-Mart's workforce is divided because it **sources** products from **all over** the globe and sells them in **many countries**.

1) Some **electronic goods** are made in factories in **China** and **Malaysia**. **Cheaper labour** and **bulk buying** mean Wal-Mart can sell these products at **lower prices** than if they bought goods made in the **USA**.

2) **Clothing** for Wal-Mart (and ASDA) is made by companies like **George**, a **British** company. Criticism of supermarkets for exploiting **cheap labour** in countries like **China** and **India** has led companies like George to **switch** some of their production to the **UK**.

There are Inequalities in Wal-Mart's Global Operation

When TNCs like Wal-Mart **divide** labour across the globe, people from different countries are **linked together** because they **work** for the **same** company. But this doesn't mean **working conditions** or **wages** are **equal**:

1) **Factories in China** — workers earn **less than $1** an hour.
2) **Factories in the USA** — workers earn the minimum wage of **around $6** an hour.
3) **Headquarters in the USA** — executives earn **hundreds of thousands of dollars** a year.

This may seem unfair, but it's the **relative amount** that matters — the **cost of living** in China is **lower** than the USA, so $1 goes **further**. Also, TNCs can offer **more reliable** wages than income from jobs like **subsistence farming**, even if the money isn't great.

I don't think you guys really understood when I said 'people are linked together'.

Practice Questions

Q1 Describe how TNCs link countries together through the production of goods.

Q2 How do trade blocs help TNCs?

Q3 Describe one inequality in Wal-Mart's global operation.

Exam Questions

Q1 Name four ways in which TNCs can create links between different countries. [4 marks]

Q2 Describe the growth and spatial division of labour of one named TNC. [10 marks]

I'm Agent Global Change from the FDI, I'd like to ask you a few questions...

If globalisation's a big juggernaut heading towards a unified world, then TNCs are in the driving seat and they're hitting the gas. They're changing the world by growing and investing their cash in loads of countries. It links together all the countries they're in, all the people that buy their stuff, and all the people that work for them. For Wal-Mart, that's basically the whole world.

Global Winners and Losers

Revising with CGP products makes you a winner. Using other, inferior brands will make you a loser.
Right, now you've got that covered let's do some geography — globalisation helps to create global winners and losers.

Some Places are Switched-on, Others are Switched-off

Air travel, **tourism**, **global businesses** (TNCs) and **communication systems** create global networks —
they **connect** different places together, accelerating **globalisation**. Global networks allow **trade**, **money**,
people and **information** to **flow** around the **world**, e.g. air travel and tourism allow **more people** to travel
to different countries, bringing **money** and **information** with them.

Global networks have helped to create places that are **switched-on** (**well connected** to global networks,
usually rich and powerful) and places that are **switched-off** (**poorly connected**, usually not wealthy or powerful).

Switched-on places	Switched-off places
1) These are the most **highly-connected countries**, as well as the **important cities** in poorer countries, e.g. **Singapore** is an important **port**, **financial centre** and **tourist destination**.	1) These are the **worst-connected countries**, as well as some **remote places** in more wealthy countries, e.g. **Bhutan** is a **landlocked** country in the Himalayan mountains, where **tourism** and access to the **internet** are **restricted**. The **economy** is based on **agriculture**, with little foreign influence.
2) Because they're **well connected**, trade, money, people and information **flow easily** between them and elsewhere — they're **global hubs** because global networks flow **through them**.	2) Some **money** does flow into switched-off places, often in the form of **aid**. Also, they may grow some crops to make money (**cash crops**, e.g. coffee), but they **trade little** and receive **very little** for the crops.
3) People in switched-on places are significant **consumers** and **producers** of goods and services because they're well connected.	3) People in switched-off places aren't significant **producers** or **consumers** because they're not well connected to global networks and aren't a **potential market** for TNCs.
4) **Energy usage** and the **ecological footprint** (how much a place **impacts** on natural resources) are **large** because of the **high levels** of production and consumption.	4) **Energy usage** and the **ecological footprint** are **low**.

You need to know the difference between places that are **interconnected** and places that are **dependent**.

1) **Interconnected** places have a roughly **equal exchange** in the flow of trade, money, people or information,
e.g. the number of tourists **visiting** a country is **equal** to the number of citizens from that country that **travel**.

2) One place is **dependent** on another if there is an **unequal exchange** in the flow of trade, money, people or information
— more is **coming in** than **going out**, e.g. **lots** of tourists **visit** a country, but **few** citizens of that country **travel** abroad.

The **multiplier effect** also helps connected places to **grow in wealth** — money **spent** in one place **causes** more money to
be **made** in that place, e.g. **more tourists** visiting a town means **more hotels** and **restaurants** are needed, so more money is
invested in the city and more local people are **employed**. They'll spend their **increased earnings** in the city, and so on...

New Technologies Make the World More Interconnected

1) **Technologies** like telecommunications, the internet and air travel create **global networks**, for example:

- **Long-distance telecommunications** began when copper **telegraph cables** were laid across the Atlantic in 1866. Now there's a **global phone network** linking all countries.

- **The internet** allows people in offices that are far apart to work together at the same time.

- Low-cost **air travel** means it's **cheap** and **easy** to travel long distances for **work** and **holidays**.

2) Global networks lead to a **shrinking world** — **distances** don't seem as far because places are very **well connected**.

3) Here's an example of how global networks can create global patterns of **connectivity**:

> **EasyJet** is a low-cost airline that helps to connect many places by making it easier
> for **more** people (not just the **wealthy**) to get to **more** places (not just **popular**
> **places**). It makes a **pattern** of connectivity, made up of all the places it flies to.
> The connections it forms can help make places **switched-on**.
>
> For example, **Tallinn** is the capital of **Estonia**, an ex-Soviet state. EasyJet has made
> Tallinn **more connected** by setting up **flights** to and from there to other European
> countries (e.g. the UK). This has **increased** the flow of **people**, **information** and
> **money** between Tallinn and other countries, helping to make Tallinn **switched-on**.

Either the world's shrinking, or this woman's enormous.

Global Winners and Losers

Physical and Human Resources Create Global Winners

The **winners** in a globalised world are countries that have **useful resources** that are in demand — this helps them **connect** to **global networks**, so they become **switched-on**.

Winners can use their **comparative advantages** (see p. 25) — they're **well connected** so they can easily **trade** for the things they **need**. This means they don't have to produce **everything**, but can concentrate on using their physical and human resources where they'd be **most useful**. The **multiplier effect** (see previous page) can also help them to become **more** wealthy.

Here are a couple of examples of how **physical** or **human resources** have helped create global winners:

Physical — Saudi Arabia

1) **Saudi Arabia** is an **oil-rich** country in the **Middle East** that gets most of its wealth (about half its GDP) from the **trade** of oil — this is called **petrodollar** wealth.

2) Saudi Arabia has **coasts** on two sides so oil can be easily **shipped** out to other countries.

3) Saudi Arabia uses the money it makes from its **comparative oil advantage** to **develop** other parts of its economy. This helps to **increase** its **global connections** and keep it **switched-on**.

Human — China

1) **China** is a **NIC** (see p. 24) with a **huge population** (more than 1.3 billion).

2) China can provide lots of **cheap** but relatively **skilled** labour, e.g. the manufacturing industry in China has **grown rapidly** because of **investment** from Chinese and foreign companies. Cheap, skilled labour means costs are **reduced** and profit can be **increased**.

3) China's **comparative advantage** in **human resources** has allowed other parts of its economy to grow because of the **multiplier effect**. This has helped to increase its **connectivity** and make it **switched-on**.

Physical Difficulties or Poor Leadership Create Global Losers

Global losers are countries that remain **switched-off** from **global networks**. This can be because of **difficult physical conditions** (e.g. landlocked countries) or **poor leadership** leading to **political isolation** (e.g. a corrupt government). For example:

Zimbabwe is a landlocked country in south-east Africa that is cut off from global networks. It has been politically isolated because of accusations of corruption and poor leadership. This has led to economic sanctions from the EU and USA, reducing the flow of trade. Also, many airlines refuse to fly to Zimbabwe, reducing its connectivity further.

The **consequences** of being switched-off from global networks mean global losers may be **left further behind**:

1) **Valuable resources** may be **wasted** or left **unused** because there's no investment to help **trade** in them.

2) **Conflict, starvation** and **disease** may make it less likely that global connectivity will **improve**.

3) Switched-on countries are more likely to work **together**, helping them to **progress** faster. This means the **gap** between switched-on and switched-off places will only **get wider**.

There are Some Odd Winners and Losers

Odd winners — some areas are in **difficult** physical locations, but are still **switched-on**. E.g. **Las Vegas** is a city in the Nevada desert (**USA**), but is a **global hub** for **tourism** (and **money**) because **gambling** is **legal** there.

Odd losers — some places are **rich** in a **natural resource** but remain **switched-off**. E.g. **Sierra Leone** (West Africa) is rich in **diamonds** but hasn't been able to generate much wealth from them due to **civil war** and **government corruption**.

Practice Questions

Q1   What factors create global winners?

Q2   What factors create global losers?

Exam Question

Q1   Describe and explain what a 'switched-on' country is.   [4 marks]

Switched-on, switched-off — wax on, wax off...

Switched-on, switched-off, winners, losers... to make some sense of all this just remember that we're still talking about globalisation here. Countries that are well connected to other countries are switched-on and will benefit from globalisation.

Consequences of Globalisation

Globalisation's brought countries together and made plenty of people rich, but as always, someone or something's gotta pay for it. There are negative consequences of globalisation for people and the environment.

There are Economic Consequences of Globalisation

For more on NICs and the OECD see p. 24.

Globalisation has caused an **increase** in **global trade** (because of the spread of global business by **TNCs**, see p. 23). Trade has increased in **most countries**, but especially in **Newly Industrialised Countries** (**NICs**) and countries in the **Organisation for Economic Cooperation and Development** (**OECD**). Increased trade has **different effects** on their **economies**:

Richer nations (e.g. OECD members)	Globalisation has caused the **deindustrialisation** of many **richer countries** — **manufacturing** industries have **moved** from richer countries to poorer countries mainly because **wage costs** are **lower**. For the **growth** of their economies to continue, rich countries have had to change to a **post-industrial economy** — one that's based mainly on the **service sector**. • **Positive consequence** — this has led to **increased wealth** for many people. One reason why many rich countries, like the UK, **educate** their population to a **high level** is that this attracts **investment** from TNCs because more people can work in the **highly paid service sector**. • **Negative consequence** — many manual workers **lost their jobs** and struggled to find new work because of **deindustrialisation**. The **economies** of some cities (e.g. **Sheffield** in the UK, famous for **steel manufacturing**) were **ruined** by deindustrialisation. Recovery has been slow because the economies were based almost **entirely** on **one industry**.
NICs	Globalisation has caused the **industrialisation** of many countries — manufacturing industries have been moved to **NICs**, changing their economy from **agriculture-based** to **manufacturing-based**. • **Positive consequence** — **increased wealth** in poorer countries. NICs, like China, **attract investment** from TNCs because of **large workforces** with **lower wage demands** than richer countries. This has brought **wealth** to **some people** in NICs. • **Negative consequence** — the **income gap** between rich and poor people has become **wider**. The wealth isn't **spread evenly** in NICs (e.g. Indonesia) — a **few people** become wealthy, while **many remain poor**.

There are Moral and Social Consequences of Globalisation

Sweatshops are crowded, dangerous factories, whose workers are paid little and work long hours.

Globalisation has meant many countries have become **more industrialised**. TNCs **move** factories from richer countries to NICs, and **sweatshops** are also set up for **sub-contract** work. Agricultural workers from **rural areas** move to **urban areas** to work in the factories and sweatshops — **rural-urban migration** (see p. 44). This can lead to the **exploitation of workers**:

1) Workers are **paid very low wages**.
2) Many workers are **killed** or **injured** in accidents because there are fewer **health and safety** regulations, e.g. **Yongkang** is an industrial city in **China** famous for the number of amputees from **factory accidents**.
3) Workers have **fewer rights**. If they **strike** because of poor conditions they may **lose their job**, or the factory may be **moved** to another place (where the workers **won't strike**).

Some people think the effects of globalisation are **morally wrong**:

1) **Dangerous**, **poorly-paid work** has just been **moved** from richer countries to poorer countries, instead of being **stopped altogether**.
2) Some sweatshops employ **children**, which is **illegal** in richer countries.
3) Products made in NICs are **cheap** because conditions are **poor** and wages are **low** — **exploitation**. Many think people in richer countries should take more **responsibility** and pay **higher prices** for products produced in NICs, so the workers get a **fairer wage**.

Other people think the effects of globalisation are **helpful** in some countries:

1) Urban **working conditions** and **standards of living** might be **better** than those in rural areas.
2) Sweatshops are the **first steps** towards a **wealthier economy**. They existed in the UK and the USA in the 19th century and helped the **economy** to **grow**.
3) Poorer countries have to focus on what they can **do best** — use their **comparative advantage** (see p. 25). They can't supply the **high levels of education** (needed for **service sector jobs**), but they can supply **cheap labour**. This means their economies will **grow** and in time conditions will **improve**.

Consequences of Globalisation

There are Environmental Consequences of Globalisation

Increase in global trade also creates environmental problems:

1) **Oil pollution** — increased global trade means **more shipping**. **Ecosystems** (the wildlife and the physical environment) are **damaged** by oil pollution from **shipping**, e.g. in the major shipping lanes near **Alaska**.

2) **Deforestation** — increased global trade has meant countries in tropical areas can **make money** by growing **crops** to sell for **profit** (cash crops), e.g. oilseed plantations for alternative fuel. They **clear forests** to make **space** for crops. **Tropical forests** are a massive **sink** of the greenhouse gas CO_2 (see p. 13). When trees are cleared by **burning**, CO_2 is released into the **atmosphere**, adding to global warming.

3) **Carbon emissions** — globalisation has meant products can be sold a **long way** from where they're made. So, they're transported a **long distance** before they're **bought**. Transporting products creates **pollution** because planes and ships release pollutants like **carbon dioxide**, which contributes to global warming (see p. 13).

   > The distance food products are transported is called 'food miles'.

4) **Waste** — increased global trade means people have access to **more products** at **low prices**, so they can afford to be more **wasteful**, e.g. people **throw away** damaged clothes instead of **repairing** them because it's cheaper to just **buy more**. Lots of waste ends up as **landfill** if it's not **recycled**.

5) **Recycling issues** — **increased waste** created by global trade means there's **more recycling**. Waste can be moved a **long way** to be recycled though, e.g. a lot of paper and plastic from the **UK** is shipped to **China** for recycling. This can lead to more **greenhouse gases** being produced, adding to **global warming**.

Solutions to the Consequences of Globalisation can be Local or Global

The problems caused by globalisation can be handled at a **local** or **global** scale, by **governments**, **businesses** and **individuals**:

Governments

Trading carbon credits — international agreements like the **Kyoto Protocol** (see p. 19) set countries **carbon emission limits** (measured in **credits**). If they emit **less** they can **sell** the extra credits, but if they emit **more** they have to **buy** credits. This **encourages** reductions in **carbon emissions** caused by transportation, and reduces the amount of **shipping** and **oil pollution**. It **discourages deforestation** as countries can **gain** carbon credits by **planting trees** instead of **cutting them down**. It takes a **long time** for governments to create these agreements, so it may not reduce emissions **quickly**.

Businesses

Stating distance transported — businesses can label products to show where they've come from. This could encourage consumers to buy products that haven't travelled as far, helping to reduce carbon emissions.

Using recycled materials — businesses can use recycled materials, e.g. recycling old drinks cans to make new ones. This reduces the amount of waste that goes to landfill, but could increase carbon emissions and oil pollution if the recycled material is shipped long distances (though it's often still better than making new products from raw materials).

Individuals

Fair trade — individuals can buy products that are **fair trade**. The producers are **guaranteed** a **fair price** for their goods (e.g. bananas). This can **increase wages** and the **security** of income for some of the poorest workers. Some argue that fair trade **prevents economic growth** — the guaranteed prices of the products are **higher** than their **market value** (what the product is **worth**). So people are encouraged to produce **too much**. This results in an **excess**, which causes the market value of the products to **fall**. Anyone who **isn't** part of the fair trade agreement will **lose out**.

Buying local — individuals can buy **local products** that haven't been transported a long way, helping to reduce **carbon emissions**. But many workers (especially in poorer countries) **rely on exporting** their goods to make money. If people **only** buy locally (especially in richer countries), millions of **workers** in **poorer countries** could **lose out**.

Recycling — individuals can **recycle more** waste, **re-use** products and **refuse** to buy products that aren't made from recycled materials. This has the **same effect** as businesses using more recycled materials (see above).

Practice Questions

Q1 How has globalisation changed the economies of richer nations?
Q2 Name one social consequence of globalisation.

Exam Question

Q1 Evaluate the strategies used to solve the problems caused by globalisation.   [15 marks]

Globalisation has econo-socio-enviro-moral consequences. Gotcha.

There's plenty of debate about whether globalisation's doing more good than bad, and how effective all the solutions to the problems really are. You need to make sure you talk about both sides of the debate to get top marks in your exam.

Migration and Globalisation

If you aren't sick of the impacts of globalisation yet, you will be soon — it also affects migration...

Migration Occurs Because of Push and Pull Factors

Migration is the (often permanent) movement of people **between** or **within** countries. **Immigration** is the movement of people **into a country** (or area) and **emigration** is the movement of people **out of a country** (or area).

The **reasons** for migration can be divided into **push** (**negative**) and **pull** (**positive**) factors:

> **Push factors** — these are things that **make** people want to **move out** of the place they're in. They're **negative factors** about the place they're **leaving**, e.g. **lack of jobs** or **poor living conditions** and **services**, fear of **political persecution**.
>
> **Pull factors** — these **attract** people to a **new place**. They're **positive factors** about the place they're **moving to**, e.g. **better jobs** and **more job opportunities**, **better** living conditions and **services**.

Hmm, he's got his own boat, but it's a shame about the beard. I'll give him a pull factor of 5.

Migration is also affected by **obstacles** and **opportunities**:

> **Obstacles** — these are things that make migration **more difficult**, e.g. the **cost** of moving.
>
> **Opportunities** — these are opportunities individuals **encounter** that mean they **stop** before they reach their **intended destination**, e.g. **Polish** migrants heading for **Ireland** for **work** might stop in **London** because there are plenty of **jobs** there.

Globalisation Can Encourage or Discourage Migration

Effects that encourage migration

1) **Open-door** policies between **EU members** — **anyone** from a country **within** the EU can **live** and **work** in **any other** EU country. (But **not all** EU countries **allow unlimited immigration** from **new** EU members, e.g. from **Poland**.)

2) **Ease of movement** of an international **elite** — **highly skilled** or **important** individuals are in **demand** around the world. **Globalisation** means they can go where they're **most needed** with **fewer restrictions** than other people, e.g. **footballers** move between **clubs** in **different countries** with relative **ease**.

3) **Increased urban investment** — investment from **Trans-National Corporations** (**TNCs**) is often **focused** on **urban areas**, which can cause an **increase** in **rural-urban migration** as people move for **new** or **better jobs**. E.g. **44%** of **Chinese** people live in urban areas **today** — it was **26%** in **1990**.

Effects that discourage migration

1) There are **restrictions** on migration **into** an **EU country** if you're **not** from one originally — **closer connections** between European countries makes migration **between** them **easier**, but makes it **more difficult** for people **outside** the EU. This is why Europe is sometimes called '**fortress Europe**' — it's **hard** to **enter**.

2) **Mexico** and the **USA** are **closely connected** by the **NAFTA trade bloc** (see p. 25), but this doesn't extend to the movement of **people** — migration **into** the USA is **strictly controlled** with a **heavily guarded border**.

Practice Questions

Q1 How do obstacles and opportunities affect migration?

Q2 Give three ways in which globalisation encourages migration.

Exam Question

Q1 Describe what is meant by push and pull factors. [4 marks]

Large, shiny tractors — rural pull factors...

Well, that page wasn't so bad — short and sweet with no case studies, just how I like them. Have another gander over it before you move on just to double check you know all about the causes of migration, and how globalisation affects it.

Population Basics

Right, before tackling the rest of the section it's a good idea to brush up on these population basics...

There are **Loads** of **Terms** and **Definitions** to Learn

1) **Birth rate** — the **number** of live **births** per 1000 people, per year.

2) **Death rate** — the **number** of **deaths** per 1000 people, per year.

3) **Fertility rate** — the **average number of children** a woman will have between the ages of **15** and **44** (**reproductive** age).

4) **Infant mortality rate** — the **number** of **children** (out of every 1000 born **alive**) who **die before their first birthday**.

5) **Life expectancy (longevity)** — the **average age** (in years) a person can **expect to live**.

6) **Migration rate** — the **difference** between the **number** of people who **migrate in** (**immigrants**), and the number of people who **migrate out** (**emigrants**) per **100 000** (or 1000) of the population, per year.

7) **Population density** — the **number** of people per **square kilometre** (km²).
It's the **total population** of an area **divided** by the **size of the area** (in km²).

8) **Changes in the population over time:**

   - **Natural change** — the change in population (**increase or decrease**) because of the **difference** between **birth rate** and **death rate** (not including changes due to **migration**). For example, when **birth rate > death rate**, the population will **grow naturally** (if migration rate is **zero**). When **death rate > birth rate**, the population will **fall** (unless enough people **migrate in**).
   - **Zero growth rate** — the population is **neither** increasing nor decreasing (e.g. **birth rate = death rate**).

< means 'less than'
> means 'more than'

The **Demographic Transition Model (DTM)** Shows **Population Change**

The **demographic transition model** (**DTM**) shows how the **population** of a country **changes** over time through **five stages**. The model shows changes in **birth rate**, **death rate** and **total population**.

'Demographic' means it's to do with human populations.

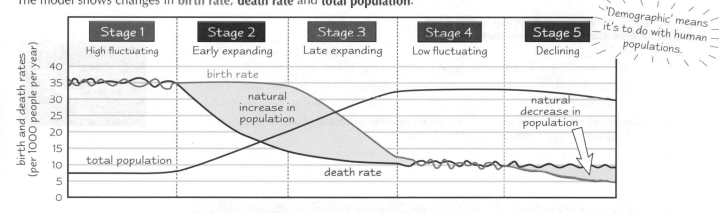

As Countries **Develop** They **Move Through** the **Stages** of the **DTM**

As countries become **more developed** their birth rate and death rate **change**, which causes the **total population to change**.

Stage 1 — high birth rate and high death rate

Birth rate and death rate **fluctuate** at a **high level** — the population remains **stable** but **low**. There **aren't any countries in Stage 1**, but some **tribes** in the rainforests of **Brazil** are in this stage.

1) **Birth rate is high** because there's **no birth control** or **family planning**, and **education is poor**.

2) It's also high because there's **high infant mortality**, so people have **more children** to replace those who've **died**.

3) **Death rate is high** and **life expectancy is low** because there's **poor health care**, **sanitation** and **diet** — leading to **disease** and **starvation**.

Population Basics

Stage 2 — high birth rate, death rate falls

Death rate **falls**, but birth rate remains **high** — the population **increases rapidly**.
Countries like **Nepal** and **Afghanistan** are in **Stage 2**.

1) **Birth rate** is still **high** as there's still **little birth control** or **family planning** and **education is poor**.

2) Birth rate also stays **high** for **labour reasons** — family members (including **children**) all have to **work**, e.g. on **farms**. A **larger** family can tend to a **larger** farm, helping to bring in **more food** and **money**.

3) **Death rate falls** and **life expectancy increases** due to improved **health care**, **sanitation** and **diet**.

Stage 3 — birth rate falls a lot and death rate falls slightly

Birth rate **declines rapidly**, while death rate **falls slowly** — the population **increases at a slower rate**.
Countries like **Egypt** are in **Stage 3**.

1) **Birth rate decreases** due to the **increased** use of **birth control** and **family planning**, and **improvements** in **education**.

2) The **birth rate** also **drops** as the **economy** moves towards **manufacturing** — **fewer children** are needed to **work** on farms, so having a **larger family** isn't as **advantageous** as it once was.

3) **Birth rate falls** further still as **more women work** rather than stay at home to have children.

4) Some countries introduce **government population policies** to try to **reduce the birth rate**.

Stage 4 — low birth rate and low death rate

Birth rate and death rate **fluctuate** at a **low level** — the population remains **stable** but **high**. Most **developed countries**, e.g. most of **Europe** and the **USA**, are in **Stage 4**. **Birth rate stays low** because **increased access** and **demand** for **luxuries** like **holidays** and **material possessions** means there's **less** money available for having children (they're **expensive** to raise). Also, there are **fewer advantages** to having children, e.g. they're **not needed** to work for the family.

Stage 5 — birth rate drops below death rate

Birth rate begins to **decline** further while death rate remains **stable** — the population begins to **decrease**. Some **highly developed** countries, e.g. **Japan**, are in **Stage 5**.

1) The **birth rate decreases** because children are **expensive** to raise and many people have **dependent** elderly relatives, so lots of people choose **not** to have children.

2) **Death rate** remains **steady** as there are **more elderly people** so more people die (of **old age**) despite **advances** in health care.

Hmm, have children or buy myself a shiny new car...

Population Structure is How the Population is Made Up

Population structure is the **number** or **%** of **males** and **females** in different **age groups** within a population. **Population pyramids (age-sex pyramids) show** population structure. You can **learn** a lot about the **demographics** of a place from its population pyramid. For example, the pyramid below shows the **population structure of France**:

(A) Some people are living to be **100**, which shows a **high life expectancy**.

(B) **Women** are living **longer** than **men**.

(C) There are **fewer** people aged **75-85**, because there was a **low birth rate** when they were **born** (around **World War 1** – WW1) and they've suffered from a **high death rate** (lots killed in **WW2**).

(D) There are also **fewer** people aged **50-60**, also because of a **low birth rate** when they were born (around **WW2**).

(E) There are **lots** of people aged **25-50** because of a **baby boom** after WW2.

(F) There are **fewer** people aged **0-10** because of a **low birth rate** for the last 10 years.

Population Basics

Population Structure Varies from Place to Place and Over Time

1) Population pyramids for **different countries** vary because of different **demographic factors** — **birth** and **death rates**, **fertility rates**, **wars**, **migration** etc.

2) A country's population structure **changes** through **time** as it moves through the **stages** of the **DTM** (see pages 33-34).

3) This means a **population pyramid shape** can show **which** stage of the DTM a country is in:

Stage 1	Stage 2	Stage 3	Stage 4	Stage 5
High birth and death rates. Low life expectancy.	High birth rate, falling death rate and long life expectancy. Population explosion.	Falling birth and death rates. More people live to be elderly.	Low birth and death rates. High life expectancy and lots of elderly people.	Birth rate drops below death rate and population declines. Increasing numbers of elderly.

Migration Can Change Population Structure

Migration can **alter population structure**, which can be seen in the **population pyramids** for the areas affected. Migration can affect **any part** of the population pyramid — it depends **how old** the migrants are. Here are some examples:

1) **Internal migration (migration within a country)**

Internal migration from **rural** areas to **urban** areas often affects the number of **young adults** (people of **working** and **reproductive age**). They **move away** from the countryside **into** the cities to find **jobs**. This is called **rural-urban migration**. This can **affect birth rate** too as the migrants are of reproductive age.

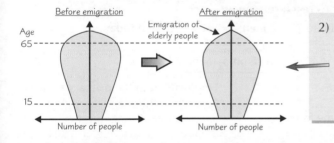

2) **Emigration away from countries at later DTM stages**

Emigration **away** from countries at **later** DTM stages **into** other countries **decreases the population** of the country they've left. E.g. **elderly people** in the **UK** retiring and emigrating to other countries. This **reduces** the number of elderly in the UK, but **increases** the number in the countries they **move to**.

3) **Immigration into countries at later DTM stages**

Immigration **into** countries at **later** DTM stages (e.g. MEDCs) **from** those at **earlier** DTM stages (e.g. LEDCs) **increases the population** of people of **working** and **reproductive age**. This **increases** the population of young people and **increases birth rate**. For example, immigration **into** the UK (Stage 4).

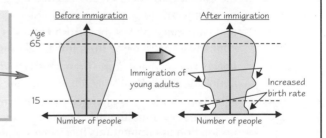

Practice Questions

Q1 What is population structure?

Q2 What do population pyramids show?

Exam Question

Q1 The table shows some population data for a country since 1600. With reference to the DTM, describe and explain the changes in the population shown by the data. [10 marks]

Date	Birth rate (per 1000 per year)	Death rate (per 1000 per year)	Population (millions)
1600	38	37	2
1800	35	18	7
1850	26	15	15
1900	18	12	21
1950	12	10	26
2000	8	10	28

Rabbits never seem to get much past Stage 2...

It's a good idea to know your way around the DTM and to understand what different population pyramids show.

Changes in the UK Population Since 1900

The population's changed loads in the last 100-odd years. Some of it's to do with stuff that's gone on in the UK (e.g. changing governments) and some of it's caused by global issues (e.g. war). Let's get factualising...

The **Population** of the **UK** Has **Changed** During the **20th Century**

The **population** of the UK has **changed** in lots of ways **since** the **1900s**:

Family size

1) **Family size fell** during the **early 20th century**, then **increased** towards the **mid-20th century**. In **1900** women had an average of **3.5 children** during their **reproductive years** (15-44), but women born in the **1920s** had only **2.07** (probably due to WW2). It rose after this to **2.46** for women born in **1934** (due to a **baby boom** after WW2).

2) Family size **fell** again **later** in the 20th century — for women born in **1955** it was **2.03** children.

3) It's expected to **fall even further** — women born in the **1980s** are **projected** to have an average of **1.74** children.

4) So women are having **fewer children** and **more women** are remaining **childless**:
   - **40%** of women born in **1934** had **three or more** children, but since then it has **fallen** to around **30%**.
   - **9%** of women born in **1945** had **no children**, but this might **rise** to **20%** for women born in the **1980s**.

Population structure

1) The **population pyramid** (see p. 34) of the UK **today** shows how the population structure has **changed**:
   - The **bulges** at **60 years old** and at **35-45** show that there was a **high birth rate** in the **40s** and **60s**.
   - The **dips** in population around **30 years** and at **5-15** show a **drop in birth rate** in the late **70s** and **90s**.

2) Today, about a **fifth** of the population is made up of the **under 16s** and about a **fifth** the over **60s**. This has changed from a **higher proportion** of **under 16s** when the larger generations were young, e.g. in the 1940s and 50s. In the future, it'll change to a **higher proportion** of **over 60s**, as the larger generations **reach retirement**.

3) **Life expectancy** has also **increased** from around **50** in **1900** to **77** for **men** and **81** for **women today**.

Migration and Ethnicity

See pages 40 and 42 for more on migration to the UK.

1) **Before WW2** many **Germans** (particularly **Jews**) and **Irish people** migrated to the UK. After the war, **immigrants** came from the countries of the then **Soviet Union**, e.g. **Ukraine**.

2) In the **50s-70s** large numbers of immigrants came from countries that were once part of the **British Empire** (**Commonwealth countries**). Most came from **India**, **Pakistan** and the **Caribbean**.

3) Lots of people have come from **central** and **eastern European** countries like **Poland** since they joined the EU in 2004.

4) All this migration has **changed** the **ethnic mix** of the UK — we're now a **multicultural country**. About **15%** of the population are **immigrants** themselves or are **descended** from immigrants. For example, there are now **over 1 million** UK **citizens** who class themselves as **Indian**.

Employment

1) **Employment** in the **primary sector** (e.g. **agriculture**) and **secondary sector** (e.g. **manufacturing**) has **declined** in the last 100 years. E.g. in **1901**, about **51%** of jobs were in the secondary sector, but this had fallen to **20%** by **2001**.

2) **Mechanisation** has meant fewer jobs in agriculture, whilst manufacturing **industries** have **moved abroad** where there's **cheaper labour**.

3) **Improvements** in **education** have led to a **rise** in **tertiary sector** jobs (e.g. **banking** and **insurance**), up from about **40%** in **1901**, to **78%** by **2001**.

Social status

Social class can be defined by things like **education** and **occupation**. The **main traditional** social classes in the UK are:

1) **Upper class** — the **nobility**, often people who hold **titles** or have **inherited wealth**.

2) **Middle class** — usually **highly educated** people with **professional** jobs and **above average** earnings, e.g. **doctors**.

3) **Working class** — **less well educated** people with **semi-skilled** or **unskilled jobs** with **below average** earnings, e.g. workers in **car assembly plants**.

It's thought that the social classes have been **changing**, e.g. the middle class is **growing** as the number of people in **higher education increases**, causing an **increase** in the **average wage** and **higher-class** activities like **skiing holidays**.

Changes in the UK Population Since 1900

Changes in Population are Caused by Internal and External Factors

Changes to the population of the UK have been caused by **internal factors** (things happening **within** the UK) and **external factors** (things happening on a **global scale** that affect the UK).

Internal factors

1) **Family size (e.g. fertility rate)**
   - The **suffragette movement** (early 20th century) — the **equal rights** movement for women led to changes in **attitude**, giving women more **freedom**. This caused a **reduction** in **birth rate** as women felt free to pursue their **own careers** and **delay** having children, or have **fewer children**.
   - **Legalisation of abortion** (1967) — more women could choose **not to have a child**.

2) **Population structure (e.g. life expectancy)**
   Establishment of the NHS (1948) — **free health care** for everyone led to **increased** life expectancy.

3) **Employment and social status**
   Increasing A-level and university take-up — greater levels of education have caused changes in **employment**, e.g. more **jobs** in the **tertiary sector**, and changes to **social status**, e.g. **increasing** numbers of **middle class**.

4) **Migration**
   More jobs created in the tertiary sector — this has been focused around the **south-east** of the UK. But the **loss of jobs** caused by the **decline** of the **secondary sector** has mostly affected the **north**. This has led to the **internal economic migration** of people to the south-east (the **south-east drift**).

External factors

1) **Family size (e.g. fertility rate)**
   - **Periods of global recession** — during global recessions (e.g. the great depression of 1929) people have **less money**, which means they **can't afford** to have lots of children. So birth rate **decreases**.
   - **Global conflict** — birth rates **fell** during the two World Wars because of the **economic stresses** of war and because men were **away from home**. After World War 2 there was a **baby boom** — birth rate **increased**.

2) **Population structure (e.g. life expectancy)**
   Decrease in dangerous jobs — the number of jobs that cause **poor health** and **loss of life**, e.g. in **mining**, has declined. Workers in the UK now carry out **less dangerous** work, so **life expectancy** has **increased**.

3) **Employment**
   Loss of manufacturing to overseas — factories have been **moved** to other countries where there's **cheaper labour**, e.g. **NICs** (see p. 24). This has caused a **decline** in the **secondary sector** in the UK, so many people have **lost** their job or have had to **change** jobs.

4) **Migration**
   Open-door policies — EU membership means people from other member countries can **live and work** in the UK. This has **increased immigration** into the UK.

You Can Research the Changes in Population in Your Local Area

The changes in population are **different** in different **parts** of the country, e.g. immigrants aren't **spread out evenly** — they tend to settle in particular areas. You can **research** how the population has changed over the last century in your **local area**:

1) Look at **census data** — a census is carried out every **10 years** in the UK. It's a survey where **data** is collected about the **whole population**, including things like **employment**, **family size** and **ethnic background**. The data goes as far back as **1841** and it's available on the internet. You can look at how the data has changed for your local area over the last 100 years.

2) Research your own **family history** (**genealogy**) — look at changes in things like **employment**, **family size** and if any members of your family **migrated** to the UK. You can research it by talking to **older members** of your family, or carry out research in a **local library** or on **genealogy websites**.

Practice Questions

Q1   Describe how family size has changed in the UK throughout the 20th century.

Q2   Outline one external factor that's caused changes to employment in the UK.

Exam Question

Q1   Describe and explain how internal factors have caused changes in the UK population in the 20th century.   [10 marks]

I say, this census makes no sense-us...

You need to learn all about the changes in population that have occurred in the UK since the 1900s, e.g. changes in family size, population structure, etc. You also need to carry out your own research into how it's been changing in your local area. What fun...

Impacts of an Ageing Population

Some countries (like Australia) are full of kangaroos and others (like the UK) are full of old people...

The **Dependency Ratio** Shows **How Much** of the **Population** is **Dependent**

The **dependency ratio** gives the **proportion** of the population that has to be **supported** by the **working population** (aged **15-64**). **Young people** (aged **0-14**) and **older people** (**over 65**) are generally **dependent** on the working population — they need to be **looked after** or **supported financially**. The **equation** for the dependency ratio is given below:

$$\text{Dependency ratio} = \frac{\text{Young people (0-14) + Old people (over 65)}}{\text{Working age population (15-64)}}$$

A **high dependency ratio** means there's a **greater proportion** of dependent people, e.g. **Uganda** has a **high dependency** ratio of **1.1** — there's **more than one** dependent person for **each** working person.

There are **Social** and **Economic** Impacts of an **Ageing Population**

An **ageing** (or **greying**) **population** means the **proportion** of older people is **increasing**, which causes an **increase** in the **dependency** ratio. This has **social** and **economic effects**:

Social

1) **Increased pressure on public services** — there's **greater demand** for services like **hospitals** and **hospices**. **More** people are needed to **care** for the elderly, so **more carers** and **nurses** will need **training**. Also, more people will act as **unpaid carers** to their **own** elderly family members, putting pressure on them **socially** and **financially**.

2) **Unequal distribution of older people** — e.g. **Eastbourne** in the UK is a **resort** with a high proportion of **retired**, older people. Areas like this may have **inadequate facilities** for **young people**, e.g. **bars** or **youth clubs**.

3) **Reduced population growth or population decline** — the working population may have **fewer children** because they already have older dependants, leading to a **reduction** in **birth rate**.

4) **Longer working life** — the **state pension** is **low** because there are **so many** retired people. It's often **not enough** to support people in their retirement so some may have to **work beyond** normal **retirement age** — to build up **personal pensions** or **savings**, or to **add to their income** from the state pension.

Economic

1) **Reduced work force** — a **smaller proportion** of the population is working, which may **slow economic growth**.

2) **Increased taxes** — **pensions** and **services** are paid for by **taxes**. A greater proportion of older people **claiming** pensions and support could mean **higher taxes** for the working population.

3) **Spending** — the elderly have **savings** and **pensions** to spend (the **grey pound**).

Case Study — The **UK** Has an **Ageing Population**

See pages 36-37 for more on how the UK population has changed.

Like most **wealthy** and **developed countries**, the population of the UK is **ageing** (it's a **greying population**) — people **over 65** make up a **large part** of the population and it's **increasing**. In **2005**, **16%** of the population of the UK were **over 65**. This is expected to rise to **25%** by **2041** — here are a few reasons **why**:

1) **Increasing life expectancy** — between **1980** and **2006** life expectancy **rose 2.8** years for **women** and **4** years for **men**. It's currently **81.3** for **women** and **76.9** for **men**. As people live **longer**, the number of older people **increases**.

2) **Baby booms** — **lots of babies** were born in the **1940s** and **60s**. These large generations are starting to **retire**, **increasing** the number of elderly people.

3) **Falling birth rate** — there are **fewer** young people, so the **proportion** of older people is **greater**.

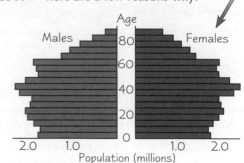

Impacts of an Ageing Population

The Ageing UK Population Causes Problems

1) **Pressure on the pension system** — there aren't enough people of **working-age** to pay for an **adequate pension** for the **retired** population. **State pensions** are paid for by the **working population** through **taxes**.

   - Today, **60%** of the population (the people of **working-age**) are paying taxes that go towards the pensions of **19%** of the population (the people of **retirement age**).
   - By **2030**, only **56%** of the population will be of **working-age** but the taxes they pay will have to pay for the pensions of the **27%** of the population of **retirement age**.

2) **More elderly people living in poverty** — the state pension **isn't very large**, and many people don't have **other savings**. The working population **isn't large enough** to provide a **better pension** (see above).

3) **Pressure on the health service** — older people often need **more medical care** than younger people, e.g. the average stay in hospital in **2005** for people **over 75** was **13** nights, but only **8** nights for the UK population **as a whole**.

Different Strategies Aim to Manage the Ageing UK Population

1 The age of retirement has been increased — retirement age in the UK is currently **65** for men and **60** for women, but it will be raised to **68** for everyone by **2050**. Increasing the retirement age means people have to work for **longer**, increasing the size of the **working population**.

2 Encouraging immigration of working-age people — the UK has allowed **unlimited immigration** of people from countries who joined the **EU in 2004**, e.g. **Poland**. In 2004, around **80%** of immigrants that came to the UK from the **new EU countries** were **34 or under**. This also **increases** the size of the **working population**.

3 Encouraging more women to have children — new UK **pension** proposals mean **women** won't lose out on **state pensions** if they take **career breaks** to have children. This could encourage women to have children. **Working family tax credits** support women (and men) who go back to **work** once their children are born, which might also encourage **more couples** to have children.

Practice Questions

Q1 What does the dependency ratio tell you about a country or area?
Q2 Give two reasons why the UK has an ageing population.
Q3 Describe one problem caused by the ageing population in the UK.
Q4 Describe one strategy aimed to manage the ageing UK population.

Exam Question

Q1 Describe and explain the social and economic impacts of an ageing population. [10 marks]

Right, time to move on — these pages are getting old...

There are plenty of undesirable impacts of an ageing population (which reminds me... you need to learn them), but lots of old people isn't all bad — they often look after grandchildren for free, which means parents can go out to work and earn more money.

Migration into Europe

Europe's totally the place to move to — it's soooooo in vogue these days, darling.

> A migrant is a person who has moved to a new area or country.

There are **Different Types** of **Migrant**

Economic migrants — people who **move abroad** to find **work** or a **better paid job**.

Voluntary migrants — people who move because they **want to**.
Involuntary migrants — people who are **forced to move** against their will.

Asylum seekers and refugees — people who move because they're at **risk**, e.g. from **war** or **persecution**. Asylum seekers apply for **permission to live** in a country (**asylum**), but if it's **denied** they're **refused entry**, or may be **sent back** (**deported**).

Illegal immigrants — people who **enter** or **stay** in a country **without permission**. Illegal immigration may be for **economic reasons**, or it may be to **escape war** or **persecution**. Illegal immigrants may be people who've applied for asylum, been **rejected** and have **stayed on**, or they may be people who've **crossed the border** without the country **knowing** about it.

Lots of People **Migrated into Europe** from **Former Colonies...**

Before the **mid-20th century**, some **European countries** had been **colonising** other places around the world, building **empires**, e.g. the **British Empire** included **India**, **Australia** and some **Caribbean** islands.
After **World War 2**, these empires **broke up** and there was a flow of people **into Europe**. This is called **post-colonial flow**.

1) Immigrants from the **former British Empire** — the **British Government invited** people from the **former colonies** to migrate to the **UK** where there was a **shortage of labour** and **lots of work** available to rebuild the **damaged economy**:

   - More than **60 000 Indians** had **migrated** to the **UK** by the **mid-1950s**. A shortage of trained UK doctors meant the NHS **recruited** many doctors from India, as well as Pakistan, Bangladesh and Sri Lanka. There are currently more than **1 million** people in the UK who describe themselves as **Indian**.
   - People from the **Caribbean islands** began emigrating to the **UK** in large numbers in **1948**. Today there are around **550 000** people in the UK who describe themselves as **Caribbean**.

2) Immigrants from the **former French empire** — from the 1950s to the 1970s loads of **people** migrated into **France** from **former French colonies** in **North Africa** (e.g. **Algeria**, **Tunisia** and **Morocco**). Many were **economic migrants** attracted by **jobs** created by **labour shortages** (lack of workers). Others were **fleeing persecution** occurring as colonies gained independence, e.g. around **1 million** people fled Algeria between 1962 and 1964 after it **became independent** in 1962.

...and from **Other Countries**

People have also migrated **into Europe** from countries that **aren't former colonies**:

1) West **Germany** made up for its **shortage of labour** in the **1960s** by **inviting** workers over from **Turkey** (**economic migrants**). **Today** there are more than **1.7 million Turks living** in Germany.

2) A lot of **asylum seekers** were created by the invasion of **Iraq** in **2003** (around **2 million** people). **Sweden** has accepted over **40 000** of these.

3) Huge numbers of **illegal immigrants** enter Europe every year, e.g. many **Africans** try to cross the **strait of Gibraltar** (the narrow gap between **Morocco** and **Spain**). It's **not known** how many people **try** to get across, but in **2001**, **45 000** people were caught and **refused entry** to Spain alone. Many people **die** in the attempt to cross.

Links Between **Europe** and the **Wider World** Explain **Migration Patterns**

1) **Former colonies** have **political links** (e.g. systems of **government**), **economic links** (e.g. flows of **trade**) and **cultural links** (e.g. a **shared religion**) with the country that used to **rule them**. People like to migrate to countries that they have some **familiarity** with.

2) Countries are **linked** by ties between **family** and **friends**, because migrants usually leave **people they know behind**. Migrants are often later **joined** by family and friends, who move to a country because they **already know someone** there.

3) Countries are **linked** by a **shared language**. For example, migrants whose **first language** is English (e.g. from **Australia** and **South Africa**) have come to Britain to **work** and **study**. Others might speak English as their **second language**, e.g. migrants from **India**. Sharing a language makes it easier to **find work** and become **integrated** into a new **society**.

Migration into Europe

Migration into Europe Has Many Consequences

A destination country is where migrants are heading to. A source country is where they've come from.

Demographic

Migration changes the **population structure** (see p. 34) of the **destination** and **source** countries.

- **Source** countries will have a **reduced proportion** of people of **working** and **reproductive age**. **Destination** countries will have an **increased proportion** of people of **working** and **reproductive age**.

- An **increase** in the number of people of **reproductive age** may **increase birth rate** in **destination** countries, e.g. around 25% of children born in the UK in 2006 had at least one parent who had migrated from another country. A **decrease** in the number of people of **reproductive age** may **decrease birth rate** in **source** countries.

Economic

Many migrant workers **send money back** to families in their **country of origin**. E.g. in **2006** over **$25 billion** was sent back to **India** from other countries. This money can form a large part of the **national income** (GDP, see p. 42) in poorer **source** countries. **Destination** countries **lose out** because the migrant workers **earn** the money in that country, but it gets **spent** in another country.

Social

Illegal immigrants (see previous page) don't have access to legal **employment**, **healthcare** or **benefits**. They live in the destination country **illegally**, so if they try to access these things they risk being **deported**. They may carry out **dangerous work** for **little pay**, e.g. in **2004 more than 20** illegal immigrants from **China drowned** when picking cockles in **Morecambe Bay** in the **UK**.

Cultural

1) Migrants bring their own **culture** (e.g. their **religion**) to the countries they move to. This has caused problems of **racial tension** in some countries, e.g. there was widespread **rioting** across **France** in **2005** because **immigrant communities** didn't think they were being treated **fairly**.

2) Where immigrant groups from several **different countries** have settled, you get a **mixture of different cultures**. This leads to new **hybrid cultures** of **music**, **fashion** and **food**, e.g. **Indian** food has become so popular in the UK that some **new dishes** have been created **specifically** for the **UK** population.

Political

1) Large numbers of immigrants can lead to **changes** in **government policies**, e.g. the UK government is changing its policy on **immigration** to a **points-based system**. Points are awarded based on an immigrant's **age**, **skills** and **experience**. They get **more points** if their age, skills and experience **match** what the **UK needs**. Migrants are allowed to **stay** and **work** if they have enough points.

2) **Racial tensions** have led to some **nationalist political parties** becoming **more popular**, e.g. the **British National Party** (**BNP**) is a political party that thinks there **shouldn't be any more immigration** to the UK. They've **become more popular** — in the 2006 local elections they **more than doubled** the number of **political seats** they held.

Environmental

Travel by planes and ships causes **pollution** and migration means a **lot of people** travel **long distances**. This leads to increased CO_2 **emissions**, which increases **global warming** (see p. 13).

Practice Questions

Q1 Describe one major migration of people into Europe from a former colony.

Q2 Explain one link between Europe and the wider world that might encourage migration to Europe.

Exam Question

Q1 Discuss the consequences of migration into Europe. [10 marks]

No Terry, this page is about Euro-revision, not Eurovision...

I'm assuming all the people that want to migrate to Europe haven't seen the Eurovision Song Contest. Most people migrate to Europe to make a better life (not for the music). This has consequences for Europe and the countries they've come from.

Intra-EU Migration

As if all this global movement wasn't complicated enough, people are dashing about within Europe too. Crikey.

Many People Have Migrated from Poland to the UK

People who come from a country **within the EU** can live and work in **any other EU country**. When **new countries** join the EU the **current members** can **choose not to allow immigration** from the new countries for a **few years**. In 2004, 10 countries in **central** and **eastern Europe** became new members of the EU, including **Poland**. Between **2004** and **2007**, more than **half a million** people from **Poland** migrated to the **UK** — most were **economic migrants**.

Here are a few reasons why they decided to **leave Poland** (**push factors**, see p. 32):

> When people move from newly joined countries it's called post-accession flow.

1) **High unemployment** — around **19%** in **2004**. People of working-age **left** Poland to **find work** in the UK — they were **economic migrants** (see p. 40).

2) **Low average wages**. People of working-age **left** Poland to find **higher wages**, e.g. the **average income** in the EU in 2004 was nearly **three times greater** than it was in Poland.

3) **Low availability of housing**. People left Poland because there **weren't enough houses** for them to move into, e.g. in **2004** there were just over **300 dwellings** for every **1000 people**.

Here are a few reasons why they decided to **come to the UK** (**pull factors**, see p. 32):

1) **Ease of migration**. Only the **UK**, **Ireland** and **Sweden** decided to **allow unlimited migration** from the new member countries in **2004**. Other countries **restricted entry**, but they will have to allow it by 2011.

2) **Good exchange rate**. A few pounds earnt in the UK were worth **lots of zloty** (Polish currency, **one pound** was worth **seven zloty** in 2004), so migrants could **send a few pounds** back to Poland and it would make a **big difference**.

3) **Plenty of jobs** and **better paid jobs**. There was a **labour shortage** for certain occupations in the UK, e.g. a shortage of **tradesmen** such as **plumbers** (who are also **paid more** in the UK than in Poland).

Migration Has Consequences for Both Poland and the UK

Demographic
Poland's population has **shrunk** because so many people have **migrated** to other countries, e.g. it **fell 0.3%** between **2003** and **2007**. The **birth rate** also **decreased** between **2003** and **2005**, partly because a lot of the people that have left are of **reproductive age**. The population of the UK has **increased** as a result (especially those of **reproductive** age).

Economic
The UK economy **loses out** because money **earnt** in the **UK** by **Polish** workers **isn't all spent** in the UK. The Polish economy **grows** because money is **sent back** to Poland by migrants, e.g. in 2006, around **€3.45 billion** was sent to Poland from abroad. Migration has also had a **bad effect** on the Polish economy — there's a **shortage of labourers** (most migrants were of **working-age**) so **less work** can be done, which means the economy **doesn't grow as much**.

Social
Migration of working-age people has **helped** the problems caused by the UK's **ageing-population** (see p. 39). Young migrant workers **pay taxes** and these are used to **support** the older retired people, e.g. they pay for **pensions**.

Cultural
Shops selling **Polish products** have **opened** in areas where lots of Polish people have **settled**, e.g. the **West Midlands**. The number of people attending **Catholic church services** in the UK has **increased** because most of the Polish migrants are **Catholic**.

Political
The **immigration policy** of the UK has been **changed** because of the **influx** of **Polish migrants**. When **Romania** and **Bulgaria** joined the EU in **2007**, the UK **didn't allow unlimited migration** like it had for Poland.

Environmental
Increased immigration from Poland has meant **more air traffic** between **Poland** and the **UK**, e.g. there were just over **500 000** passengers to and from the UK in **2003** and 3.3 million in **2006**. Increased air traffic means more **greenhouse gases** are released, making **global warming** worse (see p. 13).

Migration to the UK Might Not be Permanent

In **2008** lots of migrants **moved back** to Poland. Here are a few reasons **why**:

1) **Less work** is available in the **UK** — the economy of the UK is thought to be **shrinking**, so **less money** is being spent on things like **house renovation**, which means there's **less work** for tradesmen.

2) **More work** is available in **Poland** — the economy is **growing**, providing more work. Poland's **GDP** (the total value of goods produced and services provided) **grew by 6.5%** in 2007.

3) **Less favourable exchange rate** — **one pound** was worth about **4.5 zloty** in **November 2008**. This means the money immigrants send back **isn't worth as much** as it was in **2004**.

Intra-EU Migration

Many People Have Migrated from the UK to Spain

Lots of people **migrate** to **Spain** from the **UK** when they **retire**. The largest numbers migrated in the **1980s** and **90s**, and more are **still going**. It's difficult to know **exact numbers** because lots of people move **temporarily** — they live in **Spain** for **part** of the year, and in the **UK** for **part** of the year. It's thought that around **1 million** British people own a **property** in Spain.

There are **push factors** (see p. 32):

1) The **cost of living** is **rising** in the UK. Shopping, fuel, electricity and mortgage payments are getting **more expensive**, but people's earnings **aren't increasing** at the **same rate**, so they have **less to spend** on **other things**.

2) The **UK** has a **cool, wet** and **changeable** climate.

There are **pull factors** (see p. 32):

1) The **cost of living** is **lower** in **Spain**, so people have **more money** to spend on **other things**.

2) **Spain** has a **hot, dry** and **less changeable** climate than the **UK**. Retired people move because they **prefer the Spanish climate**.

Spain and the **UK** have become more **interlinked**, making it **easier** for people to **migrate**.

1) The increase in **budget air travel** from companies like **EasyJet** has meant that people can **afford** to visit **family** and **friends** they've **left** in the **UK several times** a year.

2) **Improved communications** such as **cheap telephone calls** and use of the **internet** means people can keep in **close contact** even when they're living **far away**, e.g. Skype™ allows people to make **free calls** over the **internet**.

There are Consequences for the UK and Spain

Demographic

The **population structure** of the UK and Spain is **altered**. The people that **retire** to **Spain** are mostly older (**over 65**) so the population structure of **Spain** will have a **greater proportion** of older people, while the **UK** will have a **reduced proportion** of older people.

Environmental

Many UK migrants don't live in Spain **all year** (e.g. there were about **230 000** part-time residents in **2008**) — they regularly **return** to the UK. This leads to **increasing air traffic**, which causes **more pollution**.

Social

A lot of migrants were in their **50s** or **60s** when they migrated in the **1980s** and **90s**. They're now reaching an age where they'll need more **long-term medical care**. It's **not known** whether the Spanish **health system** will be able to **cope**. Also, **UK-born Spanish residents** don't have the **same right** to **health care** in the **UK** as UK residents do, e.g. they don't qualify for things like **nursing home places**.

Cultural

UK migrants have set up **communities** with **British-run shops** and **restaurants**. Some **don't speak Spanish** so they don't **interact** with the **local community**. This can lead to **tensions** between UK migrants and local people.

Economic

Jobs are created in Spain to provide for the **needs** of UK migrants, e.g. more **home help** and **construction workers** to build houses. UK migrants **spend** their **savings** in **Spain** instead of the **UK**, **helping** the Spanish economy to **grow**, whilst the UK economy **loses out**.

Political

Local elections in Spain are affected by UK immigrants — they have the **right to vote**, and many are standing as **candidates** in local elections. E.g. more than **100 UK immigrants** stood as candidates in local elections in **2007**. Also, some Spanish people think the **health care** that UK migrants receive should be **paid for** by the **UK NHS**.

Practice Questions

Q1 Describe one push factor and one pull factor that help to explain why people in Poland migrate to the UK.

Q2 Describe one push factor and one pull factor that help to explain why retired people in the UK migrate to Spain.

Exam Question

Q1 Using a named example, discuss the reasons for intra-EU migration and the consequences it has for the countries involved.

[10 marks]

Entrance to the UK — if your name's not down, you're not comin' in...

People migrate when they've got good reasons to — they don't want to stay where they are (push factors), and they're drawn towards another place (pull factors). Unlike my herd of Pushmi-pullyus — they don't know whether they're coming or going.

Rural-Urban Migration

Lots of people are heading for the cities to seek their fortune where the streets are paved with gold. It's mostly happening in countries that are developing quickly, like China. Maybe I'll book a holiday to one of these cities of gold...

Most Population Movement is Rural-Urban Migration

Rural-urban migration is the **movement of people** from **rural areas** (areas with a **low population density**, e.g. the **countryside**) to **urban areas** (areas with a **high population density**, e.g. **towns** and **cities**). It causes **urbanisation**, which is the **growth** in the **proportion** of people living in **urban areas**.

More than **50%** of the world's population live in **urban areas** (**3.4 billion** people) and this is **increasing**. **Urbanisation differs** between **developed** and **developing** countries:

- **Most** of the population in **developed** countries **already live** in **urban areas**, e.g. more than **80%** of the **UK's** population live in urban areas.

- This is because most **rural-urban migration** in **developed countries** has **already happened**, e.g. in the **late 18th** and **early 19th century** in the **UK** (during the **Industrial Revolution**).

- **Less** of the population in developing countries **currently** live in urban areas, e.g. around **25%** of the population of **Bangladesh** live in urban areas.

- Most **rural-urban migration** that's happening in the **world today** is going on in **developing countries** — it's causing **rapid urbanisation** (see p. 46).

There are Many Factors Causing Rural-Urban Migration

Migration to **urban areas** in **developing** countries is **triggered** by **two** main factors:

1) **Foreign investment** from **TNCs** (see p. 26) is **concentrated** in **urban** areas because the **population density** is **high**, so there's access to a **large workforce**. This means **new job opportunities** are created in urban areas.

2) **Increased access** to **technologies** (like **television** and **radio**) as well as **transport links** (like **road networks**) mean people in **rural** areas **learn more** about the **opportunities** available in **urban areas**.

Here are a few reasons why people **leave rural areas** in **developing** countries (**push factors**, see p. 32):

1) **Inconsistent income** and **food supply** — in rural areas many people are **subsistence farmers**. They grow **food** to meet the needs of their **family** and sell any **extra** to make a **small income**. Crop failures can mean they make **no income** and even risk **starvation**.

2) **Overpopulation** in rural areas — there are **too many** people for the **resources** in many rural areas, e.g. not enough land for everyone to **farm**.

3) **Low standard of living** — there's often little access to adequate **health care** and **education**, and the **demand** is **high** because **birth rates** are **high**. Not everyone has access to **electricity** or a **clean water supply**.

Here are a few reasons why people **migrate to urban areas** in **developing** countries (**pull factors**, see p. 32):

1) **Job opportunities** — **more** jobs are available in **urban** areas.
2) **Higher wages** — jobs in urban areas usually offer a **higher** and **more stable income**.
3) **Higher standard of living** — better access to **health care** and **education**. Also, **greater access** to things like a **clean water supply** and **electricity**.

Yee-haw! We're a-heading for the city.

Rural-Urban Migration Creates Million Cities and Megacities

Increasing rural-urban migration means **metropolitan areas** (**cities** and the surrounding areas from which people commute to that city) are **growing**, helping to create more **million cities** and **megacities** around the world:

- **Million cities** are cities with a population of **1 million people or more** — there are more than **400** of them.
- **Megacities** are metropolitan areas with a population of **over 10 million people** — there are more than **22** megacities.

Most **new** million cities and megacities are being created in **developing countries** in **Africa** and **Asia** where the **greatest rates** of **rural-urban migration** are taking place.

Rural-Urban Migration

China's Experiencing Massive Rural-Urban Migration

There are a **huge number** of people migrating from rural to urban areas in **China**.

1) **300 million rural Chinese** people are now thought to live in **cities**, e.g. in **1990** around **74%** of the population lived in **rural areas**, but in **2006** it had decreased to around **56%**.

2) There's a movement of people **towards** the **east coast** because most of the **cities** in China are **concentrated** there, e.g. **Beijing** and **Shanghai**.

3) Rural-urban migration in China has helped to create lots of **million cities**, e.g. there are **more than 90** cities with a population of more than 1 million people in China **today**.

Ready, set, migrate!

Rural-Urban Migration in China is Caused by Different Factors

Rural-urban migration in China has been **triggered** by a couple of factors:

1) **Foreign investment** from **TNCs** (see p. 26) — lots of companies have opened **factories** in **urban areas** in China. This has created **jobs**, **attracting** people from rural areas, e.g. **Ford** has a large factory in **Nanjing**, north-west of **Shanghai**.

2) **Technologies** and **transport links spread knowledge** to **rural** areas about **opportunities** in **urban** areas. **China National Highway 312** is a **4800-km** road from the major urban areas in the **east** (e.g. **Shanghai** and **Nanjing**), through the **rural central areas** to the major city in the far **west** (**Urumqi**). People in **rural** areas **find out about** the **opportunities** available in the **urban** areas to the **east** and **west** because of the **highway**.

Here's why people are **leaving rural areas** in China (**push factors**, see p. 32):

1) **High unemployment** — the use of more **machinery** has made agriculture more **efficient**, which has meant **fewer workers** are needed in **rural areas**. This has created **high unemployment**, e.g. **150 million** rural people were unemployed in **2004**. So people have been **leaving** rural areas to **find work**.

2) **Poverty** — in 2004 there were **26.1 million** people in **rural areas** in **absolute poverty** (too poor to afford enough **food** and **clothing**). People have been **leaving** rural areas to **escape poverty**.

3) **Lower standard of living** — **services** like **education** and **health care** are funded by taxes collected within the **local area**. This means poor rural areas don't have the **money** to improve their **services**, so people **leave** to **improve** their standard of living.

Here's why people are **migrating to urban areas** in China (**pull factors**, see p. 32):

1) **Higher employment** — large-scale **industrialisation** since the 1970s has focused on **urban** areas. Large numbers of **manufacturing jobs** have been **created** by **foreign** companies (**TNCs**, see above) and by **Chinese** companies.

2) **Higher wages** — average income is **three times higher** in **urban** areas than **rural** areas (and the **difference** is getting **bigger**). People migrate to urban areas to **increase their income** and **escape poverty**.

3) **Higher standard of living** — the **quality** and **availability** of services like **education** and **health care** is better in urban areas because there's more **money** available to pay for **them**, e.g. in **1998** there were **7 doctors per 1000** people in **urban** areas and **1 doctor per 1000 people** in **rural** areas. People migrate to urban areas to have **better access** to **adequate** services.

Practice Questions

Q1 Define rural-urban migration.
Q2 Describe one factor that triggers rural-urban migration in developing countries.
Q3 What's the definition of a megacity?

Exam Question

Q1 Describe the push and pull factors for rural-urban migration in a named country. [10 marks]

Megacity — wasn't he a massive, seriously evil robot...

Basically, rural-urban migration is the mother of all migrations and it means loads of enormous cities are popping up in a lot of places. It happens because people are pushed out of rural areas and pulled towards urban areas. All sounds a bit rough to me.

Megacities

Remember, megacities are urban areas with a population of 10 million people or more. *The cycle of urbanisation isn't really a cycle — cities don't start back at the beginning once they've been through all four stages.*

Cities *Undergo* a *Cycle of Urbanisation*

The **different patterns** of population **movement** that happen in cities make up the **cycle of urbanisation**. Cities **don't** just go through the stages **one by one** though — **different population movements** can be happening in a city at the **same time**.

1 Urbanisation
- The **growth** in the **proportion** of people living in **urban areas**.
- It occurs because of **migration** — especially **rural-urban migration** (see pages 44-45).
- Urbanisation is happening **quickly** in **developing countries** (where most megacities have recently developed) because of the massive **rural-urban migration**. One of the ways the cities have **grown** is by poor migrants setting up **shanty towns** — **unplanned** and often **illegal** settlements where people build their own homes out of whatever they can find, usually on the **outskirts** of the city.

2 Suburbanisation
- The movement of people from the **city centre** to **lower density housing** on the **outskirts** of a city.
- As **urbanisation increases** city centres become **overcrowded** and people want **more space**. Improvements to **public transport** mean people can **live further away** but still reach the **city centre** easily.
- As megacities grow, **more suburbs** are **added** so older suburbs **aren't** on the **outskirts** any more.
- A **complex pattern** of **wealthy** and **poorer** areas develops. **Wealthy people** live in suburbs on the outskirts of the city because they can **afford** larger houses with **more space**. **Wealthy people** also **move into poorer suburbs** closer to the centre and **renovate** the houses — this process is called **gentrification**.

3 Counter-urbanisation
- The movement of people **out of the city** into surrounding **villages** and **rural areas**.
- Improvements in **transport** and **communications** mean people can **commute** to work or **work from home** over the internet.
- This happens because of **high property prices** and **overcrowding** in cities. People may also **prefer** more **quiet rural areas**.

4 Re-urbanisation
- The movement of people **back** into **redeveloped city centre** residential areas.
- In **developed countries** lots of city centres have been **redeveloped**. This attracts **young**, **affluent people** who want to be near to the **cultural activity** of the city centre, e.g. redeveloped canal areas such as **Brindleyplace** in **Birmingham**.

London *is a* Megacity *in a* Developed Country

London is a **megacity** in the south-east of the **UK**. The London metropolitan area (**Greater London** and much of the **surrounding counties**, including towns like Slough, Luton and Potters Bar) has a population of around **13 million** people. Greater London is on the **flat land** around the mouth of the river **Thames** and has a population density of about **4800** people per km². It's very **different** to megacities in other countries, e.g. **Mumbai** (see next page). Here's what's been going on in London:

Urban cycle

The population of London is growing, but not rapidly, e.g. the population of Greater London has grown by less than 1 million people since 1981. People are moving into, out of and around the city:

1) **Urbanisation** is still occurring — people are **migrating** to Greater London from **abroad**, e.g. in 2006 there was a **net gain** of almost **70 000** international migrants. **Almost all** parts of Greater London gained, but the **biggest** gains were in **central** areas, e.g. **Westminster** and **Camden**.

2) **Counter-urbanisation** is also happening — people are moving **out** of Greater London to the **rest of the UK**, e.g. in **2006** there was a **net loss** of around **80 000** people to other parts of the UK.

3) **Re-urbanisation** has happened around **London Docklands** — the area **east** of **central London** that used to be a **major port**. The port **moved upriver** between 1965 and 1980 and the area was left **derelict**. It's been **redeveloped** since the 1980s and the population has more than **doubled**.

Economy

London has a **post-industrial economy** — the economy used to be based on **industry** and **manufacturing**, but now it's mostly based on **services**, e.g. **85%** of the people employed in London work in the **service** industry.

- It's a major **financial** centre. London has one of the largest **stock exchanges** in the world. Many **global banks** have their headquarters in the centre of London, e.g. **HSBC**.

- **Tourism** is a major part of the **economy**. London is one of the **most popular** cities to visit in the world, e.g. it attracted more than **15 million foreign tourists** in **2006**.

Megacities

Housing patterns

London has a **complex residential pattern** that includes contrasting **rich** and **poor** areas.

1) **Parts** of poorer areas in the east of inner London, e.g. **Hackney**, have been **changed** because of **gentrification**. **Richer** people have moved in, making a **mixed pattern** of **rich** and **poor** people living **near** to each other.

2) **Suburban growth** has meant **villages** around London have **become suburbs** of London, e.g. **Streatham** was a **village** that became a **wealthy suburb** as London grew in the **19th century**. Other suburbs have **grown around it**. Wealthy people still live there, but it's also a **destination** for **poorer immigrants**.

Mumbai is a Megacity in a NIC

Mumbai is a **megacity** on the west coast of **India**. The **Mumbai metropolitan area** (**Mumbai city** and neighbouring areas such as **Navi Mumbai** and **Thane**) has a population of more than **20 million** people. **Greater Mumbai** is on an **island** separated from the mainland by the river **Ulhas**. It has a **high population density** — there are more than **20 000** people per km². Although Mumbai's also a **megacity**, it's very **different** to **London**.

Urban cycle

The population of Mumbai is **growing rapidly**, e.g. the population of Greater Mumbai has grown by more than **6 million** people since **1971** and people are **still moving into** the city:

- Massive **urbanisation** is occurring — people are migrating to Mumbai from **all over India**, e.g. from **1991-2001** more than **1.1 million** people migrated to Greater Mumbai from **outside Maharashtra** (the **state** Mumbai's in).

- **Suburbanisation** is occurring — some people are moving **north**, **away** from the **inner city** on the **southern tip** of the island. **Suburbs** are being built **along** the main **rail** and **road routes out** of the city.

Economy

Mumbai has a **fast growing** economy based on **manufacturing**, but the **service industry** is becoming more important:

- Until the 1980s, the economy was based mainly on **textiles manufacturing** and **shipping** (it's still a **major port**).

- There's been an increase in **IT** and **financial services** recently.

- Mumbai's a major centre for **out-sourced work** — companies in Mumbai work for **foreign companies**, e.g. the **UK-based financial services** company **Prudential** has its **call centre** in Greater Mumbai.

- Mumbai's a **major media centre** for **India**, e.g. the **Bollywood** film industry is based in Mumbai. It's one of the **largest** film industries in the world, e.g. in **2002** Bollywood films sold **3.6 billion** tickets **worldwide**.

Housing patterns

The **residential pattern** of Greater Mumbai is **complex**:

- The **wealthiest** area (**Malabar Hill**) is **near** to the **Central Business District (CBD)**.

- Around **half the population** of Greater Mumbai live in **shanty towns**. They're **squeezed in** wherever there's **space**, e.g. **Dharavi** is the **biggest** shanty town (more than **600 000** people live there) — it's **next** to the **CBD**.

- **Wealthier suburbs** have been built along the **road** and **rail routes** that run north out of the CBD, but **shanty towns** are also squeezed in as near to the **transport links** as possible.

London and Mumbai are Interlinked

> Globalisation is the process of all the world's systems and cultures becoming more integrated (see p. 22-32 for more).

Flows of **trade**, **money**, **people**, **information** and **culture link** London and Mumbai **together**, accelerating **globalisation**. For example:

1) **Cadbury** has its global headquarters in **London**, and its subsidiary company, **Cadbury India**, has its main office in Greater Mumbai. There are flows of **trade**, **money**, **information** and **people** between the two parts of the same company.

2) There are **close links** between the **film industries** in **London** and **Mumbai**, e.g. in **2006** more than **40 Bollywood films** were made in **London**. This means there's a flow of **trade** and **money** as well as **culture** between the two cities.

Practice Questions

Q1 Define urbanisation.

Q2 Define suburbanisation.

Exam Question

Q1 Compare two megacities that you have studied. [10 marks]

Urban cycle — I'm more of a mountain biker actually...

Jeez, people just can't make up their minds. They move into the city, then they move to the outer suburbs, then they move to the countryside, then they move back to the centre of the city. Why don't they just sit down and have a nice cup of tea, eh?

Urban Sustainability

Urban areas keep growing and it causes a hatful of problems. These'll only get worse unless the areas can start developing in a sustainable way. That means making sure what we're doing now isn't going to adversely affect people in the future.

There are Consequences of Urban Growth

Urban populations are predicted to carry on **growing**, e.g. the population of **Shanghai** in **China** is currently around **18 million** and it's predicted to grow to up to **25 million** by **2020**. The continued **growth** of **urban** areas will have **consequences**:

1) **Housing shortages** — there won't be **enough houses** for everyone. This will have different effects in different places though, e.g. in **developed** countries it may mean children have to live with their parents for **longer**. In **developing** countries more people could end up living in **overcrowded shanty towns** — these cause other problems such as **poor health** because of **insufficient and unclean water supplies** and a lack of **sewage removal**.

2) **Increased ecological footprints** (how much a place **impacts** on **natural resources**), e.g. **more power** will be needed as the population **grows**. This could mean that more fossil fuels are **burnt** to produce the power. This **reduces** the amount of fossil fuels **available** in the **future**.

3) **Transport problems** — lots of people use **bikes** and **scooters** to get around in **megacities** in **less developed** countries. But as **more people** move in and become more **affluent**, car ownership will **increase**. This will cause an **increase** in **pollution** and the number of **accidents**. The transport system (e.g. road networks) may not be able to **cope** so it will become **more difficult** to get around the city.

4) **Increased effect on climate change** (see p. 13) — more **greenhouse gases** will be emitted because **more power** is used as the **urban** area **grows**. This could mean that **climate change** is **accelerated**. Some natural hazards are **increasing** because of climate change, e.g. **hydro-meteorological** hazards (see p. 3), which means people may be at **greater risk**.

Innovative solutions are needed to combat growing transport problems.

Urban Areas Need to Become More Sustainable

Sustainable development means **growth** in a way that lets the people living **now** have the things they **need**, but without reducing the ability of people in the **future** to get what **they need**. Basically, it means developing in a way that **doesn't irreversibly damage** the **environment** or **use up resources faster** than they can be **replaced**. For example, an urban area that's growing by generating **all** its **power** from **fossil fuels** will **exhaust** its supply and **accelerate climate change**, so the people in the future **won't have any** fossil fuels and the **environment** will be **damaged** — it's **unsustainable**.

Megacities require so many **resources** that it's **unlikely** any megacity could ever develop in a **truly sustainable** way, i.e. develop **without depleting any non-renewable resources**. But things can be done to make them develop in a way that's **more sustainable**:

1 Build more **carbon-neutral homes** — buildings that **generate** as much **energy** as they **use** (from sources that **don't damage the environment**). They have things like **solar panels** to produce **energy**, and lots of **insulation** to reduce the amount of energy that's **lost**, e.g. **BedZED** is a carbon-neutral housing development in London with these features. Building more carbon-neutral homes provides **more housing** without increasing the **ecological footprint** of the city. However, carbon-neutral homes can be **expensive** to build so they **can't** always be used to solve **housing shortages**.

2 Generate more power from **renewable energy sources** — burning **fossil fuels** to generate power isn't sustainable because they'll **run out**. They also **increase** the rate of **climate change** because burning them produces **greenhouse gases**. Megacities could use **more power** from sources that **don't run out**, e.g. Los Angeles uses **hydroelectric power** from the **Hoover Dam**. Greater **energy needs** can be **met** without **increasing** the **ecological footprint** of the city. This means people's **ability** to generate power in the **future** is **less affected**. However, at the moment renewable energy sources can't generate **enough power** on their **own** to **support** large cities.

3 **Recycling** more **waste** — **increased** recycling means **less resources** are **used**, e.g. tin cans can be melted down and used to make **more tin cans**. **Less waste** is produced, which **reduces** the amount of waste that goes to **landfill**. Landfill is **unsustainable** because it **uses up resources** — finite resources (e.g. metal) that are thrown away and the resource of **suitable landfill sites**. **Decomposition** of landfill also releases **greenhouse gases**.

4 **Water conservation** schemes — only as much water should be **taken from the environment** as can be **naturally replaced**. If natural stores, e.g. **lakes** or **groundwater**, are reduced **too much** there **won't be enough** for future generations. Water conservation schemes reduce the amount of water **used**, but don't affect how the **needs** of people using the water are met, e.g. collecting **rainwater** for use on **gardens** or **installing toilets** that use **less water** to flush.

Urban Sustainability

(5) Improving public transport — using **buses**, **trains** and **trams** that generate **little or no harmful emissions**, e.g. some buses in London are powered by **hydrogen** and only emit **water vapour**. The **ecological footprint** of the city is **reduced** (provided the **electricity** used to produce the hydrogen fuel comes from **renewable sources**) because the buses and trains are **producing less harmful emissions**. The number of **buses** and **trains** can also be **increased**, as well as the **area they cover**. **Improved** public transport **networks** will mean **fewer cars** on the road, so **emissions** will be further **decreased**.

They're *Attempting* to *Build* a *Sustainable City* in *China*

There are **attempts** going on in the world to make **urban** areas that are more **sustainable** — in **China** they're **planning** to build an 'eco-city' — a **city** that's **as sustainable as possible**, called **Dongtan**. It's planned for the island of **Chongming** near to **Shanghai**. It's a **new city** (the island is currently a **wetland** used for **farming**) — the idea is to help solve the **problems** of **urban growth** in **Shanghai**, but in a way that will help to achieve more **sustainable development**.

Here are some of the **plans** to make it a **sustainable city**:

1) **Carbon-neutral homes** — the **housing** in the city has been designed to **generate** as much **energy** as it **uses**.
   - All the homes will produce **their own power**, e.g. using **solar panels**. They'll be **well insulated** to prevent **energy loss**, e.g. **green roofs** (with **soil** and **grass** on top) provide **good insulation**.
   - Dongtan will be more **sustainable** because it will provide **housing** to help Shanghai's **housing shortages**, but the housing won't **increase energy use** or **deplete the resources** available to the city.

2) **Renewable energy production** — the city's **designed** to **generate** all **its own** energy.
   - Power will be provided by **wind turbines** outside the city as well as **smaller wind turbines** on the **buildings**.
   - **Biofuels** will also be used — generating power by burning **waste biological material**, e.g. **rice husks**.
   - Dongtan will be more **sustainable** because **less resources** will be used, e.g. fossil fuels, but **enough power** will be produced to provide for the **needs** of the population. Using **waste biomass** to **generate energy** also means less waste goes to **landfill** so less landfill space is **used up**.

3) **Green transport strategies** — the city's designed to have **very low emissions**.
   - Vehicles that run on **petrol** or **diesel won't be allowed** in the city.
   - The city will have a **network** of **cycleways**, **walkways** and **canals**.
   - The **public transport system** will use **low-emission vehicles**, e.g. **solar-powered water taxis** along the canals.
   - Dongtan will be more **sustainable** because **few emissions** will be **produced** by the city's **transport systems**, but it **shouldn't affect** people's **ability to get around** the city.

There are **reasons** why China's plans for **sustainable urban living** might **not be achievable**:

1) There's **not enough governmental support** for **sustainable development** — **political leaders** need to **make and enforce laws** to **change** the way urban areas are **developed**. E.g. the government **hasn't renewed** the **planning permission** for Dongtan, so some people **don't think** it'll **ever happen** as it's been planned.

2) It **costs a lot** and takes **a long time** to build **more sustainable** urban areas. Shanghai's **urban growth problems** may need **cheaper** and **quicker** solutions, so **plans** for Dongtan may be **compromised** to get it finished **sooner**.

3) Even if all the plans were carried out **in full**, Dongtan still wouldn't be **truly sustainable** — **huge resources** would be used to **construct** the city, and **some emissions** would be caused by **housing** and **transport**.

4) It's **difficult** to make **existing urban areas** sustainable. Even if **new** urban areas are made to be **more sustainable**, old urban areas are still **unsustainable** — they're **using up resources** and **damaging the environment**.

Practice Questions

Q1 Describe one problem caused by urban growth.
Q2 Define sustainable development.

Exam Question

Q1 Describe and explain how an urban area could become more sustainable. [10 marks]

If I can sustain this revision it'll be a miracle...

Sustainability's a tough cookie, but the overlords of geography just love it to bits. In a more sustainable city, people can get what they need without reducing the ability of people in the future to get what they need, so it's about preserving the environment.

Extreme Weather Events

Some extreme things are fun, like extreme sports and, um, extreme ironing (yes, it exists, honest).
Other extreme things, like extreme weather events, really aren't. Read on...

Extreme Weather is Severe or Unexpected

1) **Extreme weather** is weather that's **unusually severe** (e.g. when hot weather turns into a heatwave) or that occurs in an area **where** it **isn't expected** (e.g. drought in a usually wet area).

2) There are many different **types** of extreme weather — **temperate storms**, **tornadoes**, **tropical cyclones**, **heatwaves**, **droughts**, **blizzards** and **ice storms**.

Temperate Storms are Caused by Depressions

1) **Temperate storms** are **weather systems** with **strong winds** and **heavy rainfall**.

2) They're **caused** by **extreme low pressure systems** called **depressions**. Here's how a depression forms:

1) **Warm air** constantly moves **out of tropical areas, towards** the **poles**. A **warm front** is the **leading edge** of a **warm air mass**.

2) **Cold air** moves **out** of **polar regions, towards** the **tropics**. A **cold front** is the **leading edge** of a **cold air mass**.

3) Where the air masses **meet** (in the **temperate zone**) the **warm air** heading towards the pole **rises** above the cold air heading towards the tropics (because **warm air** is **less dense** than cold air).

4) The rising **warm air** means there's **less air** at **ground level**, so atmospheric **pressure** is **reduced**.

5) **Strong winds** blow into this area of low pressure in a **spiral fashion**.

6) The direction of these winds combined with the fact that **cold fronts move more quickly** than warm fronts leads to the cold front **catching up** the **warm front**.

7) When this happens the **warm air** behind the warm front is **undercut** by the incoming cold front and is **lifted** away from the ground entirely. It now sits **above** the **cold air** — this is an **occluded front**. The warm air rises into the **upper atmosphere** and the depression **dissipates**.

3) **Depressions** are **common**, but some **cause strong winds** (due to extremely low pressure) and **heavy rainfall** (due to cooling and condensation when warm air rises).

4) When the winds get **stronger** and rainfall **heavier** they are classed as **temperate storms**, e.g. the Great Storm of October 1987 in the UK. The diagram on the right ⟹ shows the weather conditions of a temperate storm.

5) Temperate storms occur in **temperate areas (25-65° latitude)** where the **winds** come mainly **from** the **west**. This means they're **common** in **north-west Europe** and **North America**.

1) As the **warm front** passes there is **light rain**.

2) Rain **stops briefly** as the warm air mass passes.

3) The **cold front** brings **heavy rain**.

Tornadoes Form Inside Massive Storms

1) A tornado is a **rotating column of air** that is **in contact** with the **ground surface** and the **clouds** above.

2) Tornadoes have **wind speeds** of **up to 480 kph** and can **travel over land** for **many kilometres**.

3) They **form** when **rotating air** high in the **atmosphere** gets **turned on** its **side** into a **vertical column** and is **dragged down** to the **surface** by **descending air**. This happens in **large storms** (e.g. temperate storms or tropical cyclones).

They're visible because a funnel of condensation forms along with strong winds.

4) This means tornadoes occur anywhere there are **temperate storms** — they're most common in the **USA** (there were over 1000 tornadoes there in 2007) but also occur in **north-west Europe**.

5) Tornadoes can also be found where **tropical cyclones hit land** — **south-east Asia**, **Australasia** and **southern Africa**.

Extreme Weather Events

Tropical Cyclones Form Over Warm Water

Tropical cyclones are also called hurricanes or typhoons.

1) Tropical cyclones are **huge spinning storms** with **strong winds** and **torrential rain** that **develop over water**.
2) Scientists don't know exactly **how** cyclones are formed but they do know the **conditions** needed. These include:
   - A **disturbance** near the sea-surface that triggers the cyclone (e.g. an area of low pressure).
   - **Sea water** that's **warm** (above **26.5 °C** at the **surface**), so that it will **evaporate**.
   - The **Coriolis effect** (see page 5) — to make the **winds spin**.
3) Tropical cyclones form around the **tropics** because the water there is **warm** (as it receives a lot of **solar radiation**).
4) They **don't form below 5° latitude**, because the **Coriolis effect isn't strong enough** to make the winds **spin**.
5) The **energy** that keeps the cyclone going comes from the **condensation** of **water vapour**, so tropical cyclones maintain **strong winds** over **warm water** (due to high levels of evaporation from the sea).
6) Tropical cyclones **dissipate** over **land** (because the **supply** of **warm**, **moist air** is **cut off**).

Tropical cyclone **Katrina** developed in the **south-eastern Bahamas** in **August 2005** and **moved** over **land** in **Florida**, where it **weakened**. It then **strengthened** as it moved over the **warm waters** of the **Gulf of Mexico** and **struck land** again in **Louisiana**, southern USA.

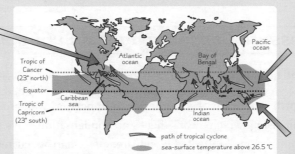

path of tropical cyclone
sea-surface temperature above 26.5 °C

Tropical cyclones **move westwards** due to the **east-west winds** in the **tropics**, e.g. the trade winds move cyclones west across the Atlantic ocean.

They **move away** from the **equator** because of the **Coriolis effect**.

Extreme Weather Events can Cause Flooding

Flooding isn't a type of extreme weather, but it's often caused by storms and cyclones.

Flooding is when an area of **land** that **isn't** usually covered in **water** becomes **submerged**. **Different types** of flooding occur in **different places** including:

River Flooding — **Rivers flood** when the **water level** becomes **so high** that the river **spills** over its banks onto the **flood plain**. This can be caused by **constant rainfall** over a **long period** of time or a **massive input of water** over a **short period** of time (e.g. heavy rainfall in a **temperate storm** or **cyclone**). Any **low-lying area near** to a **river channel** is **at risk** from **river flooding**, e.g. large areas of China are flooded by the river Yangtze.

Coastal Flooding — **Coastal areas** can **flood** when the **sea surges** onto the **land**. This can happen when **temperate storms** or **cyclones** cause a **storm surge** — they reduce the atmospheric pressure on the sea surface, causing it to **rise**. Strong **onshore winds** associated with storms can also force water to higher levels along the coast. Any **low-lying area** near the **coast** is potentially **at risk** from coastal flooding, e.g. a storm surge in 2004 off the west coast of Indonesia caused widespread flooding in south-east Asia.

Flooding can be particularly **severe** when **several factors** are **combined**, e.g. **melting ice** and **snow** in the **Himalayas**, **high rainfall** from the **monsoon** and **tropical cyclone Yemyin** together caused **widespread flooding** in **southern Asia** in **2007**.

Practice Questions

Q1 What is the definition of 'extreme weather'?
Q2 Briefly explain how a depression forms.

Exam Question

Q1 Describe the conditions needed for tropical cyclones to form and explain their distribution. [10 marks]

Toto, I've a feeling we're not in Kansas anymore. We must be over the rainbow...

Well, there may have been a tornado in the Wizard of Oz, but there certainly wasn't any depression — bit annoyingly optimistic that Dorothy, don't you think? You need to know what different types of extreme weather there are and where they occur. Easy.

Extreme Weather Events

Oh joy, there's more. We've done too windy and too wet, now we're on to too dry and too cold.

Drought is When Conditions are Drier than Normal

1) A drought is a **long period** (weeks, months or years) during which **precipitation** is **consistently below average**.

2) The **conditions** of a drought are **different** in **different places**, e.g. the worst drought in Britain since records began lasted 16 months (from May 1975 to August 1976), whilst droughts in some African countries can last for more than a decade.

3) The **map** on the right shows the **areas** of the world that were **affected** by **drought** in **November 2008**.

4) Areas **most at risk** from drought are **north-eastern Africa**, the **Sahel**, **southern Africa**, the **Middle East**, **Australia** and parts of **eastern South America** and **Indonesia**.

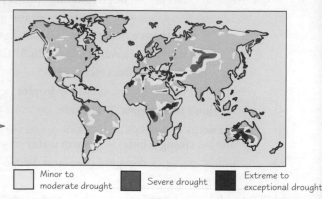

Minor to moderate drought | Severe drought | Extreme to exceptional drought

Areas of High Pressure Cause Drought in Subtropical and Temperate Zones...

1) **Air circulates** around the Earth as weather systems — in some places it **rises** and in others it **sinks**. Where air **sinks** an area of **high pressure** called an **anticyclone** is formed. Anticyclones commonly occur over **Europe** and **North America** in the **northern hemisphere**, as well as across **most** of the **southern hemisphere**.

2) Anticyclones **stop air rising**, which means there's **no condensation**. This leads to **clear skies** and **no precipitation**.

3) The **position** of an anticyclone is **affected** by **jet streams** — **narrow currents** of **fast moving air** high up in the **atmosphere**. When an **anticyclone** is **cut off** from a **jet stream** it can remain **stationary** for **long periods** (days or weeks). These anticyclones **block incoming depressions** (they're diverted around them) — so they're called **blocking anticyclones**. This results in **no precipitation**, and possible **drought** conditions (e.g. drought in the UK in 1979).

...and also in Tropical Regions

1) Some **tropical regions** (e.g. the Sahel in northern Africa and Malawi in southern Africa) are already **very dry** because **rain only falls** during the **wet season**. Seasonal rainfall is caused by the **Intertropical Convergence Zone** (ITCZ) — a zone of **low pressure** created by air circulation patterns, **moving north** in July and **south** in January.

2) The **rest** of the **year** the **climate** is **dry**. This is due to **bands of high pressure** present at around **30° north** and **south** of the equator. Here, **sinking dry air** causes continually **dry conditions** in tropical regions.

3) **Changes** in **atmospheric circulation** can cause the **ITCZ** to **stay closer** to the equator than normal for the time of year, or cause the band of high pressure to move. This can cause some regions to receive a lot **less rain** during the wet season, leading to **drought**.

4) These atmospheric conditions may last for **several years** causing a **long-lasting** and **severe drought**, e.g. the ITCZ shift contributed to the **drought conditions** in the **Sahel** that lasted from the **1960s** to the **1980s**.

A Heat Wave is when Conditions are Hotter than Normal

1) A **heat wave** is a **long period** (days or weeks) during which the **temperature** is much **higher** than **normal**.

2) The **conditions** of a **heat wave** are **different** in **different places**, e.g. the conditions considered a heat wave in the **UK** would be much **cooler** than in a country like **Spain**, where higher temperatures are **expected**.

3) Heat waves are also caused by areas of **high pressure**.

4) In **temperate areas**, **blocking anticyclones** (see above) in summer can result in **reduced cloud cover**. This means **less** solar radiation is **reflected back** into space and **more** is **absorbed** by the land, causing an **increase in temperature**. Blocking anticyclones can last for a long period of time, leading to a **heatwave**.

5) Another way a heatwave can occur in temperate zones is due to **shifts** in **bands of high pressure**. Changes in **atmospheric circulation** can cause the bands to **move polewards**, bringing **hot, dry conditons** with them. For example, in 2003 the northern band moved further north and brought conditions commonly found in **north Africa** to **southern Europe**. These conditions were **abnormal** in Europe and led to the **2003 European heatwave**.

Extreme Weather Events

Drought and Heat Waves can Cause Wildfires

1) Wildfires are **uncontrolled fires** that usually **start** in the **natural environment** (e.g. **forests, grassland**) and can **spread** into **human environments** (buildings and land).

2) Wildfires are a **natural phenomenon**. However, these fires can spread rapidly and cause **widespread destruction**.

3) Fires often **start** during **droughts** and **heat waves** (see previous page) because **low precipitation** and **high temperatures dry out vegetation**. Vegetation can then **easily be ignited** by many things, e.g. **lightning strikes**.

4) Wildfires **spread quickly** where there are **warm, dry winds**.

5) They're common in **environments** where there's **lots of vegetation** and **dry weather**, e.g. parts of **Australia**, **South Africa** and **North America**.

Winter Weather Happens Where Temperatures Fall Below Freezing

1) Winter weather includes **low temperatures**, **ice** and **snowfall**.

2) In areas at **high altitude** and **high latitude** winter weather is **expected**.

3) Winter weather occurs at **high latitudes** (**above 40°**) because **less solar radiation** is received than at lower latitudes. **Temperatures** fall **below freezing**, resulting in **ice** and **snow formation**. E.g. **northern** parts of **Asia**, **Europe** and **North America** and **southern** parts of **South America** and **New Zealand** experience winter weather every year.

The extreme winter weather called for extreme winter clothing.

4) Winter weather occurs at **high altitudes** because **temperature decreases** by about **6-10 °C** for every **1000 m** gained.

5) Winter weather can become **extreme** when conditions are **more severe** than usual (e.g. **blizzards** and **ice storms**) or when they're very **prolonged**, or they occur in **places** that **don't** usually **experience them** (e.g. **lower latitudes**).

6) More **severe conditions** can happen when **temperate storms** (see p. 50) occur during **winter**, resulting in a **blizzard** or an **ice storm**:

Blizzard
- A blizzard is a **winter storm** with **high winds** and **snowfall**.
- They happen when an **intense low pressure system** forms during **winter**.
- Blizzards occur in the **higher latitudes** of the **temperate zone** (**40° to 60° latitude**) where there are **freezing temperatures** and **low pressure systems**, e.g. **Canada**, **northern Europe** and **southern New Zealand**.
- For example, in the 'storm of the century' (USA, March 1993) a **huge low pressure system** formed over the **east coast** of the USA. It caused **massive snowfall**, **low temperatures** and **high winds**, from **Canada** down to **Cuba**.

Ice Storm
- An ice storm is a **storm** in which the **ground** and **surfaces** (e.g. of buildings) get **covered** in a layer of **ice**.
- This happens when **rainfall** (from a **storm**) **passes through** a **layer** of **cold air** at (or near to) the **ground**. So the **rain freezes** as it **hits** the **surface** covering everything in **ice**.
- For example, in the 'Great Ice Storm' of 1998 in North America, warm, moist air from the Gulf of Mexico rose above cold air trapped at ground level. This caused an ice storm for several days over a wide area.

Practice Questions

Q1 Explain how drought can lead to wildfires.
Q2 Explain why winter weather commonly occurs at high latitudes.

Exam Question

Q1 Describe how an anticyclone can lead to extreme weather events. [10 marks]

I don't like extreme weather — I'm anti-cyclone...

This stuff isn't too bad really — high pressure leads to anticyclones, which cause bad things like droughts and heatwaves to happen. Simple. OK, there's a bit more to it, but that's the general idea. All you have to do now is go back and learn the details.

Extreme Weather — Fieldwork and Research

Weather diaries aren't exactly fascinating. I can't see 'The Secret Weather Diary of Joe Bloggs Aged 17¾' becoming a bestseller. Synoptic maps are a tad better — they're the funny-looking ones that weathermen use. Ooh, the excitement...

A **Weather Diary** is a **Primary Source** of **Data** on **Weather Patterns**

A **weather diary** is a **record** of the **weather conditions** (e.g. temperature, precipitation, air pressure, wind speed) over a **period of time** in a **specific area**.

Making your **own weather diary** is one way of collecting **primary data** (first-hand information). You can use this data to help you **understand** the **weather patterns** you've studied, like **depressions** and **anticyclones**.

Here's how to make a weather diary...

1) **Choose** the **elements** of the **weather** you're going to **observe**, e.g. pressure and wind direction. The **more elements** you record the **more detailed** your **data** will be, which is **helpful** when you're looking for **patterns** in the weather.

2) You need to **take** and **write down** readings for **each element** you're observing.

3) Take your readings at the **same time** each day, or at **set time intervals** over the course of the day.

4) Take your readings in the **same place** each day — **avoid** anything that would **affect** the readings. E.g. do it in an **open space** away from buildings that could affect the wind, and **surfaces** that **reflect** lots of **heat** (like tarmac).

5) It's best to take **readings** for a **few days** or even **weeks** because it's more likely you'll record **different weather conditions** and be able to see **distinct patterns**.

A **Weather Diary** Should **Look** Something **Like This**...

By carrying out **fieldwork** like making a weather diary, you can see when a **front** is **passing**, what kind of **pressure system** (high or low) is present and what kind of **air mass** the area's in (warm or cold).

Here's an **example** of a **weather diary** that shows the **weather conditions** as a **depression** (see p. 50) passes over:

Your weather diary can be used alongside secondary sources (e.g. news reports and synoptic maps — see next page) to help you understand what your observations show.

1 Ahead of the **warm front**:
- Temperatures **begin to rise**.
- **Drizzly rain**.
- Pressure **falls**.
- Wind speed **increases** and direction **begins to turn**.

2 As **warm front** passes:
- **Temperatures rise**.
- Rain becomes **heavier**.
- Pressure **falls**.
- Wind is strong and **blustery**. Wind **turns** direction.

3 Warm air overhead:
- Temperatures remain steady.
- Rain is **light** and **may stop**.
- Pressure remains **steady**.
- Wind speed **decreases**, turns direction **slightly**.

Time	Temp (°C)	Rainfall (mm)	Pressure (millibars)	Windspeed & direction (Beaufort scale)
6.00	9.8	0.0	990	South-easterly 4
8.00	10.2	2.8	986	South-easterly 4
10.00	11.6	4.6	979	Southerly 5
12.00	12.2	7.3	974	South west 6
14.00	12.3	0.9	975	South west 4
16.00	11.9	1.1	975	South west 5
18.00	8.2	9.5	984	North-westerly 9
20.00	8.6	1.5	990	North-westerly 9
22.00	9.7	0.8	994	North-westerly 7
0.00	10.1	0.0	998	North-westerly 4

4 As **cold front** passes:
- Temperatures **drop** suddenly.
- **Heavy rain**, **storm** conditions.
- Pressure **rises** suddenly.
- Wind speed **increases** to **gale force**, **turns** direction **sharply**.

5 Cold air overhead:
- Remains **cold**.
- **Rain showers**.
- Pressure continues to **rise**.
- Wind speed **falls gradually**.

Extreme Weather — Fieldwork and Research

Synoptic Maps Display Weather Data from Different Primary Sources

1) **Synoptic maps** are a type of **secondary data** (second-hand information) about the weather.
2) They **display** weather data from a **range** of **primary sources** (e.g. weather stations).
3) You can **use** them to **find** the **positions** of **fronts**, **air masses** and **pressure systems** (see p. 50).

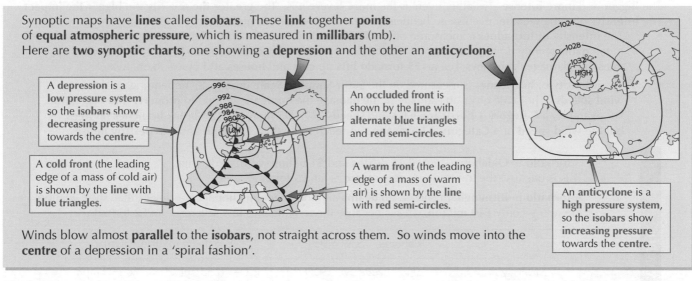

Synoptic maps have **lines** called **isobars**. These **link** together **points** of **equal atmospheric pressure**, which is measured in **millibars** (mb). Here are **two synoptic charts**, one showing a **depression** and the other an **anticyclone**.

A **depression** is a **low pressure system** so the isobars show **decreasing pressure** towards the **centre**.

A **cold front** (the leading edge of a mass of cold air) is shown by the **line** with **blue triangles**.

An **occluded front** is shown by the **line** with **alternate blue triangles** and **red semi-circles**.

A **warm front** (the leading edge of a mass of warm air) is shown by the **line** with **red semi-circles**.

An **anticyclone** is a **high pressure system**, so the isobars show **increasing pressure** towards the **centre**.

Winds blow almost **parallel** to the **isobars**, not straight across them. So winds move into the **centre** of a depression in a 'spiral fashion'.

Synoptic maps use a variety of symbols:

Some symbols show the **type** of **weather**.

Wind speed, wind direction and **cloud cover** are all **combined** in one symbol.

You can Use Other Secondary Sources to Research Weather Patterns

You can **use secondary sources** of weather data to **find out** about **extreme weather events** in the **past**:

Example: To research a **storm** (e.g. the Great Storm of October 1987) find **synoptic maps** (from the Met Office), **satellite images**, and **newspaper** and **online articles** about the storm. The **synoptic maps** will show the **position** of the **warm** and **cold fronts** (and air masses). If you look at synoptic maps for different times you can see the **development** of the **low pressure system**. **Articles** and **satellite images** will tell you about the associated **weather patterns** (heavy precipitation, strong wind). Using these together you can show the **progressive nature** (i.e. the stages) of the **depression** as it passes across the country.

Practice Questions

Q1 Why is it important to take measurements for a weather diary in an open space?
Q2 What do isobars show?

Exam Question

Q1 Describe and explain a programme of fieldwork and research you would use to investigate the links between weather conditions and a depression. [15 marks]

What do people drink at the iso-bar? Strong gale...

The examiners think 'examining a developing depression, cold snap or heatwave' is an 'ideal scenario'. It doesn't seem like an ideal scenario for a Sunday afternoon, or a hot date, so I guess it means fieldwork.

The Impact of Extreme Weather

Now you know why extreme weather events occur, it's time to take a look at their impact. And it's not pretty.

Three Key Factors Influence the Impact of Extreme Weather Events

(1) The Severity of the Extreme Weather Event

The **bigger** and **more intense** a weather event is the **more severe** it is. The **greater the severity** the **bigger the impact**. The **intensity** of some weather events can be measured on a **scale**, for example:

- The **intensity** of **tornadoes** is measured on the **Fujita Scale** (from F0 to F5). They're categorised by how much **damage** they do to **property** and **vegetation**. For example, an **F0 tornado breaks** the **branches** off trees and **damages chimneys**, but an **F5 tornado lifts** up **cars** and **houses** and blows them away.

- The **intensity** of **hurricanes** is measured on the **Saffir-Simpson Scale** (from 1-5), depending on their **wind speeds**. The scale gives an estimate of the **damage** the hurricane will do to **property** and **vegetation**. For example, a **Category 1 hurricane** has **wind speeds** of **74-95 mph** and can **break branches** off trees, but the **wind speed** of a **Category 5 hurricane** can reach more than **155 mph** and can **destroy houses**.

EXAMPLE

1) A **tornado** in **Oklahoma** caused **41 deaths** and **$1 billion** worth of damage. This is because the tornado was **very severe** — an **F5** tornado.

2) A **tornado** in **Birmingham** caused **no deaths** and the **economic impact** was **lower** than the Oklahoma tornado — only **£40 million**. This is because the tornado was **less severe** — an **F2** tornado.

	Oklahoma, USA (1999)	Birmingham, UK (2005)
Severity	F5 — Wind speeds over 300 mph	F2 — Wind speeds up to 130 mph
Death toll	41 dead, 583 injured	O dead, 19 injured
Economic impact	$1 billion (£620 million), 4300 houses damaged or destroyed	£40 million, 4449 houses damaged

(2) The Level of Economic Development in the Affected Area

Generally, the **economic impact** of an extreme weather event is **greater** in **more economically developed areas**. But, the **social impact** is **greater** in **less economically developed areas** because people have a **lower capacity to cope** with extreme weather events (they're **more vulnerable**).

EXAMPLE

1) **Hurricane Mitch** hit **less economically developed** areas, e.g. Honduras. The **death toll** was **high** for a number of reasons. **Inadequate roads** and **bridges** were **quickly destroyed** so people **couldn't evacuate** easily and there were **shortages** of **food** and **water** immediately after the hurricane. **Poor sanitation systems**, e.g. broken sewers, meant flood water became contaminated, which **spread disease**. The **poor infrastructure**, **poor sanitation** and **poor emergency responses** (common in less economically developed areas due to lack of money), meant that the **impact** of the hurricane was **high**.

2) **Hurricane Wilma** hit **more economically developed** areas, e.g. Florida. The **death toll** was **lower** because these areas are better **able to cope** with the **disaster**, e.g. by providing **warnings**, **shelters** and quick **evacuation**. But the **financial cost** of the hurricane was much **higher** because the property and infrastructure destroyed was **more valuable**.

	Hurricane Mitch (1998)	Hurricane Wilma (2005)
Areas hit worst	Honduras and Nicaragua	Mexico, Cuba, Florida
Severity	Category 5	Category 5
Death toll	Over 11 000	63
Economic impact	US$6 billion	US$29 billion

The Impact of Extreme Weather

③ The *Vulnerability* of *People* in the *Affected Area*

The **poorer** the country is, the **more vulnerable** the population, but some **groups** of people **within** a population also have a **lower capacity to cope**, so are **more vulnerable**. The **impact** is **greater** on vulnerable people. They have a lower capacity to cope with extreme weather because of...

- Their **age**, e.g. the elderly are more susceptible to the effects of a heatwave.
- Their **health**, e.g. disruption of health care affects people who need regular medication more than those who don't.
- Their **wealth**, e.g. hurricane evacuation is more difficult for those who don't own a car because they're poor.
- Where they **live**, e.g. tornadoes affect people who live in mobile homes more than people in permanent homes.

EXAMPLE

The **heatwave in England** and **Wales** in **2003** lasted for 10 days and may have caused over **2000 deaths**. In southern England **excess mortality** (the percentage extra deaths during that time, compared to previous years) was **33%** for people **aged 75 and over**, compared to **13.5%** for those **under 75**, during the heatwave. Therefore the **elderly** were **more vulnerable** during the heatwave, possibly because dehydration has more serious effects on the elderly.

Use *Fieldwork* and *Research* to *Investigate* the *Impact* of *Extreme Weather*

Fieldwork and **research** can be carried out to measure and predict the impact of extreme weather events on an area. This could include investigating the **severity** of the event, the level of **economic development** of the area affected and the **vulnerability** of people in the area. It's most likely that any **fieldwork** you'll do in this country will be on **flooding**:

Fieldwork

- **Visit** an **area** that's **prone** to **flooding**. Use a **land-use map** of the **flood plain** to **count** how many **houses** and **businesses** could be flooded.
- Design a **questionnaire** asking **local** people and businesses about the impact of previous flooding. You'll need to ask **closed** questions like *'How much did it cost to repair the damage?'* to get specific, detailed responses.

However, you can carry out **research** on lots of extreme weather events:

Research

- Study (online) **newspaper articles** to find out about the **intensity** and **amount of damage** of a past **hurricane**.
- Look at the **flood reports** and **maps** on the **Environment Agency website**, to find out about the **physical extent** of past UK floods.
- Visit the **Met Office Library** in Exeter, or look at its **website** to find **meteorological data** (e.g. rainfall data) on previous UK extreme weather events (e.g. storms, droughts).
- Look at the USA's **National Oceanic & Atmospheric Administration** (NOAA) **website** for **official reports** and **interactive maps** on past and current extreme weather events.
- Look at recent reports and the current drought monitor map on the **website** of the **UCL Department of Space and Climate Physics**.

Practice Questions

Q1 Describe a scale used to measure the intensity of an extreme weather event.
Q2 Give an example of a vulnerable group of people.
Q3 Give an example of how you could research the impact of hurricanes.

Exam Question

Q1 Explain the factors that influence the impact of extreme weather events. [10 marks]

The Fajita Scale — used for measuring the spiciness of Mexican food...

I always thought the severity of tornadoes was measured by how many cows they could pick up. As in, "Did you see that tornado? Must have been a 3 cow-er, at least." Guess not. The important thing to remember from these pages is that the effect of an extreme weather event is always dependent on three key factors — severity, economic development and vulnerability. Sorted.

The Impact of Extreme Weather — Case Studies

*Learning some theory about the impacts of extreme weather is one thing, but nothing beats a nice, juicy case study.
Except for maybe three nice, juicy case studies. Handily, that's exactly what's coming your way...*

Case Study — Major Drought in South-Eastern Australia Since 2002

Australia is suffering from **severe, long-term drought**. The **worst hit** area is the **Murray-Darling Basin** in south-east Australia, which is Australia's most **important agricultural region**. This drought has many **social, environmental** and **economic** impacts:

1) The drought has led to **water use restrictions**. The **3 million people** who rely on the **River Murray** for their water supplies have had their **allocation reduced**.

2) Over **10 000 farming families** have been **forced** to **leave** the Murray-Darling Basin in the **last five years** because they can **no longer make a living** from **agriculture**.

3) The drought is **increasing groundwater salinity** in **over 35 towns** in the river basin. This causes **structural damage** to homes. Many **properties** are **losing value**.

4) **Financial hardship** caused by the drought is affecting the **mental health** of many people. The **Government** has spent over **$10 million** on strategies, such as **mental health workshops**, to help communities cope with mental health issues.

5) The drought has caused **vegetation loss** and **soil erosion**, as well as increased **wildfires** and **dust storms**. Depleted rivers and lakes are suffering from **outbreaks** of **toxic algae**. This damage is **threatening** the **habitats** of many species, some of which are **endangered** (e.g. the **Purple-spotted gudgeon**).

~All these impacts are <u>ongoing</u>~ because Australia is still suffering from drought.

6) Agricultural production of **cereals, fruit, vegetables, dairy** and **livestock** has **decreased** due to lack of water. Crops that rely on **irrigation** (watering) have been particularly badly affected, e.g. **rice production** has fallen to just **2%** of pre-drought totals. All of this has **increased food prices**.

7) Many **farms** and **small businesses** have **closed**. **Production levels** and **incomes** of many other businesses have **decreased**. This has caused **unemployment** levels to rise to **7% above** the **national average**.

8) More than **23 000** rural families and **1500 small businesses** receive **income support** to help them survive.

Three Factors Influence the Impact of the Drought

(1) Severity of the event

1) It's Australia's **worst drought** on **record** — rainfall in **June 2008** was the **lowest** recorded in **117 years**. This has increased the **severity** of the impacts shown above.

2) Parts of the Murray-Darling Basin have been in **drought** since **2001** and water levels are now **so low** that it'll take **years of high rainfall** for the basin to **recover**. Therefore even after the drought some of the impacts will be ongoing.

~Severity is the most influential factor.~

(2) Level of economic development

1) Australia is a **more economically developed** country, so it's **more able** to **cope** with some of the **impacts** of drought (e.g. the Government can afford to spend money on **tackling mental health problems**).

2) However, the Murray-Darling Basin is a **rich agricultural area** (responsible for **34%** of Australia's gross value of **agricultural production** in **2000/2001**) — so drought in this region is having a huge impact on Australian agriculture as a whole and is causing **large financial losses**.

(3) Vulnerability of the affected populations

1) **Poorer people** are badly affected by the drought because they **can't afford** the **high prices** of food.

2) The large numbers of **farmers** in the area are also badly affected as they depend on water for their **livelihood**.

The Impact of Extreme Weather — Case Studies

Case Study — Hurricane Katrina hit South-eastern USA in August 2005

In **August 2005**, the USA was hit by **Hurricane Katrina** — a **Category 5** hurricane. **Louisiana** was the worst hit — over 85% of deaths occurred there. The hurricane had many **social**, **environmental** and **economic** impacts:

1) The **death toll** was **1836**, with about **700** people still **missing**. Many people **lost family members, homes** and **jobs**. Over **1 million** people **moved** to other parts of the USA following the hurricane.

2) Around **300 000** homes were **destroyed** and many **more** were **damaged**.

3) People were **injured** directly by the hurricane. At one hospital emergency department the **number** of **patients treated rose** by **83.6%** in the week following the hurricane.

4) **Storm surges** caused substantial **beach erosion**. Many **coastal habitats**, which were **breeding grounds** for sea turtles, marine mammals and migrating birds and fish were **lost**.

5) Many major **highways** and **bridges** were **damaged**, e.g. the **Rigolets Bridge** in New Orleans. Some were completely **destroyed**, e.g. the **Biloxi Bay Bridge** on the US Route 90 highway.

6) Agricultural **crops** (e.g. cotton, sugar cane) and **forests** were **destroyed**. The **oil** and **gas industry** was **disrupted** (30 oil platforms were destroyed and **9 refineries** closed).

7) In **Louisiana**, over **70 000 businesses** were affected. Around **230 000 jobs** were **lost**.

8) The hurricane caused around **$300 billion** of **damage**.

LOUISIANA

MISSISSIPPI

New Orleans

There are Three Reasons why Katrina's Impact was so High

(1) Severity of the event

Hurricane Katrina was a **Category 5** storm, but weakened to **Category 3** before it hit land. This is still fairly severe, which meant that its **social**, **environmental** and **economic impacts** were **high**.

(2) Level of economic development

Hurricane Katrina affected **more economically developed** areas, so the **economic impact** was **high**.

(3) Vulnerability of the affected populations

Hurricane Katrina hit **poorer areas** of New Orleans. People from these regions **weren't able** to **evacuate** as easily and the **buildings** and **infrastructure** were of a **lower quality** and therefore more easily damaged. The **ill** were also **badly affected**, with **hospitals flooding** and **equipment failing**.

The Impact was Made Worse by Inadequate Levees

1) Most of **New Orleans** lies **below sea level**. It relies on **levees** (see p. 67) to **protect** the city from **floods**.

2) During Hurricane Katrina, **storm surges** generated **waves** about **8 m** high. The **levees** catastrophically **failed**, causing **80%** of **New Orleans** to be **flooded** — this was blamed for much of the damage and loss of life.

3) **Reports** found that **faulty design, incomplete sections** and **poor construction** all contributed to **levee failure**.

4) It's been estimated that if the **levees** had **not failed**, up to **two-thirds** of the **deaths** could have been **avoided**.

Flooding in New Orleans after Hurricane Katrina.

The Impact of Extreme Weather — Case Studies

If you thought you'd got away with two case studies, think again. I promised you three and three you'll get. Enjoy.

Case Study — Flooding of Carlisle, Cumbria, January 2005

The **River Eden** runs through **north Cumbria** and reaches the sea near **Carlisle**. On **8th January 2005**, after hours of heavy rainfall, the **River Eden** flooded **Carlisle**. The flood had many **social**, **environmental** and **economic** impacts:

SOCIAL IMPACTS

1) **Three people died** in the floods.

SIMON FRASER / SCIENCE PHOTO LIBRARY

A residential area in Carlisle during the flood.

2) **Over 3000 people** were made **homeless** for up to a **year** and thousands of **personal possessions** were **damaged**. Living in **temporary accommodation disrupted lives** in many ways, e.g. **travel arrangements** were **disrupted**, people were **separated** from **community networks** and **friends**, and they had **problems receiving post**.

3) Children **lost** out on **education** as **four schools** were **severely flooded**. **Newman Catholic School** didn't re-open until **Easter**.

4) There was an **increase** in **stress-related illnesses** following the floods.

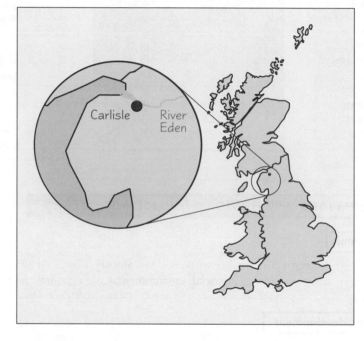

Carlisle River Eden

ENVIRONMENTAL IMPACTS

1) The flooding **increased river bank erosion** in some areas.

2) **Rivers** were **polluted** with rubbish and sewage.

ECONOMIC IMPACTS

1) It took about a **year** to **repair** the **damage** to homes and repairs **cost over £100 million**.

2) **350 businesses** had to **shut down** as there was **no electricity**, **telephone service** or **transport**. **Trade activities** from Carlisle **railway** station were **suspended**.

3) **70 000 addresses** had **no power**. The **sewage works**, **police station**, **fire station** and **council offices** were **severely flooded**.

4) **80 buses** (most of the public transport fleet) were **destroyed**. Many **roads** and **bridges** were **damaged**, e.g. **Warwick Road**.

It was just too much. The ladies of Carlisle started to desperately hope for a drought.

5) **United Biscuits**, the **largest employer** in Carlisle, was **flooded** with **3 m** of water that caused **over £5 million damage**. **33** out of 1100 employees **lost** their **jobs**.

The Impact of Extreme Weather — Case Studies

Three Factors Influenced the Impact of the Flood

1) Severity of the event

1) The **River Eden** flowed at its highest recorded level of **1520 cumecs** — this would be expected **about once every 200 years**. At **Eden Bridge**, flood waters rose **over a metre higher** than the **previous highest waterline**.

2) The **severity** of the flood meant that its **impact** was **high**.

Severity influenced the impact of the flood the most.

2) Level of economic development

1) Carlisle is an urban area in a **more economically developed** country so **money** was spent on **flood defences**. These performed well, protecting over **6000 properties**. **Emergency services responded well** after the flood, **decreasing** its **impacts**.

2) Most people's **financial needs** (e.g. to repair houses) were met by **insurance** companies, **decreasing** the **economic impact** on **individuals**.

3) However, the economic impact was **high** because Carlisle has a lot of **high value property** and **infrastructure**. Some businesses were **badly hit**, e.g. **United Biscuits**, Carlisle's largest employer, had **over £5 million** pounds worth of **damage**.

3) Vulnerability of the affected populations

1) The **failure** of **landlines** and **mobile phone networks** meant that people were unable to call for **assistance**. This particularly affected the **elderly** and **ill** as they had the **most difficulty evacuating**.

2) People on **lower incomes** were **less likely** to have had **insurance** and so they suffered the most from **property damage**.

3) The increased **costs** of living in **temporary accommodation** also particularly affected **people** on **lower incomes**.

Practice Questions

Q1 Describe the environmental impact of the drought in south-eastern Australia.

Q2 Identify one group of people who are particularly vulnerable to the drought in south-eastern Australia.

Q3 Give two social impacts of Hurricane Katrina.

Q4 Give two economic impacts of the Carlisle flood.

Q5 Describe the severity of the 2005 Carlisle flood.

Exam Question

Q1 With reference to one or more named examples, describe and explain the impact of an extreme weather event. [15 marks]

Best way to learn about flooding? Give it some welly(s)...

It's a bit grim this stuff. Seems unfair that some people get way too much water and others don't have enough...
There's quite a bit to learn here, but it's not actually too bad once you get going. Start by jotting down the social, economic and environmental effects of these extreme weather events — then see if you can remember how the three factors affect the impact.

Increasing Risk from Extreme Weather

It's not good news, I'm afraid — extreme weather events across the world are becoming more common.

Extreme Weather *is Getting* More Frequent *and* More Severe

International weather records show that **extreme weather events** have **increased** in **number** and **severity** during the **last 50 years**. For example:

1) The graph below shows the **global frequency** of **hurricanes** (an extreme weather event) and **floods** (an event that can be caused by extreme weather), compared to the frequency of **earthquakes**, which are **not** weather related. It shows that the **frequency** of **hurricanes** and **floods** has **increased** since **1980**, while the **frequency** of **earthquakes** has stayed more **constant**.

2) Globally, the **proportion** of **Category 4** and **5 hurricanes** has **risen** from **20%** in the **1970s** to **35%** in the **1990s**.

3) The **frequency** of **heavy rainfall** and **severe floods** has **increased** over **most land areas** in recent years. In the **UK**, the **frequency** of **intense winter rainfall** events and the **risk of flooding** have **increased** over the **last 40 years**. British **insurance companies** paid out **£6 billion** on **weather damage claims** between **1999** and **2004** — over **twice** the amount paid during the **previous 5-year period**.

4) Worldwide, the **percentage** of **land** area affected by **serious drought** more than **doubled** between the **1970s** and the early **2000s** — going from **10-15%** to **30%**.

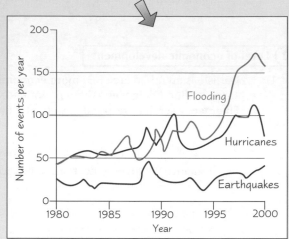

The more **frequent** and more **severe** the events, the **greater** the **risk** of them **affecting humans**.

Global Warming *is* Increasing *the* Risk *of Some* Extreme Weather

Global warming (see p. 10) is a type of **climate change**. Many scientists think that global warming is **contributing** to the **increasing frequency** and **severity** of **extreme weather events**. Here are some of the most **common arguments** for a **link** between the two:

DROUGHTS

Higher temperatures due to **global warming** cause **changes** in **global air circulation** and **ocean currents**. This means some areas will experience **less rainfall** than usual, and some areas will experience **more rainfall**. Areas experiencing **less rainfall** may have **more frequent** and **more severe droughts** (e.g. the long-lasting drought in the Australian Murray-Darling River Basin — see p. 58).

They didn't care that it increased the risk of hurricanes, it was soooo warm...

HURRICANES

1) **Hurricanes** can **only form** when the sea surface **temperature** is **warmer than 26.5 °C**. Global warming **increases ocean temperatures**, making the **conditions** hurricanes need to form **more frequent**.

2) **Increased temperatures** also **increases** the **energy supply** for **hurricanes**, making them **more severe**. One study found that for **every 1 °C rise** in **sea surface temperature**, **hurricane rainfall increased** by **6-18%** and **wind speed increased** by up to **8%**.

STORMS

Higher temperatures due to **global warming** cause **changes** in **global air circulation** and **ocean currents** (see above). This means **some places** will have a **higher frequency** of storms and get **more severe storms**.

Climate change can increase the risk of flooding in other ways that aren't related to weather, e.g. causing ice caps to melt, leading to a rise in sea level.

An **increase** in the **frequency** and **severity** of **storms** and **hurricanes** can lead to an **increase** in **flooding**.

Increasing Risk from Extreme Weather

Poor Land Management Increases the Risk of Flooding Occurring

1) An increase in **storm frequency** or **severity increases** the **risk** of **flooding**.
2) But **poor land management** increases the risk of an extreme weather event **resulting in flooding**:

> 1) **Urbanisation** on flood plains **increases** the area of **impermeable surfaces** (e.g. concrete), which **increases surface runoff**, leading to **higher river levels**.
> 2) **Agricultural practices** can **affect** the **volume** and **rate** of water reaching a river, e.g. **drainage systems** allow water to flow more quickly into a river channel. Other farming practices (e.g. **removal of vegetation**, **overgrazing**, use of **heavy machinery**) increase **soil erosion**, which leads to more soil being **deposited** in a river. This **lifts up** the **river bed**, **decreasing** the **capacity** of the **channel** and increasing the risk of flooding.
> 3) **Deforestation reduces interception** and **evapotranspiration**. This **increases** the **volume of water** that reaches the river channel, which **increases discharge** and the risk of flooding.

Page 64 explains interception and evapotranspiration.

Population Growth Along Rivers and Coasts Increases the Number at Risk

1) As the **world's population increases**, **more people** will be **at risk** from **extreme weather** events and **flooding**.
2) One reason for this is that a **large proportion** of the **world's population** lives near **rivers** or **coasts**, which are **prone** to **flooding**. Some **coastal areas** are also at **risk** from **hurricanes**. As the population **grows**, **more people** live in these areas, which **increases** the **number** of people experiencing **flooding** and **hurricanes**.
3) In **2006/07**, local **planning authorities** in **England** gave **permission** for **13 major developments** to go ahead **against Environment Agency advice** on flood risk. Around **two million properties** in England and Wales are on the **flood plains** of rivers or on low-lying land **close to the coast**, so are **at risk** from **flooding**. For example, the UK city of **York** is built on the **flood plain** of the **River Ouse** and despite severe floods, several **new housing developments** have been built on the **flood plain** in recent years.
4) Some people believe there's **no alternative** to using **flood plain land** for **development** because sometimes it's the **only land** available to support a **growing population**.

Various Factors may Contribute to Increased Risk from Extreme Weather

EXAMPLE — Flooding along the River Ouse, UK

1) **Various factors** have been **blamed** for the **increase** in the **frequency** and **severity** of **flooding** along the **River Ouse** in **Yorkshire**. These include **global warming**, **housing developments** on the **flood plain**, **overgrazing** in the **drainage basin** and **poor flood defences**.
2) The **relative importance** of each of these **factors** is **disputed** by **different groups** including the **Environment Agency**, **farmers**, **developers** and **local councils** — partly because all these groups have **different self-interests**.
3) There's **evidence** to suggest **all these factors** may play a part — but **proving** that **one factor** is the **most important** is **very difficult**. Most people now recognise that a **range of factors** all have **some impact** — so **each factor** is addressed in **flood management strategies**.

There's more information about factors that increase the risk of flooding on page 64.

Practice Question

Q1 Give two ways in which global warming is thought to lead to an increased risk of hurricanes.

Exam Question

Q1 Explain the factors that may have led to an increased risk of flooding in the UK. [10 marks]

Extreme weather is getting more violent — now it's sandbags at dawn...

Bad news, it's getting worse... Extreme weather that is, not this book. You need to learn what makes it worse, what's making it more likely to cause flooding, and why it's not always great to live by water. So, what are you waiting for — cover the page and get scribbling.

Increasing Flood Risk — Fieldwork and Research

Next up, you need to know the causes of flooding and how you can investigate them. Oh yes, it's fieldwork and research time.

You Need to be Able to *Investigate Why* a *River Floods*

To investigate why a river floods you need to know the **factors** that **increase flood risk**. These include **meteorological** factors such as heavy or prolonged rainfall, other **physical characteristics** of the area and some **human activities**.

Meteorological Factors are the *Main Cause* of *Flooding*

1) **Flooding** occurs when the **discharge** of a river is **so high** that the **river spills over** its **banks** onto the **flood plain**.

2) A **major cause** of **flooding** is **prolonged rainfall**. After a **long period** of **rain**, the **ground** becomes **saturated** (it **can't absorb** any more water). Any further rainfall **can't infiltrate**, which **increases surface runoff**, which **increases discharge**.

3) **Heavy rainfall** (e.g. the rain you get with **thunderstorms**) can lead to **rapid surface runoff** if the rainfall is **too intense** for **infiltration** to occur. This can lead to a **sharp rise** in **river discharge** called a **flash flood**.

4) **Melting snow** and **ice** also lead to a **huge increase** in a river's **discharge**. For example, **melting snow** in the **Himalayas** contributes to the **annual summer flooding** of the **River Ganges** in **Bangladesh**.

If you're not sure of your **technical terms**, fear not...

Discharge	The **amount** of water that **flows** in a river **per second**. It's measured in **cubic metres per second** (m³/s), or **cumecs**.
Evapotranspiration	The combination of **evaporation** (water turning into **water vapour**) and **transpiration** (evaporation from plant leaves).
Infiltration	Water **soaking** into the **soil**.
Interception	When some precipitation **lands on vegetation** or other structures **before** it reaches the soil.
Lag time	The **delay** between **peak rainfall** and **peak discharge**.
Precipitation	Includes **all** the ways **moisture** comes **out** of the **atmosphere**, e.g. rain, hail, dew, frost...
Surface runoff	Water flowing **over** the **ground**.

There are Other *Physical Factors* That *Increase* the *Risk* of *Flooding*...

Some **physical characteristics** of **drainage basins** can **increase** the **risk** of **flooding**:

Sparse vegetation or deciduous trees

- **Sparse vegetation** in the drainage basin means **little rainfall is intercepted**, so **more rain** reaches the **ground**. This **increases** the **volume of water** reaching the river, which **increases discharge**.
- **Deciduous trees** have **no leaves** in **winter**, which has the **same effect** as sparse vegetation — little rainfall is intercepted.

Impermeable ground

- **Clay soils** and some **rocks**, such as **granite** and **shale**, are **impermeable** — they **don't allow infiltration** of **surface water**. This **increases surface runoff**, which **increases discharge**.
- If the ground has been **baked hard** by the heat of the summer, or it's **frozen**, the **same thing happens** — water can't infiltrate, increasing surface runoff and discharge.

Circular drainage basins

Water draining into the main river channel will **all arrive** in a **short space of time** because all points in the basin are a similar distance from the river. This **increases discharge**.

High drainage density

Drainage basins with a **high drainage density** (lots of streams) drain **quickly**, so have **short lag times**. Lots of water flows from the streams into the main river in a **short space of time**, **increasing discharge**.

Steep slopes

If the **drainage basin** has **steep-sided valleys**, water will reach the **river channel** much **faster** because water flows **more quickly** on **steeper slopes**. This **increases discharge**.

...and *Human Factors*

Humans often make flooding more **frequent** and more **severe** by **changing things** in the **drainage basin**. See page 63 for how urbanisation, agricultural practices and deforestation can increase the risk of flooding. But that's not all...

- **Flood management strategies** (see page 67) can actually end up making **flooding worse**. For example, if **dams fail** they release a **huge volume** of **water all at once** — giving a huge **increase** in **discharge**.
- **Climate change** could cause an **increase** in **rainfall** and **more storms** in some areas, which could **increase flooding**.

Increasing Flood Risk — Fieldwork and Research

Fieldwork Can Provide Primary Data on Factors That Lead to Flooding

1 You can do Fieldwork to Show the Link Between Precipitation and Flooding

A good way to investigate the **link** between **precipitation** and **flooding** is to **measure precipitation** and **estimate river discharge**. It's best to do this at **one or more locations** along a river, over a **period of time** (hours or days).

1) You can **measure** the amount of **precipitation** (in mm) using a **rain gauge**.
2) You can **measure water velocity** (in m/s) by **timing** how long something that floats takes to **pass between two points**.
3) You can **estimate** the **cross-sectional area** (in m²) by taking **depth measurements** at **several points** across a river. You can use these to draw the river's **cross section** on **graph paper**, and **count** the **squares** to work out the area.
4) To **calculate river discharge** (in m³/s), multiply the **water velocity** by the **cross-sectional area** of the channel.
5) Once you've recorded precipitation and river discharge **over a period of time**, you can plot them both on one graph called a **hydrograph**. A hydrograph allows you to see the **link** between **precipitation** and **river discharge**, and from your hydrograph you can work out the river's **lag time**.
6) If you carry out your fieldwork when a river floods you'll be able to **estimate** the **discharge** needed for the river to **flood**. This is called the **bankfull discharge** — the discharge at which the water level reaches the top of the river channel. If the **discharge** of the river **rises above** the **bankfull discharge**, the river will **flood**.

2 You can Measure Physical Factors that Affect Flooding

Some of the **physical factors** that affect flooding can be **easily measured**:

1) **Surface runoff** — the **amount** and **speed** of **surface runoff** affects the risk of flooding because the **sooner** precipitation reaches the river channel, the more chance there is of the river level rising above **bankfull discharge**. Surface runoff can be **measured directly** by digging a ditch of a known area and using a container to **collect runoff**. You need to **divide** the **amount of runoff** collected **by the rainfall** at each location so you can **compare** locations **fairly**.
2) **Infiltration** — a **high infiltration** rate **reduces surface runoff** and vice versa. **Infiltration rates** can be measured using an 'infiltration ring' that you push into the soil — you pour a **known volume** of water into the ring and then **record the time** it takes to **soak away**.
3) **Vegetation cover** — the **more vegetation** cover there is, the **more rainfall** will be **intercepted**, and so **less water** will **reach** the **channel** (and vice versa). You can **map** the **vegetation cover** of an area of land.

3 You can Monitor how Changes in Land Use are Increasing Risk

Fieldwork can also be carried out to determine the impact that **human activities** have on flood risk. For example:

Land use can be **mapped** to record the **amount of urbanisation** (e.g. developments on flood plains, areas of impermeable surfaces like concrete), **agricultural land** and **deforestation**. This can then be **combined** with **research** (see next page) to investigate the **link** between **flooding** and **changing land use**.

Increasing Flood Risk — Fieldwork and Research

Research can be Used to Gather Reliable Long-Term Data

Fieldwork provides you with **primary data** about factors that affect flooding, but you'll also need to do some **research** to gather reliable **long-term**, **secondary data** to support your **conclusions**.

1 You can Research the Link Between Precipitation and Flooding

1) You can get **rainfall data** from **local weather stations** or the **Met Office** — meteorological data and **weather reports** go back to the **1860s**. You can also look at **weather diaries** from the **18th century**. You can use this data to investigate the **long-term links** between **precipitation** and **flooding**, e.g. you could see whether **historical flood events** occurred in periods of **high rainfall**.

2) You can get **river discharge data** (including **hydrograph records**) from the UK **National River Flow Archive** (NRFA) or **local gauging stations**. These records often go back **many years**. You can use this data to **investigate the long-term links** between **river discharge** and **flooding**, e.g. you could find out **how high** the **river discharge** was when **past floods** occurred.

3) Information about the **size** and **impact** of **previous floods** can be found in **newspaper archives**, **council reports** and **National Water Archive sources**. This information can be useful in calculating **flood return intervals** (how often a flood of a **certain magnitude** is likely to **occur**).

2 You can Research How Physical Factors Affect Flooding

1) You can use **Ordnance Survey®** maps to work out the **size** and **gradient** of river **drainage basins** you're studying. Rainfall in drainage basins with **steep slopes** will reach the river more quickly, **increasing discharge**.

2) Look at **maps** on the **British Geological Survey** website to find out the **rock type** in different areas. Rocks like **granite** are **impermeable** (don't allow infiltration), which **increases surface runoff**.

3) You can use maps to investigate the **link** between **vegetation cover** and **flooding**. **Woodland** areas **reduce river discharge** because the vegetation **intercepts** precipitation before it hits the ground.

3 You can Research How Changing Land Use Affects Flooding

1) You can look for **historical maps**, **land use surveys**, **old photographs** and **historical diaries** (e.g. Samuel Pepys' diary) in **libraries** and **online**. These sources can show how land use has changed over the years, so you can **investigate the links** between **land use changes** (e.g. urbanisation) and **flooding**.

2) There are **flood risk maps** on the **Environment Agency** website. The maps show **areas at risk** from **flooding**, areas benefiting from **flood defences** and **flood management plans** for the future. You can use this data to see if flood defences have reduced the risk of flooding in some areas.

3) The **Environment Agency** also produces **reports** giving details about **previous floods**. You can use these reports to look at the **human factors** associated with **previous floods**, e.g. floods that have been made worse by **blocked drains** and **concrete driveways**.

Practice Questions

Q1 Why is prolonged rainfall a major cause of flooding?

Q2 Name three physical factors that increase the risk of flooding.

Q3 What data do you need to plot a hydrograph?

Q4 Where can you obtain long-term rainfall data from?

Exam Question

Q1 Describe and explain a programme of fieldwork and research you have carried out to investigate the physical factors that affect flooding. [15 marks]

I'm a meteorological dater — I just love Siân Lloyd...

Yup, you guessed it — it's another one of those exciting fieldwork and research topics. And I bet you've been lucky enough to go out and play pooh sticks in a river somewhere. So make sure you put that information to good use — if you get a question about fieldwork and research, dazzle the examiners with your detailed methods... they'll just love it.

Managing Extreme Weather

On to something a bit more optimistic now — strategies that help to manage floods, droughts and hurricanes.

Flood Prevention Strategies *Include* Hard Engineering *and* Soft Engineering

1 Hard Engineering *Defences Involve* Built Structures

Hard engineering defences are **man-made structures** that **reduce flooding**. Here are some of the **most common** types:

Scheme	How it works	Extra benefits	Disadvantages
Dams	Dams are huge walls built across rivers. A reservoir (artificial lake) is formed behind the dam. Flood water is caught by the dam, which prevents flooding downstream. The water is released as a steady flow throughout the year.	• Turbines are often built into the dams, which generate electricity. • Steady water release allows irrigation of land below the dam throughout the year. • People can use the reservoir for recreational activities, e.g. sailing.	• They're very expensive. • Land is flooded when a reservoir is created. This often destroys farmland and forces people to move elsewhere. • They affect wildlife, e.g. they can prevent salmon migrating upstream to breeding grounds. • They trap sediment normally carried in rivers. This can cause the dam to fail. It can also cause increased erosion downstream, as there's less protective sediment being deposited.
Levees	Levees are embankments built along rivers. The river can hold more water without overflowing and so it floods less often.	They allow the flood plain to be built upon.	• They're quite expensive. • There's a risk of severe flooding if the levees are breached.

2 Soft Engineering *Defences* Work With, *Not Against, the* Basin Processes

Soft engineering defences use **knowledge** of the **whole river basin** and its **processes** to **work with nature** to reduce flooding. Here are some of the **most common** types:

Scheme	How it works	Extra benefits	Disadvantages
Land use management	Planning restrictions prevent buildings or roads being constructed on the flood plain. Use of the flood plain is restricted to things like playing fields, allotments or parks. More water can infiltrate so there's less surface runoff, which reduces discharge and flooding.	• There are no new buildings or roads on the flood plain to be damaged, so the impact of any flooding is reduced. • It provides recreational opportunities, e.g. football fields.	• It restricts development. This is especially a problem where there's a shortage of housing. • It can't be used in areas that are already urbanised.
Alteration of urban surfaces	Building porous pavements or soakaways increases infiltration, which reduces rapid surface runoff to the river channel. This increases lag time, which reduces discharge and flooding.	Any pollutants in the water are filtered out by the soil before the water reaches the channel.	It's expensive.

Soft Engineering *is* More Sustainable *than* Hard Engineering

Hard engineering is often **expensive** and **disrupts natural processes**. Soft engineering tends to be **cheaper** and requires **much less time** and **money** to **maintain** than hard engineering. Soft engineering is designed to **integrate** with the natural **environment** and it creates areas like **wetlands**, which are important **habitats** for **wildlife**. So soft engineering's a **more sustainable management strategy** than hard engineering because it has a **lower economic cost** and **environmental impact**.

There are Strategies *that* Reduce *the* Impacts *of* Floods

If flooding does occur, there are ways to **reduce** the impact (to **minimise loss of life** and **property damage**). Strategies include:

1) **Forecasting** and **warning systems** — **weather forecasts** are used by **government organisations** to **predict flooding events**, so **warnings** can be given for people to **protect** their **property** or **evacuate**. E.g. before Carlisle flooded in 2005, the **Environment Agency** issued **flood warnings** via the **media** and direct **door knocking**, and sent **automatic voice messages** to over **5000 properties** at risk.

2) **Emergency plans** — **rescue plans**, **evacuation routes** and **emergency supplies** are put in place in areas **vulnerable** to **flooding**, to **minimise loss of life**. E.g. the **RAF** are **trained** in how to **rescue** people from floods using helicopters.

3) **Community education** — **information** about **what to do** in the event of a flood and how to **protect** your **home** is provided by organisations like the **Environment Agency** and **local councils**.

You can do **fieldwork** on flood strategies, e.g. **mapping where** they are and **recording** the **types**.
You can **research** flood strategies **online**, e.g. on the **Environment Agency** and **local UK councils'** websites.

Managing Extreme Weather

There are *Strategies* that *Reduce* the *Impacts* of *Droughts*...

1) **Conservation** of **surface water** and **groundwater** — e.g. **water use restrictions**.

2) **Changing agricultural practices** — e.g. planting crops **less dependent** on **water**, encouraging practices that **improve infiltration** and **retention** of **soil moisture, avoiding overgrazing** and **minimising erosion.**

3) Building **canals** or **redirecting rivers** to **irrigate** areas suffering from **drought**.

You can **research** drought strategies **online**, e.g. at the **Food & Agriculture Organisation website**.

...and *Strategies* that *Reduce* the *Impacts* of *Hurricanes*

1) **Forecasting** and **warning systems** — national weather forecasting bodies (such as the **National Hurricane Center** (**NHC**) in the USA) issue **hurricane warnings** via **radio** and **television** so people can get **supplies, secure** their **homes** and prepare to **evacuate.** E.g. the **NHC** issued **warnings** two days **before Hurricane Katrina** hit New Orleans, so a lot of people were able to **evacuate**, which **saved** many **lives.**

2) **Emergency plans** — **rescue plans, evacuation routes** and **emergency supplies** are put in place in areas **vulnerable** to **hurricanes**, to **minimise loss of life.** E.g. **refuges** with **emergency supplies** were set up for people who couldn't leave **New Orleans.**

3) **Community Education** — **governments** provide **information** about **what to do** and how to **protect** your **home.**

You can **research** hurricane forecasting systems **online**, e.g. at the **National Hurricane Center** website.

Some *Strategies* are *More Successful* than *Others*

You can use **fieldwork** and **research** to **evaluate** the **success** of existing **disaster management strategies**, for example:

1) You could visit somewhere that suffers from **frequent extreme weather events**, e.g. York suffers from flooding.

2) You'll need to **compare** the **impact** of **similar extreme weather events** — **before** and **after** the **management strategies** were put in place. E.g. **compare** the **impact** of the **1982 flood** in York (before river embankments were raised and sluice gates constructed) with the impact of the **2000 flood** (which happened after their construction).

3) Find **data** to help your **comparisons.** E.g. look at the **Environment Agency website** and **newspaper articles** to find the **size** of the **area flooded**, the **cost** of the damage and the **number** of **houses flooded** in the 1982 and 2000 floods.

4) Using the **data**, decide whether or not the **impact** was **lower** when the management strategies were in place (**not** all strategies are **successful**). Also look for any **unwanted side effects**, e.g. damage to natural habitats.

New *Technology* and *More Powerful Technology* has *Led* to...

① Better Coordinated Disaster Response

A **Geographic Information System** (**GIS**) is **software** that's used to **compare** and **analyse** different **sets** of **geographical data** — different maps are **overlaid** on top of each other. GIS can be used to **highlight densely populated areas** that are most **at risk** from an extreme weather event, so **search and rescue teams** can be **sent** to these areas and the **right areas** can be **evacuated.** For example, the **Federal Emergency Management Agency** (**FEMA**) can use GIS to **map** where **populations** are at **most risk** from **river flooding.** It does this by mapping the **flood plains**, then mapping the **densely populated areas** near to them and putting both maps **together** — the **overlap** shows the areas where most people are at risk.

Managing Extreme Weather

2 More Accurate Weather Forecasts

As **computers** and **radars** get **more powerful**, **forecasts** of **extreme weather** become **more accurate** and **more detailed**. This means **earlier warnings** can be given, so people have **more time** to **protect** their **property** or **evacuate**, which **reduces damage** and **loss of life**. Here are some **examples** of how technology is improving the accuracy of forecasts:

1) The **Met Office** is responsible for UK weather forecasting. It uses **supercomputers**, which are **more powerful** and have **faster processing speeds** than previous models. This means scientists can run **more complex weather models**, making the forecasts **more accurate**. Forecasting **accuracy** (e.g. correctly predicting the next day's rainfall in a particular place) rose from **79%** in **1980**, to **86%** in **1996**, because of **computer upgrades**.

2) The **National Oceanic and Atmospheric Administration** (**NOAA**) in the **USA** warns of **dangerous weather events** such as **storms** and **hurricanes**. In the **1980s** and **1990s**, NOAA **replaced** its **conventional weather radars** with radars, which can **measure** the **speed** of **precipitation particles** as well as their **position** and **intensity**. Scientists can now **identify wind patterns** that could cause **tornadoes**. By **2011**, NOAA will have a network of **radars** that will help scientists identify **rain**, **hail** and **snow**, allowing **more accurate predictions** of extreme weather.

3 Better Communications

New **communication technologies** include **portable cellphone towers** and **communications support trucks** with **satellite uplink**. These all help provide **better communication** during extreme weather events, **reducing loss of life** and **minimising damage**. For example, communications support trucks help **emergency services** stay in **contact** with **each other** and **weather forecasters**. This helps them perform **rescue operations efficiently** and keeps them **updated** on the **progress** of the **weather event**.

4 Drought-resistant crops

Advances in **genetic engineering technology** have led to the development of **drought-resistant crops**, which can **withstand long periods of drought**. They can help to **reduce loss of life** (from starvation) in drought-prone areas by providing **food**. However, many of these crops are still in the **experimental stage**, e.g. some don't grow well when it does rain.

5 Hurricane-Proof and Flood-Proof Buildings

Hurricane-proof and **flood-proof buildings** are buildings that have been **designed** to **withstand** floods or hurricanes. This means that when a flood or hurricane occurs there's **less structural damage**, leading to **reduced financial cost** and **loss of life**. At the moment the **technologies** involved are **expensive**, but in the **long-term** they may work out **cheaper** than the cost of **rebuilding** after disasters.

Practice Questions

Q1   What is hard engineering? Give an example of a hard engineering flood defence.
Q2   What is soft engineering? Give two advantages of using soft engineering rather than hard engineering defences.
Q3   Briefly describe two strategies that reduce the impacts of droughts.
Q4   Briefly describe two strategies that reduce the impacts of hurricanes.

Exam Question

Q1   Outline the ways in which new technology and more powerful technology have improved the management of extreme weather events.   [10 marks]

NOAA uses powerful computers to ensure the animals come in two by two...

Crikey, there seems to be an awful lot of text on these three pages... Don't worry, just make sure you know the strategies used to reduce the impact of extreme weather, how you can investigate if they're successful and how new technology is helping us. Phew.

Drought and Water Management

Droughts tend to last for longer than other extreme weather events, like tornadoes — in fact droughts can last for years. So their impact needs to be managed using sustainable strategies.

Managing Drought Involves Physical, Social, Economic & Political Responses

Governments, **water authorities**, **agricultural organisations**, **businesses**, **communities** and **individuals** all have **different strategies** for **reducing** the **impacts** of **drought** by **managing water supply** and **use**. Strategies include:

- **Physical responses** — e.g. **diverting** rivers and canals from wetter areas to **drier areas**.
- **Social responses** — e.g. **recycling water** from treated waste to use for flushing toilets.
- **Political responses** — e.g. **policies** to **regulate** water **supply** and **use**.
- **Economic responses** — e.g. **grants** to help **farmers** introduce **water-saving technologies**.

A drought management strategy is **sustainable** if it **permanently reduces water use** and **doesn't deplete resources** (e.g. money).

Case Study 1 — Drought And Water Management In Australia

A sustainable solution works in the long-term.

Parts of **Australia** have been suffering from **severe drought** for **several years** (see p. 58). Various **strategies** have been used to try to **reduce its impact**:

1) **Perth** has a **desalination plant** that supplies the city with **17%** of its **water**. The plant continuously **filters**, **treats** and **desalinates** (removes the salt from) **seawater** and **mixes** it with the **public water supply**. It's **powered** by **renewable energy** from **wind farms** and seawater is a **renewable resource** — so it's a **sustainable** strategy. **More** desalination plants are **planned** in Australia.

2) Many Australian regions have **temporary** or **permanent water use restrictions**, e.g. the **Murray-Darling Basin** region. **Water restrictions** include **banning** people from **watering lawns**, **washing vehicles**, **cleaning windows** and **refilling swimming pools**. Permanent water restrictions will **permanently reduce water use**, so they're a **sustainable** strategy.

3) Over **500 sewage treatment plants** in Australia now **recycle** some of their **treated wastewater** and **sewage**. **Households** have both a **drinking water supply** and a **recycled water supply**, which is used for **watering gardens**, **washing cars** and **flushing toilets**. Water recycling schemes **permanently reduce water use** and so are a **sustainable** strategy.

Mmm, tasty recycled water.

4) The Australian **Government** has introduced **rules**, **guidelines** and **educational programmes**, e.g. **labelling schemes** — products like washing machines must have a label showing their **water efficiency**. These schemes aim to **permanently reduce water use**, so they're a **sustainable strategy**.

5) The **Government** provides **direct economic assistance** (e.g. income support, interest rate subsidies) to **farmers**, **rural communities** and **small businesses** that are **dependent** on **agriculture**. Over **$1000 million** was provided in **drought assistance** in **2007**. These assistance schemes have a **high financial cost**, which **can't** necessarily be **maintained** in the long-term, so they're **not sustainable**.

6) Many people believe that **farming certain crops** (e.g. cotton) in **some areas** of Australia **can't** be **maintained**. So, the Government offers 'exit grants' of up to **$170 000** to **help farmers leave** their **land**, **relocate** and **retrain**. Exit grants can **permanently reduce water use** so they aim to be **sustainable**, but they have a **huge financial cost** so will only work as long as the Government can **afford** them.

7) The **Government** also **funds research** into **strategies** such as **cloud seeding** (dispersing substances such as sliver iodide into clouds, to induce rainfall), **water-conserving agricultural techniques** and growing **drought-resistant crops**. These strategies may be **sustainable** if they **permanently reduce water use** but it depends on how **expensive** they are to introduce.

These strategies have some **disadvantages**:

1) The **cost** of **building** the **desalination plant** in Perth was **very high**.
2) Many people **dislike** the **idea** of using **recycled water** as **drinking water**. E.g. **people** in **Toowoomba**, in the Murray-Darling Basin, **rejected** a proposal (**62%** against) to use **recycled water** for **25%** of the town's **drinking water** supply.
3) **Not many farmers accept exit grants**, e.g. because they may feel **forced** into **abandoning** a **family history** of **farming**.
4) **Cloud seeding doesn't work** in **cloudless skies**, which **limits** its use.

Drought and Water Management

Case Study 2 — Drought in South-East England

South-east England is prone to **dry weather** and **water shortages** — a recent **drought** lasted from **2004** to **2006**. Various **strategies** are being used to **reduce its impact**:

1) **Water companies** are trying to **fix leaking pipes**, which **waste** huge amounts of **water** — over **900 million litres** of water are lost **every day** in **London** through **leaking pipes**. This is a **sustainable** strategy because it **permanently reduces water wastage**.

2) The UK's first **desalination plant** has been approved for **east London** and is expected to be completed in **2009**. It will only operate in **periods** of **drought** or **low rainfall** and will treat **Thames estuary water** to provide almost a **million people a day** with **drinking water**. Even though it's **costing a lot** (an estimated **£250 m**) to build the plant, **Thames Water** are committed to running the plant on **100% renewable energy** (initially **biodiesel**, with wind power a possibility in the future). They also plan to use **waste energy** to **provide heating** for nearby homes. The desalination plant **won't deplete resources** so will be **sustainable**.

The real culprit of drought...

3) When **water levels** are **low**, **water companies restrict public water use** (e.g. hosepipe bans, sprinkler bans, car-wash bans) and the **Environment Agency restricts water** being used for **agriculture**. If these water restrictions are only **temporary**, they won't permanently reduce water use so **won't be sustainable**.

4) The **Government**, **Environment Agency** and **water companies** encourage **water conservation** through **campaigns** to **educate** people and **promote water efficiency** in homes, businesses and industry. For example, companies offer **free devices** to place in **toilet cisterns**, so **less water** is used when **flushing**. These **schemes** aim to **permanently reduce water use** so are **sustainable**.

5) The **Government** plans to **review water tariffs** and install **water meters** in areas **worst affected** by drought. Water metering means that people are **charged** for the **exact amount** of water they **use** — so they create a **financial incentive** to **use less** water. It's hoped the plan will **permanently reduce** water use and be a **sustainable** strategy.

These strategies have some **disadvantages**:

1) It's **not** always **easy** for water companies to **repair leaks**, e.g. because they might need **council permission** to **close roads** while the leaks are fixed. Fixing leaks can also be **expensive** and can take a **long time**.

2) Desalination plants are **very expensive** and some people think there's **no need** to spend such a huge amount of money building one in London — they think **fixing** the **leaking pipes** will **solve** the **water shortage**.

3) Some people argue that **compulsory water meters** are **unfair** to families living on a **low income** because they **won't** be able to **afford** the amount of water they **need**.

Practice Questions

Q1 What's meant by a 'sustainable' drought management strategy?
Q2 List five strategies used in Australia to manage the impacts of drought.
Q3 Give two disadvantages of Australia's drought management strategies.
Q4 List four strategies used in south-east England to manage drought.
Q5 Why do some people object to London's new desalination plant?

Exam Question

Q1 With reference to at least two named examples, discuss the sustainability of a range of drought management strategies. [10 marks]

Exit Grant — not just a stage direction from Eastenders...

I think I might be behind the times with that gag — he's not been in it for years, has he? Anyway, exam questions on drought are likely to ask you to compare the sustainability of drought management strategies, so make sure you know if they permanently reduce water use or if they deplete resources. Desalination plant or recycled water — it's a tough call...

Coastal Population Growth

Coastal environments are the areas where the land meets the sea, and it seems that everyone wants to be there...

Different Physical Factors Create Different Coastal Environments...

1) **Different rock types** and the process of **erosion** produce features like **cliffs**, **arches** and **stacks**.

2) Coastal **erosion** can also create **sheltered inlets** and deep **natural harbours**.

3) Where big **rivers** flow into the sea, wide tidal **estuaries** are formed.

See page 79 for more on coastal erosion.

4) **Beaches** are formed where the sea **deposits** eroded material, e.g. pebbles or sand.

5) **Flood plains** are wide, flat valley floors that are **regularly flooded** by a river.
Deltas form at a river **mouth** when sediment is deposited by the river faster than the sea removes it.

6) Certain **coastal ecosystems**, such as **mangrove swamps**, are valuable natural environments, providing important **breeding grounds** for many species of fish and shellfish.

...Which Encourage Different Types of Development

1) The **dramatic scenery** of some coastlines **attracts tourists**, e.g. the **Jurassic Coast World Heritage Site** in Dorset and East Devon attracts thousands of visitors each year.

2) Natural harbours allow **easy access** for the **import** and **export** of raw materials and manufactured goods by ship, which **attracts industry** to the area, e.g. companies such as **Shell** and **Esso** have located in **Rio de Janeiro**, Brazil.

3) **Estuaries** also allow **easy access** for ships, so encourage **port development** and **attract industry** to their **hinterlands** (the area surrounding the port), e.g. the **Port of Shanghai** on the **River Yangtze estuary** is the busiest port in the world.

4) Attractive **beaches** in areas with an **equable** (warm, temperate) climate will **attract tourists**, e.g. Costa Brava in Spain.

5) The nutrient-rich **alluvium** deposited by rivers on flood plains and deltas makes the **soil** very **fertile**. This **attracts agriculture**, e.g. the Nile Delta in Egypt has been farmed intensively for over 6000 years.

6) Some **coastal ecosystems** have a **high biodiversity**, which attracts **fishing** and **tourists**, e.g. the **Great Barrier Reef** in Australia attracts over a million tourists per year.

Increased Development Causes Coastal Population Growth

1) The physical factors of accessibility, fertile soil, equable climate, dramatic scenery and high biodiversity lead to an increase in fishing, tourism or industry.

2) An increase in **fishing**, **tourism** or **industrial/port development** in an area causes an **increase** in **population** because people are **attracted** to live there by the **opportunities for employment**.

3) Also, the **land** is often **flat** by the coast which means **homes** and **businesses** can be built much **more easily**. This **encourages** people to **live** and **locate businesses** in these areas, causing population growth.

Case Study 1: Brighton

Brighton is a coastal city in **East Sussex** on the **English Channel coast**.
Brighton has seen population growth for many years due to different factors:

Location

1) **Potential for fishing** — Brighton initially grew as a fishing village. People moved to the area because of the jobs available as fishermen.

2) **Tourism** — In the 18th century, it was believed that bathing in seawater was good for your health. Rich people, including the Prince of Wales, began to go to Brighton to be cured. This 'celebrity effect' saw Brighton attract wealthy tourists. People migrated to the area, attracted by the jobs that this new-found tourism provided.

3) **Accessibility** — In the Victorian period, a railway was built linking Brighton and London. Improved accessibility meant that working class people could travel to Brighton on day trips. This saw the growth of **mass tourism** and **exponential** population growth. Between 1841 and 1881, Brighton's population rose from **15 000** to over **135 000**.

4) **Industrial development** — Since the 1970s there has been a decline in tourists holidaying in British resorts. To fight this, Brighton has redeveloped itself as a centre for other **tertiary** and **quaternary** industries. It's now attracting large numbers of people who work in the **media** sector, particularly in "new media" such as the internet.

Coastal Population Growth

Case Study 2: Dubai

Dubai is in the **United Arab Emirates**, on the **Persian Gulf coast**.
It has experienced different periods of growth for different reasons:

Location of Dubai

1) Dubai's **geographical proximity** to India made it an important **trading centre** between Asia and Europe and many traders eventually **settled** in the city. Until the 1930s it was known for its pearl exports.

2) In **1966 oil** was discovered. **Industrial** and **port development** followed as Dubai Creek was dredged to improve **accessibility**. This allowed large ships access to the city and a **new port** was built at **Jebel Ali**, the biggest in the Middle East. The population of Dubai City **quadrupled** from 1968 to 1975 as **foreign workers**, largely from India and Pakistan, flooded into the city to work in **construction** and **oil production**.

3) It was known that Dubai's oil reserves would not last, so money from oil exports was used to **diversify the economy** to promote continued growth. As well as the building of the port at Jebel Ali, a **Free Economic Zone** was set up adjacent to the port, offering tax incentives to international businesses. Global businesses such as Microsoft®, IBM®, CNN and Reuters located there, attracting both **domestic** and **international workers** to the area.

4) Over the last 10 years, **tourism** has become important to the growth of Dubai. In contrast to British resorts, which are having to diversify because of a drop in tourist numbers, the Dubai government is **investing heavily** in tourist **infrastructure** and hopes to attract 10 million tourists per year by 2010. Huge construction projects, which require a **skilled foreign labour** force, have contributed to a **doubling** in Dubai's population since 1993. **Less than 20%** of the 1.4 million people who now live in Dubai are **native**.

You Need to Know How to **Research** Factors Affecting **Population Growth**...

1) You could look at **historical documents** and **maps** to see how **land use** has changed over time. This may indicate a change in the factors influencing the growth of the population.

2) If you want to find out **population numbers** and how quickly populations have grown, look at **census data**.

3) You should check out **local newspapers** for the areas you're studying as they may have information on **development projects**, which could be tied to an increase in population. Foreign newspapers may have English language websites.

4) If the location being studied is a tourist destination, then you could look at **holiday brochures** to identify factors that attract people to the area.

...and Do **Fieldwork** to **Investigate** It

1) You could do **land use surveys** and look for **visible evidence** of economic development in a UK location, and then try to link the results to the factors on the previous page.

2) To find people's **reasons for moving** to an area, you could **survey** local people of a range of ages. Tourists can also be surveyed to find out what **attracted** them to the area.

The results of the survey were unanimous — not biodiversity, but bikinis...

Practice Questions

Q1 Explain how soil fertility can influence coastal population growth.
Q2 List four factors, other than soil fertility, that can increase population growth at the coast.

Exam Question

Q1 For two contrasting coastal locations, explain why their population has grown rapidly.   [10 marks]

You say Dubai, and I say hello...

Make sure you learn the physical and economic factors that influence population growth at the coast and can relate them to two contrasting case studies. You might also get asked a weirdy fieldwork and research question on all this stuff, so make sure you know what methods you used to investigate coastal population growth. All this talk of Dubai has made me fancy a holiday...

Coastal Development and Conflict

Ahhh land use models. Bet you thought you'd left all that behind at GCSE. Nope. Mwahahaha...

A **Land Use Model** is a Diagram That Shows **How Land is Used** in Different Areas

Land use models contain a number of different **zones**. They're **simplified** diagrams showing typical **patterns of land use** in an area (the zones are defined according to the **major** land use in that area). There are three popular urban land use models:

1) **Burgess** — The Burgess model shows a settlement growing out in concentric zones from the centre.

2) **Hoyt** — Hoyt's model also has concentric zones, but adds sectors that grow along linear features, like main roads or rivers.

3) **Harris and Ullman** — This land use model shows multiple nuclei of different land uses. It assumes that similar industries with common land use and financial requirements develop near to each other.

Krystal, 28, a coastal land use model.

Burgess

Hoyt

Harris & Ullman

☐ Central Business District   ☐ Outlying Business District
☐ Low-quality residential   ■ Residential suburb
☐ Medium-quality residential   ■ Heavy manufacturing
☐ High-quality residential   ☐ Industrial suburb
☐ Wholesale light manufacturing

Coastal Developments **Distort** Land Use Models

Coastal development creates patterns of land use **zoning**. The diagram below shows a generalised land use model for a UK **seaside resort**. There are a number of characteristics to note:

1) **Shape** — The shape of land use zones is **distorted** in a coastal settlement, as the sea **limits growth** in that direction. **Linear zones** develop along the **sea front** and **main roads** away from the sea, similar to Hoyt's model. **Semicircular** zones may then grow **away from the coast**.

2) **Accommodation** — Hotels are attracted to sites with sea views or close to a promenade. The **larger hotels** will be based on the **sea front**, closest to the **Tourist Business District** (TBD). **Smaller hotels** will also try to locate on the sea front, but will be **further from the TBD**. This may lead to **multiple nuclei** of land use, like in Harris and Ullman's model. **Guesthouses** and bed and breakfasts, which can't charge as much for rooms, will be located **further** from the sea front, where land is **cheaper**. Residential housing will also be found further from the sea.

3) **Open spaces** — There may be **parks** or **pleasure gardens** on the sea front. Although land prices are now high, they will have been set aside at a time when prices were **lower**, e.g. during Victorian times. Strict **planning policies** prevent them from being developed.

> The Peak Land Value Intersection (PLVI) is the point in the resort which has the highest land prices.

4) **Entertainment** — Most tourist and recreational attractions are linked to key sites such as **piers**. They want to attract tourists, so they need to locate where tourists gather at the **sea front**. The **TBD** will usually be found along the **main street** running inland from the **Peak Land Value Intersection**. Sites that need a lot of **space**, such as golf courses, will be located near to the **edge** of the urban area.

Coastal Development and Conflict

Coastal Development Has Led to the Need for Planning Control

The rate of **development** at the coast is **increasing** as the coastal population continues to grow (see p. 72). However, the area of land available for development is decreasing and **fierce competition** is driving land prices up. To prevent unchecked growth of coastal areas and the possible destruction of important coastal ecosystems, strict **planning controls** are needed. The controls have to **balance** the **economic advantages** of development against the **environmental damage** caused.

Coastal Development Can Cause Conflict with Coastal Conservation

Different people have **different ideas** of how development should take place at the coast. These people are called **stakeholders** (and include tourists, small business owners, industrialists and conservationists). There's often **conflict** between stakeholders over **activity at the coast**. Some of the activities likely to cause conflict are:

1 Tourism

Tourism brings with it job opportunities and increased spending in local businesses (e.g. shops, cafés). However, there can be conflict between tourists and locals over traffic congestion, parking and noise. Tourism can also bring with it an environmental impact, as demand for access to tourist areas increases road building and construction of other amenities. These may be built on ecologically important land, leading to the destruction of valuable coastal ecosystems. Tourists can also contribute to coastal erosion by walking over sand dunes and destroying the plants that stabilise the dunes. This causes conflict between tourists and those responsible for protecting the ecology of the coast.

2 Overfishing

Fishing brings **jobs** and **money** to coastal areas but **overfishing** can lead to rapid decline and even **extinction** of fish populations. Efforts to conserve fish stocks cause conflict with the fishing industry. Treaties have been agreed by many countries to try to stop fish stocks from collapsing, e.g. the **EU Common Fisheries Policy**. But because these treaties **limit** the amount of fish that can be caught, they can lead to **job losses** and the **decline** of fishing communities.

3 Aquaculture

Demand for affordable fish and shellfish has led to the cultivation of aquatic animals in '**fish farms**'. This leads to **conflict** between the **producers** and **environmentalists**, due to the potential **negative effects** aquaculture can have on the surrounding ecosystem. High levels of fish waste can **decrease** dissolved **oxygen levels** in the water, which can lead to the **death** of **other fish** and plant life in the area. **Diseases** can spread **from farmed fish to wild fish**, which can then have a devastating effect on the natural population of certain species.

4 Industrialisation

As **ports** have **expanded** because of **industrial growth**, coastal **ecosystems** have come under threat. There's pressure to develop **salt marshes** at the coast as they provide flat land and sheltered water, ideal for ports and industry. There's a **conflict** between **industry** wanting to exploit the advantages of locating at the coast, and those trying to **protect** salt marshes and other **Sites of Special Scientific Interest** (SSSIs).

Pollution of both the sea and beaches from **industrial waste** has harmful effects for **swimmers** and **marine creatures**. This causes conflict between the **coastal industries** who are responsible for much of the pollution, and both **tourists** and **environmentalists**.

Practice Questions

Q1   Annotate a diagram to show the main land use zones of a seaside resort.
Q2   Describe the characteristics of the TBD.
Q3   Give a definition of the PLVI.

Exam Question

Q1   Examine the environmental impact of development at the coast and the conflict this causes.   [10 marks]

Aquaculture — not an underwater opera...

There's quite a lot to learn on these pages, but it's all good nuts 'n' bolts geography stuff — land use models, development, conflict. Make sure you know the characteristics of the coastal land use model, and the issues surrounding rapid development of the coast.

Coastal Development and Conflict

Sorry to break the bad news, but there's even more on coastal development and conflict.

Development in Dubai Has Caused Conflict

Dubai is in the **United Arab Emirates** (UAE), on the Persian Gulf coast. Page 73 outlines how and why Dubai developed.

The **rapid** coastal **development** since the 1970s has led to **conflict** in Dubai. This is because the **stakeholders** have **different opinions** and **ideas** about how development should proceed.

There are a number of **different activities** that cause **conflict** between stakeholders:

(1) **OIL PRODUCTION** — Dubai produces over **150 000 barrels** of oil a day. Oil is very important to the **economy** of UAE as a whole, making up around a **third** of the country's **GDP**. Conflict between **oil companies** and **conservationists** occurs because **oil tankers** cause **pollution** in the Gulf. This can take 5-8 years to flush out because the Gulf is a semi-enclosed body of water. The pollution of the sea around Dubai also causes conflict with the **fishing industry** as it can affect **fish stocks**.

(2) **FISHING** — Overfishing in Dubai is a problem as there are **no quotas** set to limit the numbers of fish that can be caught. Increasing **demand** from **tourists** for fresh local fish is putting further strain on fish stocks (certain species, such as the **hamour**, are in danger of being fished to **extinction**). Also, illegal **drift nets** are sometimes used, which affect **endangered species** such as the **hawksbill turtle**. This creates conflict between **conservation** agencies such as the **Environmental Research and Wildlife Development Agency (ERWDA)** and the **fishing industry**.

(3) **TOURISM** — In **2007** the number of **hotel guests** staying in Dubai was about **7 million**. It's estimated to reach **14 million** by **2015**. This causes conflict between the **tourist industry** and **conservationists** because the increase in tourists will lead to **more sewage, litter**, and more **erosion** of the coastline. **Four-wheel-drive vehicles** used for tourist excursions have also **damaged turtle nesting beaches**.

(4) **PROPERTY DEVELOPMENT** — Several 'mega projects' are being constructed in Dubai such as **The Palms** and **Waterfront** (artificial islands with houses, hotels and leisure facilities). They can **damage coastal habitats**, e.g. **Palm Jebel Ali** is being **built over coral reef**. Some of these developments are also being built on **land reclaimed** from the Persian Gulf using material **dredged** from the seabed. Dredging **destroys** the **seabed environment**. Many developments also **increase** the **number of tourists** and so increase the problems they cause. This creates conflict between **property developers** and **conservationists**.

A **conflict matrix** can be used to **record** the conflicts between **different stakeholders**.

For Dubai it would look something like this. ⟹

	Oil companies	Fishing industry	Conservationists	Property developers
Oil companies				
Fishing industry	-1			
Conservationists	-1	-1		
Property developers	0	0	-1	
Tourist industry	0	+1	-1	+1

+1 = interaction is positive
-1 = interaction is negative (conflict)
0 = no direct interaction

Tools Can be Used to Assess Conflict and Evaluate Developments

1) An **Environmental Impact Assessment** (EIA) is a process to determine the **environmental consequences** of a development project.

E.g. an EIA was undertaken for a proposed **combined power station** and **desalination plant** at **Hassyan** in **Dubai**. Data from **publications, internet research** and **satellite imagery** was studied. **Government officials, local interest groups** and **international experts** were consulted. An **ecological survey** to gather information on plants, animals, habitats and water quality was undertaken. A number of issues were identified, including:

1) **Seawater quality changes** — e.g. increased temperature and salinity.

2) **Modification** or **loss of coastal habitats** — e.g. **coral reefs** could be lost due to the seawater changes (corals are very sensitive to temperature changes).

3) **Loss** of the **Jebel Ali Wildlife Sanctuary**.

Coastal Development and Conflict

2) A **Cost-Benefit Analysis** (CBA) is a process that allows the **costs** and **benefits** of any development to be examined to see if it should go ahead. It can also be used to **compare different developments** to see which is best. All aspects of the development are given a **monetary value**, e.g. how much it costs to build, how much money it would bring to the area per year, etc. Then you can see if the total benefits **outweigh** the total costs. But, it's **difficult** to give a monetary value to **all** costs and benefits (e.g. the economic value of hamour fish is difficult to figure out), so it can be inaccurate.

3) **Values analysis** is another way of deciding if a development should go ahead. It's similar to a cost-benefit analysis, but involves examining the **viewpoints** of **different stakeholders** as well.

> E.g. after analysing the costs and benefits of the **combined power station** and **desalination plant** at **Hassyan** in **Dubai**, it was **approved**. The viewpoints of different stakeholders were considered, but the decision was largely due to the **huge increase in the demand for water**. Dubai currently has the capacity to supply **260 m gallons/day**, but demand is expected to increase to **800 m gallons/day** by **2015**. The new desalination plant will be able to provide an extra **600 m gallons/day**.

Charlie built a moat to protect his coastal development from conflict.

You Need to be Able to *Investigate Coastal Development* and *Conflict*

FIELDWORK

1) To assess the **environmental value** of an area that may be affected by development you could **survey** the **biodiversity** of the area, e.g. by counting the number of **different species** present.

2) To assess the **recreational value** of an area that may be affected by development you could **survey** the **different recreational activities** on offer there.

3) To **assess** the **impact** of **tourists** attracted by a development, you could **survey** the amount of **litter**, **trampling of vegetation** and **erosion** in the area.

> Don't forget that this would have to be done before and after the development, or you'd have to compare it to a similar area away from the development.

RESEARCH

1) To **identify** any **new developments** you could look at **planning applications**, or look in **newspapers** for articles about proposed developments. Looking at **land use maps** could also indicate new developments.

2) To **assess** the **environmental value** of an area that may be affected by development (e.g. fragile habitats like **dunes**, **salt marshes** and **SSSIs**) you could research if it **provides habitats** for **endangered species**.

> SSSIs are Sites of Special Scientific Interest.

3) To **assess** the **impact** of **fishing**, **aquaculture** and **tourism** you could look for **newspaper articles** or look on the internet for **reports** from the government or conservation groups.

Practice Questions

Q1 List the four main activities that cause conflict between stakeholders in Dubai.

Q2 What is an Environmental Impact Assessment?

Exam Questions

Q1 Explain, with reference to one or more named areas, how economic development has threatened the coastal environment. [10 marks]

Q2 Describe and explain the fieldwork and research you could do to investigate development and conflict at the coast. [15 marks]

...hello, hello. I don't know why you say Dubai, I say hello...

See what I did there? Very clever. Well, at least I thought so. Anyway, back to you being clever — or, more precisely, proving to the examiners that you're clever. The best way to do that is to learn all the lovely facts, figures and other bits of thrilling information on these two pages. Then we can move on from coastal development and conflict. Thank goodness for that.

Coastal Processes

All kinds of processes occur in coastal environments. If you're not up to speed on the basics, then have a read of this...

Coasts are Systems — They Have Inputs, Processes and Outputs

1) **INPUTS** — **river sediment**, sediment from **cliffs** that have been **eroded** or suffered **landslides**, and sediment that has been **transported** by waves from **offshore** (out at sea).

2) **PROCESSES** — **wave action**, **tidal movement**, **erosion**, **weathering**, **transportation**, **deposition**.

3) **OUTPUTS** — sediment **washed out to sea**, or deposited **further along** the coast.

> **Coastal sediment cells** (also called **littoral cells**) are lengths of coastline that are pretty much entirely **self-contained** for the movement of sediment. Each one is a **coastal system**. So **processes** going on in **one cell** don't affect the movement of sediment in **another** cell.

Sediment cells in England and Wales

Waves are Responsible for Erosion and Deposition of Beach Sediment

1) **Waves** are created by the **wind** blowing over the surface of the sea. The **friction** between the wind and the surface of the sea gives the water a **circular motion**.

2) The **effect of a wave** on the **shore** depends on its **height**. Wave height is affected by the **wind speed** and the **fetch** of the wave. The fetch is the **maximum distance of sea** the wind has blown over in creating the waves. A **high wind speed** and a **long fetch** create **high** waves.

3) As waves approach the shore they **break**. **Friction** with the sea bed **slows** the bottom of the waves and makes their motion more elliptical (squashed and oval-shaped). The **crest** of the wave rises up and then **collapses**.

4) Water washing **up** the beach is called the **swash**. Water washing **back** towards the sea is called the **backwash**.

5) There are **two types** of wave:

Constructive waves have a **low frequency** (only around **6-8** waves per minute). They're **low** and **long**, which gives them a more **elliptical** cross profile. The powerful swash carries material up the beach and **deposits** it.

Destructive waves are **high** and **steep**, with a more **circular** cross profile. They have a **higher frequency** (**10-14** waves a minute). The strong backwash **removes** material from the beach.

6) The waves in an area are usually mainly constructive or mainly destructive.

Wave frequency is how many waves pass a point in a particular time.

Tides Affect Where Waves Break

Tides are the periodic **rise** and **fall** of the **ocean surface**. They're caused by the gravitational pull of the **Moon** and the **Sun**. Tides affect the **position** at which **waves break** on the beach (at high tide they break higher up the shore). The area of land between **maximum high tide** and **minimum low tide** is where landforms are created and destroyed.

Sub-aerial Weathering Occurs Along the Coastline

1) **Sub-aerial weathering** describes coastal processes that are **not linked** to the action of the sea. It includes **freeze-thaw weathering** and **salt weathering**. Weathering **weakens cliffs** and makes them **more vulnerable** to **erosion**.

2) **Throughflow** (the flow of water through the cliffs) and **runoff** (the flow of water over the land) caused by **heavy rain** can also make cliffs more **unstable** and increase the likelihood of **mass movement**.

3) Mass movement is the **movement** of material **downhill** due to gravity. It includes **landslides**, **slumping** (a type of landslide) and **rockfalls**.

Coastal Processes

There are **Five** Main Ways **Waves Erode** the **Coastline**

Waves don't just erode beaches — they also erode **rocks** and **cliffs**. Here are the five main ways they do it:

1) **Abrasion/corrasion** — Bits of rock and sediment transported by the waves smash and grind against rocks and cliffs, breaking bits off and smoothing surfaces.
2) **Hydraulic action** — **Air** in cracks in cliffs is **compressed** when waves crash in. The pressure exerted by the compressed air breaks off rock pieces.
3) **Quarrying** — The energy of a wave as it breaks against a cliff is enough to detach bits of rock.
4) **Corrosion/solution** — **Soluble rocks** (e.g. limestone, chalk) get gradually **dissolved** by the seawater.
5) **Attrition** — Bits of rock in the water smash against **each other** and break into smaller bits.

The **Rate** at Which a Stretch of Coastline is Eroded Depends on **Several Factors**

1) **The width of beach** — i.e. the distance between high and low tide marks. Beaches slow down waves, reducing their erosive power. So a wide, flat beach will protect cliffs more than narrow, steeper beaches.
2) **The breaking point of the waves** — a wave that breaks directly at the foot of a cliff transfers the most energy to the cliff and causes the most erosion. Waves that hit the cliff before they break, or break further offshore will erode much less.
3) **The aspect** — if the coastline faces the dominant wind and wave direction, erosion will be faster.
4) **The fetch of the waves** — waves with a longer fetch are much higher and steeper, and have more energy, so will cause the most erosion.

See page 84 for a case study of coastal erosion.

5) **Rock type** — hard rocks like granite are much more resistant to erosion than softer rocks, e.g. clay.

Currents Transport **Sediment**

1) A **current** is the general flow of water in one direction.
2) Currents move material **along** the coast — this is called **longshore drift**.
3) **Swash** carries sediment (e.g. shingle, pebbles) **up** the beach, **parallel** to the prevailing wind. **Backwash** carries sediment back **down** the beach, at **right angles** to the shoreline.
4) When there's an **angle** between the prevailing wind and the shoreline, a few rounds of swash and backwash move the sediment **along** the shoreline.

Practice Questions

Q1 Draw a table to show the main inputs, processes and outputs of a coastal system.
Q2 Sketch a diagram to show how longshore drift works.

Exam Questions

Q1 Describe the characteristics of constructive and destructive waves. [4 marks]
Q2 Outline how cliffs are eroded along the coastline. [6 marks]

What did the sea say to the beach — nothing, it just waved...

It's a good idea to get your head around all the processes going on at the coast — cliffs are eroded and weathered, currents carry sediment about and constructive waves deposit it. Then there are destructive waves that annoyingly remove prime sunbathing spots.

Coasts Under Threat — Erosion and Flooding

Ah, to live by the sea. The fresh air... the views... the erosion and flooding... hold on a second, what was that last one?

Coastal Development is Threatened by Erosion and Flooding

Coastal environments are vulnerable to physical processes such as **erosion** and **flooding**. This means that **coastal developments** are also **at risk**. As the level of development in coastal areas **increases** (see page 72), so does the potential **impact** of erosion and flooding in these areas.

Coastal Flooding Occurs Naturally Due to Physical Causes

Coastal lowlands (such as coastal plains, salt marshes and deltas) are liable to flooding when the sea rises above normal high-tide level. There are several **physical causes** of this:

1) **Low pressure atmospheric systems** such as **hurricanes** (cyclones) reduce atmospheric pressure on the sea surface, causing it to **rise**. This is called a **storm surge**.

2) **Strong onshore winds** can force water to higher levels along the coast, allowing waves further inland.

3) **Tidal currents** and **surges** may be funnelled into a coastal bottleneck such as the Bay of Bengal, or English Channel, forcing sea levels higher.

4) **High rainfall** may cause **high river discharge**. If sea level at the river mouth is high, e.g. due to high spring tides or storm surges, the large volume of river water may be **unable to drain** into the sea and can cause flooding.

5) When a **combination of the above factors** coincide. E.g. a hurricane making landfall in Florida may cause a storm surge and high rainfall (which may be unable to drain to the sea). The storm surge and wave energy may both be intensified by strong onshore winds.

6) **Tsunamis** are huge ocean waves caused when water is displaced by **landslides**, **volcanic eruptions** or **submarine earthquakes** that shift the ocean floor. When travelling in open water (i.e. out at sea) they have a very small wave height (less than a metre) and travel at hundreds of kilometres an hour. As the waves approach the coast, the bottom of the waves slow considerably due to friction with the sea bed, causing the wave height to increase enormously.

Coastal Flooding May Also be Caused or Intensified by Human Activity

1) **Management of river systems** — some management strategies (e.g. dams) trap sediment and so reduce the amount being deposited at the river's mouth. This causes deltas and salt marshes to shrink, providing less protection against high tides and storm surges.

2) **Management of coastal systems** — some management strategies alter sediment movement, reducing the amount of protective beach material further along the coast. E.g. coastal defences at Barton in Hampshire have reduced sediment transport to the east, allowing Hurst Spit to be breached more often, flooding lowlands behind.

3) **Building on coastal lowlands**, especially sand dunes, has restricted sediment supply to protective beaches and marshes. Development of coastal lowlands, such as Florida, also **increases** the **impact** of any coastal floods.

4) **Reclamation of coastal lowlands**, such as the Dutch polders, and reclaimed marshes along the east coast of England. Draining this land to reclaim it causes the land to shrink to become lower than sea level.

Coastal Flooding is Now More Likely Because of Rising Sea Level

1) Sea level **varies** on a daily basis with the **tidal cycle**. **Onshore winds** and **low atmospheric pressure systems** also cause the sea surface to rise **temporarily**.

2) On a much longer time scale, global sea level is rising at almost **2 mm** each year, which is forecast to **increase** to **4 or 5 mm** a year by 2100.

3) This will increase both the **frequency** and **severity** of flooding in low-lying coastal areas.

Recorded and predicted sea level change

- Recorded rise in sea level
- Average predicted rise
- Max. and min. predicted rise

88 cm
49 cm
9 cm

Coasts Under Threat — Erosion and Flooding

Sea Level Changes are Either Eustatic or Isostatic

EUSTATIC

Eustatic sea level change is caused by a change in the **volume of water** in the sea, or by a change in the **shape** of the **ocean basins**.

The effects are always **global** and the main **causes** are:

1) **Tectonic movements** of the Earth's crust that alter the shape (and so the volume) of ocean basins. E.g. sea floor spreading **increases** the **volume** of the basin and so **decreases** sea level.

2) **Changes in climate.** Different changes affect sea level in different ways:

   - An **increase** in **temperature** causes **melting** of **ice sheets**, which **increases** sea level. It also causes water to **expand**, which **increases** sea level further.

   - A **decrease** in **temperature** causes more precipitation to fall as **snow**. This increases the volume of water **stored** in **glaciers** and so reduces the volume of the sea, which **decreases** sea level.

ISOSTATIC

Isostatic sea level change is caused by **vertical movements** of the land **relative** to the sea.

Any **downward** movement of the land causes sea level to **rise** locally, while **uplift of land** causes sea level to **fall**.

The effects are always **local** and the main **causes** are:

1) **Tectonic** (crustal) uplift or depression, which occurs mostly at plate boundaries.

2) **Compression** or **decompression** of the Earth's crust due to accumulation or melting of **ice sheets**. Slow uplift of land can continue for thousands of years after the weight of a **retreating glacier** has gone. **Accumulation of sediment**, mostly at the mouths of major rivers, can also cause **compression**.

3) **Subsidence** of land due to shrinkage after **abstraction of groundwater**, e.g. drainage of marshland.

Sea Level Rise Can Have a Variety of Impacts

1) **More frequent** and **more severe coastal flooding**.
   Flooding of low-lying areas has increased with sea level rise and it will increase more with further rises. For example, at the beginning of the 20th century **St Mark's Square** in **Venice** flooded less than **10** times per year, and in **1996** it was flooded almost **100** times.

2) **Submergence of low-lying islands**.
   Lots of low-lying islands have **disappeared** as sea level has risen, and loads more are **at risk** of disappearing. For example, if the sea level rises by just **0.5 m** from the current level then most of the **Maldives** would be submerged.

Barry and Ami wish they hadn't delayed their holiday to the Maldives.

3) **Changes in the coastline**.
   As sea levels rise the coastline changes — **islands** are **created** and the **area** of **land** is **decreased**. E.g. over the last 10 000 years sea level rise has separated Britain from mainland Europe. If the sea level rises **0.3 m** from the current level **8000 km²** of land in **Bangladesh** will be lost.

Don't forget that all these impacts have **further impacts**, e.g. damage to coastal **infrastructure**, decrease in **tourism**, decrease in **agriculture**, loss of **homes** etc.

Practice Questions

Q1   What is a storm surge?

Q2   Briefly describe three physical and three human causes of coastal flooding.

Q3   Briefly describe two causes of eustatic sea level change and two causes of isostatic sea level change.

Exam Question

Q1   Briefly describe the possible impacts of sea level rise.   [10 marks]

I'd start moving up onto high ground now...

You need to know the causes of coastal flooding, and you need to know them well. Also, examiners love asking questions about current issues and rising sea levels are a hot topic at the moment — so make sure you're hot on all the details too.

Coastal Flooding — Case Study

Case study time again, and it's not a particularly jolly one I'm afraid. But then coastal flooding never is that jolly...

A *Tsunami* Struck *Southern Asia* on *26th December 2004*

The **tsunami** that devastated areas of **Indonesia**, **Sri Lanka**, **Thailand** and **India** in December 2004 was caused by a submarine **earthquake** in the Indian Ocean. The earthquake is estimated to have measured **9.0** on the Richter scale, making it one of the **strongest earthquakes** ever recorded. The map below shows some of the countries **most affected** by the tsunami.

The tsunami travelled across the **Bay of Bengal** at speeds up to **800 kilometres per hour**. The waves struck south-eastern India just **two hours** after the earthquake.

The tsunami reached more than **2 km inland** at Trincomalee in the north-east of **Sri Lanka**.

Waves up to **30 m high** struck the Indonesian island of **Sumatra** within **minutes** of the earthquake.

The **epicentre** of the earthquake was off the **western coast** of **Sumatra** in Indonesia.

The Tsunami Had Severe *Economic, Environmental* and *Social Impacts*

The *Economic Impacts* Were *High* and *Long-Lasting*

A destroyed fishing boat on a beach in Phuket, Thailand.

1) Estimates of the **cost** of the initial **damage** caused by the tsunami are between **$8 billion** and **$15 billion**.

2) **Fishing** is a large part of the economy for many of the areas hit by the tsunami. **Boats**, **nets** and other **equipment** were **destroyed** or **lost**, severely affecting the livelihood of fishermen.

3) **Salinisation** (increase in salt content) of land has severely **reduced soil fertility**. **Crop production** will be **lower** for several years to come.

4) **Tourism** is important to the economy of many of the countries affected. **25% of hotels** in southern **Thailand** were **closed** for at least **6 months** because of damage and the number of **foreign visitors** to the island of **Phuket dropped 80%** in **2005** as the area was perceived to be less safe.

Coastal Flooding — Case Study

Environmental Impacts Included Habitat Destruction and Pollution

Mangrove trees uprooted by the waves.

1) **8 million litres of oil** were released into the environment after **two oil plants** in Indonesia were **destroyed**. The oil caused widespread **pollution** at sea and **contamination** of the soil, posing **health risks** to humans in the area.

2) **Mangrove forests** as far away as the **East African coast** were **damaged** by the force of the waves, or **covered in layers of silt**.

3) The **high salt content** of the floodwater **destroyed** the natural balance of many **ecosystems**, e.g. the **Karagan Lagoon** in southern **Sri Lanka**.

The Social Impacts Were the Highest Recorded for a Tsunami

1) It was the **deadliest** tsunami **ever recorded**, with an estimated **230 000** people **killed** or **missing**.

2) It's estimated that **1.7 million people** were made **homeless**.

3) Many sources of fresh **drinking water** were **polluted**, either by **sewage** or by **saltwater**.

4) An estimated **400 000 lost their jobs** in **Sri Lanka** alone.

The remains of a house in a destroyed village in Indonesia.

Human Activity Increased the Impact of the Flooding

1) **Mangrove forests** protected parts of the **Sri Lankan coast** by **absorbing wave energy**. Pressure for **tourist development** and the creation of intensive **prawn fisheries** has led to the **destruction** of mangrove forests in other areas around the Indian Ocean. It's estimated that **Thailand** has lost up to **half** of its mangrove forests since **1975**. The lack of protection meant that waves could reach **further inland** and the **flooding** was **much worse** than in areas protected by mangroves.

2) It's thought that healthy **coral reefs** surrounding the **Maldives** acted as a **breakwater** (reducing the power of the tsunami waves) and prevented the complete destruction of the low-lying islands. Illegal **coral mining** and the use of dynamite in explosive **'blast fishing'** has **destroyed** many offshore coral reefs in the Indian Ocean. This reduced the level of natural protection from the waves.

In the absence of a natural breakwater, Nancy was sent in to hold back the waves.

Practice Questions

Q1   On what date did the south Asia tsunami happen?

Q2   Name three countries that were badly affected by the south Asia tsunami.

Exam Question

Q1   Describe and explain the causes and effects of coastal flooding in a named coastal area.   [15 marks]

Coastal flooding — it really is no joke...

You can see from these pages the huge impact of coastal flooding on humans and the environment. Make sure you know a case study of the causes and effects of coastal flooding in a specific area — it's one the examiners love to ask you about.

Coastal Erosion — Case Study

The Holderness coastline in East Yorkshire is the fastest eroding coastline in Europe (what a claim to fame).
If you get a case study question in the exam you need to have a bagful of juicy facts at the ready, so get learnin'.

The Average *Rate of Erosion* at Holderness is About *1.8 Metres per Year*

The Holderness coastline is **61 km long** — it stretches from Flamborough Head to Spurn Head. In some places, e.g. **Great Cowden**, the rate of erosion has been over **10 m/year** in recent years. The main **reasons** for this rapid erosion at Holderness are shown in **purple**. Some of the possible **social**, **economic** and **environmental impacts** of the erosion are also shown.

1) **Easily eroded rock type** — the cliffs are mostly made of **till** (or 'boulder clay'). Not only is till **easily eroded** through **corrasion**, but it's also prone to **slumping** when wet.

2) **Narrow beaches** — beaches slow the waves, **reducing** their **erosive power**. Narrow beaches **protect** the cliffs **less**. Beaches along the Holderness coast are narrow for two main reasons:
   - **Flamborough Head stops sediment** from the north replenishing the beaches along Holderness. It's also made of **chalk**, which dissolves when eroded rather than making sand for the beaches.
   - **Coastal defences**, e.g. at Mappleton (see p. 86 for why these lead to narrow beaches). This is a **human** cause of erosion.

3) **Powerful waves** — the waves are powerful because of:
   - The **long fetch** (all the way from the **Arctic Ocean**).
   - The coast faces the **dominant wind** and **wave direction** (from the **north-east**).

1) **Property prices** along the coast have **fallen** sharply for those houses at risk from erosion.

2) Around **30 villages** have been lost since **Roman times**.

3) **Visitor numbers** in **Bridlington dropped** by over **30%** between **1998** and **2006** (though this could have been due to other reasons).

4) Many **caravan parks** are at risk from erosion, e.g. **Seaside Caravan Park** at **Ulrome** is losing an average of **10 pitches a year**.

5) **£2 million** was spent at **Mappleton** in **1991** to **protect** the coast.

6) The **Gas Terminal** at **Easington** is at risk (it's only **25 m** from the cliff edge). This terminal accounts for **25%** of **Britain's gas supply**.

7) **80 000 m²** of good quality **farmland** is lost each year. This has a huge effect on **farmers' livelihoods**.

8) Some **SSSIs** (Sites of Special Scientific Interest) are threatened — e.g. **The Lagoons** near **Easington** are part of an SSSI. It has a colony of over 1% of the British breeding population of **little terns**. The lagoons are separated from the sea by a narrow strip of sand and shingle. Erosion of this would connect the lakes to the sea and 'The Lagoons' would be destroyed.

Map labels: CHALK, Bridlington, Flamborough Head, Ulrome, longshore drift, Mappleton, BOULDER CLAY, Easington, Humber Estuary, Spurn Head

You Need to Know How to *Research Erosion Rates* and *Causes*

CAUSES
1) Research what the **cliffs** are **made from** at **different locations**. E.g. in Holderness the cliffs are all made of till, but the different tills (e.g. Withernsea Till, Skipsea Till) will erode at different rates.
2) Research the effect of **coastal defences** on erosion rates. E.g. for Holderness you could compare erosion rates before and after the defences were built at Mappleton in 1991 — both at Mappleton and a little way to the south (down-drift), e.g. at Great Cowden.

EROSION RATES
1) A great way to calculate the erosion rate is to **compare** the **position** of the **coastline** on maps (or **satellite photos**) from **different years**. Don't forget that the maps and photos need to be at the **same scale** for easy comparison.
2) You could also simply research erosion rates on the **internet**. E.g. there's data available for sites all along the Holderness coast.

Coastal Erosion — Case Study

You Also Need to Know Fieldwork Methods for Erosion Rates and Causes

CAUSES

1) You could **compare erosion rates** for locations just up-drift and down-drift of **sea defences** (e.g. at Mappleton) to tell you if sea defences are affecting erosion rates.

2) You could **measure** the **width** of **beaches** at different points to investigate whether width of beach affects the rate of erosion.

Make sure other factors (e.g. sea defences, type of till) are as similar as possible and measurements are taken at the same stage of the tide.

EROSION RATES

You could **compare** the **position** of the **present-day cliff-line** with recent **satellite photos** or **local maps** to estimate the rate of erosion.

You Need to be Able to Research the Impacts of Erosion...

SOCIAL

1) Use **old maps** and **historical records** to identify **villages** that have disappeared into the sea.

2) Research **census data** for the past 100 years to find changes in **population size** and **structure** for coastal areas.

3) Research **land** and **property values** to see if they've gone **down**.

Don't forget that you need to compare the trend to a similar area (so you can tell that the trend is due to erosion, not just general change in population in coastal areas).

ECONOMIC

1) Contact **insurance companies** to ask for data about **changes in premiums** for settlements along the coast.

2) Research **trends** in **tourist visitor numbers** to see if fewer tourists are visiting the area.

3) Research the impact on **industry** and **jobs** in the area.

For all these things, don't forget that you need to compare the trend to a **similar** coastal area.

ENVIRONMENTAL

Contact **Natural England** (the government body responsible for conservation) for information and data about how erosion is affecting the **environment** in the area.

The **local newspapers** will contain stories about all the different impacts. Watch out though — they can be unreliable.

You could also contact **local politicians** for their own and local residents' views on the impacts of erosion.

...And Do Fieldwork to Investigate Them

SOCIAL

1) Use a **questionnaire** to **survey local people**, asking how it's affected them. You could **analyse** the answers to find out **who's affected the most**, e.g. farmers, pub owners, retired people etc.

2) Use a **questionnaire** to **survey tourists** (e.g. in the main resorts of Bridlington or Hornsea), asking their opinions about whether coastal erosion has affected them or whether they will continue holidaying there.

ECONOMIC

Arrange to **visit** any **businesses** affected. E.g. go to a caravan park in Holderness and find out how it's affected their business.

Visiting businesses affected by coastal erosion was more pleasant than Raj originally thought...

Practice Questions

Q1 Describe how you could research the social impacts of coastal erosion.

Q2 Why do you need to compare the trends you find in your research to a similar area?

Exam Question

Q1 With reference to one named area describe and explain the causes of coastal erosion. [10 marks]

Like easily eroded till, I'll be gone when the morning comes...

You need to know a case study of coastal erosion as well as you know how to make beans on toast. Draw an annotated diagram to refresh your memory... toast, then butter, then beans, er... sorry, I mean label the physical causes, human causes and impacts.

Coastal Management

Coastal management is a complex thing. Fixing up one coastal area can have the unintended effect of messing up another area nearby.

See pages 82-84 for some examples of the impacts of coastal erosion and flooding.

Only **Some Parts** of the **Coast** are **Managed**

The aim of coastal management is to **protect homes**, **businesses** and the **environment** from **erosion** and **flooding**.

This is because flooding and erosion of the coastline can have severe **social**, **economic** and **environmental impacts**.

All coastal settlements want to be defended, but the amount of **money available** is **limited** so not everywhere can be defended. Choosing which places are defended (and how) is based on a **cost-benefit analysis**. The money available is usually used to protect **large settlements** and important **industrial sites**, rather than isolated or small settlements.

There are **Four Options** for **Coastal Management**

1) **Hold the line** — maintain the **existing** coastal defences.
2) **Advance the line** — build **new** coastal defences **further out to sea** than the existing line of defence.
3) **Do nothing** — build **no** coastal defences at all, and deal with erosion and flooding **as it happens**.
4) **Retreat the line** — build no coastal defences, but **move people away** from the coast.

Coastal Defences *Include* Hard Engineering *and* Soft Engineering

Hard Engineering *Defences Involve* Built Structures

Defence	How it works	Cost	Disadvantage
Sea wall	The wall reflects waves back out to sea, preventing erosion of the coast. It also acts as a barrier to prevent flooding.	Expensive to build and maintain	It creates a strong backwash, which erodes under the wall.
Revetment	Revetments are slanted structures built at the foot of cliffs. They can be made from concrete, wood or rocks. Waves break against the revetments, which absorb the wave energy and so prevent cliff erosion.	Expensive to build, but relatively cheap to maintain	They create a strong backwash, as above.
Gabions	Gabions are rock-filled cages. A wall of gabions is usually built at the foot of cliffs. The gabions absorb wave energy and so reduce erosion.	Cheap	Ugly
Riprap	Boulders piled up along the coast are called riprap. The boulders absorb wave energy and so reduce erosion.	Fairly cheap	Can shift in storms.
Groynes	Groynes are fences built at right angles to the coast. They trap beach material transported by longshore drift. This creates wider beaches, which slow the waves (reducing their energy) and so gives greater protection from flooding and erosion.	Quite cheap	They starve down-drift beaches of sand. Thinner beaches don't protect the coast as well, leading to greater erosion and flooding.
Breakwaters	Breakwaters are usually concrete blocks or boulders deposited off the coast. They force waves to break offshore. The waves' energy and erosive power are reduced before they reach the shore.	Expensive	Can be damaged in storms.
Earth bank	Mounds of earth act as a barrier to prevent flooding.	Quite expensive	Can be eroded.
Tidal barrier	Tidal barriers are built across river estuaries. They contain retractable floodgates that can be raised to prevent flooding from storm surges.	VERY expensive	Really, VERY expensive.
Tidal barrage	Tidal barrages are dams built across river estuaries. Their main purpose is to generate electricity. Water is trapped behind the dam at high tide. Controlled release of water through turbines in the dam at low tide generates electricity. They also prevent flooding from storm surges.	VERY expensive	They disrupt sediment flow, which may cause increased erosion elsewhere in the estuary.

Coastal Management

Soft Engineering Defences Involve Coaxing Natural Processes Along

1) **Beach nourishment** is where **sand** and **shingle** are added to beaches from elsewhere (e.g. **dredged** from offshore). This creates **wide** beaches, which **reduce erosion** of cliffs more than thin beaches.

2) **Beach stabilisation** can be done by **reducing the slope angle** and planting **vegetation**, or by sticking **stakes** and **old tree trunks** in the beach to stabilise the sand. It also creates **wide** beaches, which **reduce erosion** of cliffs.

3) **Dune regeneration** is where sand dunes are **created** or **restored** by either nourishment or stabilisation of the sand. Sand dunes provide a **barrier** between land and sea, **absorbing wave energy** and preventing flooding and erosion.

4) **Land use management** is important for dune regeneration. The vegetation needed to stabilise the dune can easily be **trampled** and destroyed, leaving the dune **vulnerable** to **erosion**. Wooden **walkways** across dunes, and **fenced-off areas** that prevent walkers, cyclists or 4×4 drivers from gaining access to the dunes, all **reduce vegetation loss**.

5) **Creating marshland** from mudflats can be encouraged by **planting** appropriate vegetation (e.g. glassworts). The vegetation **stabilises** the sediment, and the stems and leaves help **reduce the speed** of the waves. This **reduces** their **erosive power** and **how far** the waves reach **inland**, leading to **less flooding** of the area around the marsh.

6) **Coastal realignment** (also known as **managed retreat**) involves breaching an existing defence and allowing the sea to flood the land behind. Over time, vegetation will colonise the land and it'll become **marshland**.

Soft Engineering is More Sustainable than Hard Engineering

Hard engineering is often expensive, and disrupts natural processes. Soft engineering schemes tend to be cheaper and require much less time and money to maintain than hard engineering schemes. Soft engineering is designed to integrate with the natural environment and it creates areas like marshland and sand dunes, which are important habitats for coastal plants and animals. So soft engineering is a more sustainable management strategy than hard engineering because it has a lower environmental impact and economic cost.

Management Strategies for the Future Must be Sustainable

1) **Rising sea level** means **more** coastal management will be **needed** to protect coastal settlements and developments. **Storms** also seem to be getting **more frequent** and **more severe**, increasing the need further.

2) There's growing emphasis on the need for **more sustainable management strategies**, i.e. soft engineering.

3) Deciding how to manage a coastline is now done in a more **integrated** way to **improve sustainability**. For example, a **Shoreline Management Plan** (SMP) is a plan for how the coastline in one **sediment cell** (see p. 78) should be managed. SMPs are developed by **local authorities**. All the local authorities in one sediment cell **co-operate** when planning their coastal management strategy, so that defences in one area don't increase erosion in an adjacent area in the same cell.

4) The **process** of trying to come up with an integrated, sustainable management plan is called **Integrated Coastal Zone Management** (ICZM).

Practice Questions

Q1 What is the aim of coastal management?
Q2 What are: a) gabions,
              b) groynes,
              c) revetments?
Q3 What other options are there for coastal management, apart from hard and soft engineering?

Exam Question

Q1 Explain why soft engineering schemes are more sustainable than hard engineering schemes. [10 marks]

Do nothing? Retreat? Sounds like a lousy revision strategy to me...

Coastal management sounds like a difficult and unending job. Even after spending hundreds of thousands of pounds on a nice big concrete wall to keep the waves out, and some wooden groynes to hold the beach in place, it can still all go horrendously wrong. When it goes wrong, it costs even more money. These days they try to use sustainable methods instead, but it's still hard.

Coastal Management — Case Studies

You need to know case studies of coastal management. Wait a minute, what's this I see...

Hard Engineering Has Been Used Along Holderness

The Holderness coast is the fastest eroding coastline in Europe. Page 84 outlines the main reasons for the rapid erosion and the social, economic and environmental impacts of the erosion. A total of **11.4 km** of the 61 km coastline is currently protected by **hard** engineering:

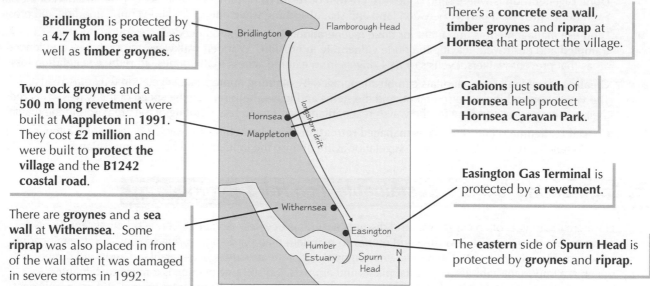

Bridlington is protected by a **4.7 km long sea wall** as well as **timber groynes**.

Two rock groynes and a **500 m long revetment** were built at **Mappleton** in **1991**. They cost **£2 million** and were built to **protect the village** and the **B1242 coastal road**.

There are **groynes** and a **sea wall** at **Withernsea**. Some **riprap** was also placed in front of the wall after it was damaged in severe storms in 1992.

There's a **concrete sea wall**, **timber groynes** and **riprap** at **Hornsea** that protect the village.

Gabions just **south** of **Hornsea** help protect **Hornsea Caravan Park**.

Easington Gas Terminal is protected by a **revetment**.

The **eastern** side of **Spurn Head** is protected by **groynes** and **riprap**.

The Schemes are Locally Successful but Cause Problems Down-drift

1) The groynes **trap sediment**, increasing the **width** of the **beaches**. This **protects** the **local area** but **increases erosion** of the cliffs **down-drift** (as the material eroded from the beaches there isn't replenished). E.g. the Mappleton scheme has caused **increased erosion** of the cliffs **south** of Mappleton. **Cowden Farm**, just south of Mappleton, is now at risk of falling into the sea.

2) The **sediment** produced from the erosion of the Holderness coastline is normally washed into the **Humber Estuary** (where it helps to form **tidal mudflats**) and down the **Lincolnshire coast**. Reduction in this sediment **increases the risk of flooding** along the Humber Estuary, and **increases erosion** along the Lincolnshire coast.

3) The protection of local areas is leading to the **formation of bays** between the areas. As bays develop the wave pressure on headlands will increase and eventually the **cost** of maintaining the sea defences may become **too high**.

4) All these problems make the existing schemes **unsustainable**.

Possible Schemes All Have Problems

See p. 87 for more on SMPs.

1) The **SMP** for Holderness for the next 50 years recommends '**holding the line**' at **some settlements** (e.g. at Bridlington, Withernsea, Hornsea, Mappleton and Easington Gas Terminal) and '**doing nothing**' along more **unpopulated stretches**. However, this is **unpopular** with owners of land or property along the stretches where nothing is being done.

2) **Coastal realignment** of businesses has been suggested, e.g. relocating **caravan parks** further inland. This would be a **more sustainable** scheme as it would allow the coast to be eroded as normal without endangering businesses. However, there are issues surrounding how much businesses will be **compensated** by for relocating. Also, relocation isn't always possible, e.g. farmland can't be 'relocated', and there may be no land for sale to relocate buildings to.

3) A **sea wall** has been proposed to better protect **Easington Gas Terminal**. This would cost **£4.5 million**. The problem is that it would reduce sediment flow to the south, **increasing erosion** at the **village of Easington** (with a population of **700 people**). A **longer sea wall** could be built that would protect the village as well as the gas terminal, but that would cost **£7 million**.

4) **Offshore reefs** made from **concrete-filled tyres** have been proposed to protect the coastline. They act like **breakwaters**. Similar reefs have been built in the USA and have reduced erosion. Some people think that the reefs will **harm the environment** though (although there's currently no evidence of this).

Coastal Management — Case Studies

Soft Engineering Has Been Used Along Blackwater Estuary

Blackwater Estuary is part of the **Essex** coastline. Land in the estuary is being eroded at a rate of **0.3-1 m/year**. In some exposed areas (e.g. **Cobmarsh Island**) the erosion rate is **2 m/year**. The area is also **at risk from flooding** as sea level is rising and the **South** of England is **sinking** relative to the sea. There are some hard engineering schemes in the estuary, but these are becoming too expensive to maintain, so **soft** engineering approaches are now being implemented:

Coastal realignment was implemented at **Tollesbury Fleet** in **1995**. An existing **sea wall** was **breached** and **21 hectares** of farmland were flooded to encourage a **marshland** to form. A **new lower sea wall** was built **further back** on higher ground to protect from flooding.

Beaches have been **nourished** along the estuary, e.g. at **Mersea Island**.

Marsh stabilisation has been carried out by planting **stakes** and **brushwood** on the water line to encourage sediment to build up, e.g. at **Ray Creek**.

In **1991** an **existing sea wall** was **lowered** and **breached** flooding **0.8 hectares** of land at **Northey Island**.

In **1995** a **sea wall** was **breached** and **40 hectares** of farmland at **Orplands** were flooded as part of **coastal realignment**.

Coastal realignment has been carried out at **Bradwell-on-Sea** by **breaching** an **old sea wall**.

The Schemes are More Sustainable than Hard Engineering Schemes

1) The schemes are **more sustainable** in the **long term**. E.g. to repair the sea wall at Orplands would have cost more than £600 000 (and it would only last for 20 years). The 40 hectares of farmland flooded was valued at around £600 000, but the marshland created would defend the coast for **longer** as it's **self-repairing**.
2) The schemes have created **more marshland**, which provides a larger **habitat** for **wildlife**.
3) However, some areas **haven't changed** to marshland (e.g. parts of the Orpland site are still bare mud, which is easily eroded). Also, **grazing land** has been **lost**.

The Success of Coastal Management Schemes Can be Investigated

RESEARCH
1) Research the **rates of erosion before** and **after** the scheme was implemented (both **at the site** of the scheme and **down-drift**). Data and maps could be obtained from **local agencies** (e.g. the **Council**) or from the **Environment Agency**.
2) Research the **flood risk before** and **after** the scheme was implemented — again using data and maps.
3) Search **local newspapers** to see whether local people have been positively or adversely affected by the scheme.

FIELDWORK
1) Visit the scheme and **record** the **structures** there, then **observe** the **effects** of the schemes **at the site** and **down-drift**.
2) Use a **questionnaire** to find out how the scheme has affected **local residents**, **business owners** and **tourists**.

Practice Questions

Q1 List the types of hard engineering used along the Holderness coast.
Q2 List the types of soft engineering used along the Blackwater Estuary in Essex.

Exam Question

Q1 Evaluate the success of a named coastal management scheme. [15 marks]

More case studies — what a pain in the groyne...

The best thing to do here is learn the annotated map for each case study. Draw them out over and over again until they're practically tattooed on the inside of your eyelids (it'll hurt a lot less than missing a load of easy marks in the exam, I promise).

Introduction to Inequalities

Calling all human geographers... Here's a nice section for you — lots of rural and urban differences, some causes and effects, and a little bit of economics thrown in. Dosage: take two pages at a time with a large cup of tea.

Unequal Spaces are Areas That are Unbalanced

Unequal spaces are **areas** with **uneven levels** of **wealth**, **social opportunity** and **environmental quality**. They're caused by **movements** of **people** and **money**, and **changing opportunities** between different areas. The **differences** between unequal spaces need to be **recognised** in order for the **balance** to be **restored** and people's lives to be **improved**.

Differences Between Areas are Called Inequalities

1) The **differences** in levels of **wealth**, **social opportunity** or **environmental quality** between different areas are called **inequalities**. For example, the south of England is **more wealthy** than the north, which means there's **economic inequality** between these two areas.

The word 'disparity' can be used instead of difference.

2) All inequalities can **contribute** to a person's **quality of life** (degree of **wellbeing**).

3) The table below shows examples of how different inequalities can be **measured**.

Inequality	Includes differences in...	Examples of measures
Economic (wealth)	Income, economic assets (e.g. house, pension, inheritance)	Average income, average house price, proportion of people on benefits, car ownership
Social	Type of employment, education, amenities, access to services, health, incidence of crime, community life	Unemployment level, proportion of GCSE passes, number of people per doctor, burglary rate
Environmental	Pollution, green spaces/gardens, housing quality	Air quality, area of green space/number of parks, proportion of buildings with graffiti

4) A single **measure** can show **more than one** type of **inequality**, e.g. **vandalism** is a **crime** (creating **social inequality**) but it also **damages** the environment people live in (creating **environmental inequality**).

5) Some **measures** are **more useful** than others depending on the **areas** you're studying. E.g. the **number of people per doctor** is a useful measure of social inequality **between countries**, but it **isn't** very useful when comparing **different regions** of the **UK** because the figures are fairly **similar**.

6) **Indexes of inequality** have been developed to take into account **several different measures**. E.g. the **Human Development Index** (**HDI**) includes measures of life expectancy, literacy, education, standard of living and GDP (Gross Domestic Product — the total value of goods and services produced in a country in a year).

7) '**Spatial inequalities**' are **inequalities** between **different geographical areas** (it's a fancy geography term). E.g. the inequalities that exist between the **north** and **south** of **Cardiff** (see page 96).

Inequalities Exist on Global, Regional and Local Scales

The following table gives examples of **different inequalities** and their **measures** at **different scales**:

INEQUALITY	GLOBAL SCALE	REGIONAL SCALE	LOCAL SCALE
Economic (wealth)	Japan has greater wealth than Central Africa. E.g. in 2005, the GDP per person was $32 000 in Japan, compared to $1000 in Central Africa.	The north of England is more wealthy than the south. E.g. in 2004, average gross disposable household income (per person) was £15 300 in London and £10 900 in the north-east of England.	Differences in wealth exist between different areas of a city. E.g. the estimated average weekly household income in 2001/02 for Bristol was £640 in Redland and £470 in Southville.
Social	Japan has greater social opportunity than Central Africa. E.g. in 2002, enrolment in primary education in Japan was 99%, compared to 44.4% in Central Africa.	The incidence of disease varies across the UK. E.g. in 2005 the incidence of tuberculosis was 14.8 per 100 000 in England, compared to 6.3 in Scotland, 5.4 in Wales and 3.9 in Northern Ireland.	Urban areas have more services and amenities than rural areas. E.g. in January 2004 the road distance to a supermarket was 20 km for the village of Cartmel and only 0.6 km for the town of Ulverston.
Environmental	There's greater access to clean drinking water in Japan than in Central Africa. E.g. in 2000/02, 50% of people in Central Africa had no access to clean water, compared to 0% of people in Japan.	River quality varies across the UK. E.g. in 2006, the percentage of rivers that had 'good chemical quality' was 95% in Wales, compared to 66% in England.	Inner city areas often have less green space than suburban and rural areas. E.g. the City of London has 5% green space, compared to South Lakeland (Cumbria) that has 86% green space.

Introduction to Inequalities

There are **Many Causes** of Inequality

1) There are **many different causes** of inequality, but most can be **linked** to the **economy**. For example, **economic decline** in an urban area causes a **decrease** in **employment** in particular industries (**social inequality**), which **leads to** lower average family incomes (**economic inequality**) and **dereliction** as industries and people move away (**environmental inequality**).

2) Inequalities are usually **interlinked** — the **effect** of one inequality can **cause** another inequality. E.g. **economic inequality** in an urban area means that people have **less money** to spend in shops in that area, so businesses may **collapse** or **move away**, causing **social inequality** (because of a lack of amenities).

3) All this interlinking can lead to a **cycle of decline** — one inequality causes **deprivation**, which leads to **more inequalities**, which cause **more** deprivation, leading to more inequalities, and so on. A cycle of decline can also be called a **vicious cycle**, **negative feedback** or a **cycle of inequality**.

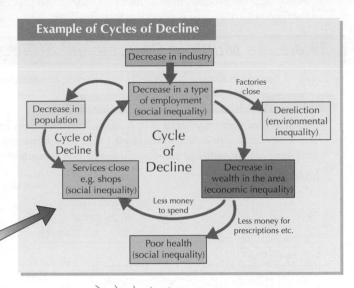

Example of Cycles of Decline

Deprivation is where there are social, economic and environmental problems in an area, e.g. poor housing, lack of services.

Inequalities Lead to **Reduced Opportunities**

One **effect** of inequalities is **reduced opportunities**. For example, people living in an area that has **economic inequality** caused by **low incomes**, are **less likely** to go on to **further education** (e.g. university, which is expensive) — so economic inequality leads to **reduced education opportunities**. Reduced opportunities include:

- Reduced **employment** opportunities — caused by many different social inequalities, e.g. lack of jobs in a particular field, lack of access to the internet to look for jobs, lack of transport to get to jobs.

- Reduced **housing** opportunities — caused by economic and social inequalities, e.g. low incomes, lack of affordable housing.

- Reduced **education** opportunities — caused by economic and social inequalities, e.g. low incomes, lack of good teachers, lack of local funding.

Fashion inequality has always existed between Essex and the rest of the UK.

Practice Questions

Q1 What are unequal spaces?
Q2 What are the three main types of inequality?
Q3 Give one measure of social inequality.
Q4 What are spatial inequalities?
Q5 Give one example of global economic inequality.
Q6 Give one example of regional social inequality.

Measure	Bradford	Harrogate
Total population (2001)	467 665	151 336
Average detached property selling price (Aug 2001)	£112 723	£191 024
% unemployed (2001)	4.4	1.8
% people of working age claiming a key benefit (Aug 2001)	17	8
% people with 'not good' general health (2001)	10.2	7.21
Police recorded offences of theft from a motor vehicle (Apr 01 - Mar 02)	9961	698
% 15 year old pupils achieving 5 or more A* - C GCSE grades from schools within the area	37.3	68.6
Total number of students aged 16-17 (2001)	10 256	3041
Area of green space (km²) (Jan 2005)	0.27	1.25

Exam Question

Q1 Outline how well the information in the table shows the inequalities between Bradford and Harrogate. [10 marks]

Unequal spaces — so that's why I can't parallel park...

I reckon if you tell anyone that you're studying 'Unequal Spaces' they won't have a clue what you're going on about — it might make you sound intellectual though. When they find out what it really is, they may just fall asleep. Unfortunately you need to learn this basic stuff really well 'cause it'll make the rest of this section much easier to understand.

Causes and Effects of Urban Inequalities

Now that you know what inequalities are, you can apply the ideas of inequality to different areas.
First up, urban areas — a round of applause please...

There are **Multiple Causes** and **Effects** of **Urban Inequalities**

Some of the **main causes** and **effects** of different **inequalities** are shown below:

1 Cause: INCREASE in Urban Employment

When **businesses** move **into** urban areas, they cause an **increase** in employment in one or more industries.
This can cause a population **increase** (as people **move into** the area for **work**), affecting **services**, **housing**
and people's **incomes** (wages) — all leading to **inequalities**.

<u>EXAMPLE</u>

CAUSE:
New factories built
in cities during
Industrial Revolution
in UK (1800s), e.g.
new pottery factories
in Stoke.

Increase in wealth
in the area
(economic inequality)

People have
more money
to spend

Increase in services, e.g. shops,
schools (social inequality)

Greater
demand for
services

Increase in
employment
(social inequality)

Rapid increase
in population

Services
can't cope

Lack of basic amenities,
e.g. water, electricity
(social inequality)

Lack of sewage disposal
(social inequality)

Poor health
(social
inequality)

Housing
supply can't
cope

Overcrowding
(social inequality)

Disease
spread by
sewage

Increase in pollution,
e.g. smoke from factories
(environmental inequality)

Poor health
(social inequality)

Disease spreads
more easily

2 Cause: DECREASE in Urban Employment

When **businesses shut down** in urban areas, they cause a **decrease** in employment in one or more industries, which can
cause a population **decrease**, affecting **services**, **housing** and people's **incomes** (wages) — all leading to **inequalities**.

<u>EXAMPLE</u>

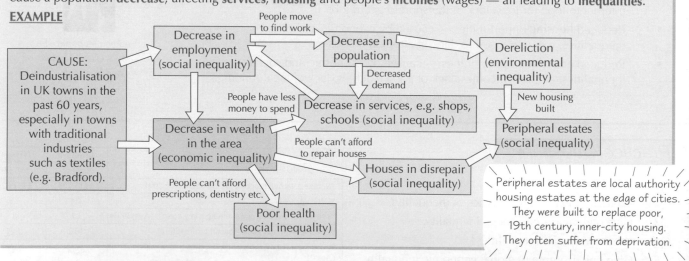

CAUSE:
Deindustrialisation
in UK towns in the
past 60 years,
especially in towns
with traditional
industries
such as textiles
(e.g. Bradford).

Decrease in
employment
(social inequality)

People move
to find work

Decrease in
population

Dereliction
(environmental
inequality)

Decreased
demand

New housing
built

People have less
money to spend

Decrease in services, e.g. shops,
schools (social inequality)

Decrease in wealth
in the area
(economic inequality)

People can't afford
to repair houses

Houses in disrepair
(social inequality)

Peripheral estates
(social inequality)

People can't afford
prescriptions, dentistry etc.

Poor health
(social inequality)

Peripheral estates are local authority
housing estates at the edge of cities.
They were built to replace poor,
19th century, inner-city housing.
They often suffer from deprivation.

3 Cause: Rural-urban Migration

In many countries there's **mass
migration from** rural areas **into**
urban areas, due to **push factors**
(reasons people leave, e.g. lack of
employment in rural areas) and
pull factors (things that attract
people, e.g. perceived better quality
of life in urban areas). This can
cause many **urban inequalities**.

<u>EXAMPLE</u>

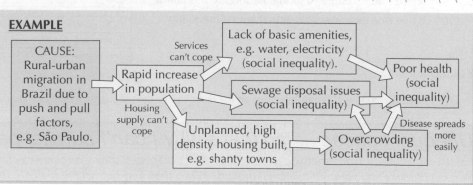

CAUSE:
Rural-urban
migration in
Brazil due to
push and pull
factors,
e.g. São Paulo.

Rapid increase
in population

Services
can't cope

Lack of basic amenities,
e.g. water, electricity
(social inequality).

Poor health
(social
inequality)

Sewage disposal issues
(social inequality)

Housing
supply can't
cope

Unplanned, high
density housing built,
e.g. shanty towns

Overcrowding
(social inequality)

Disease spreads
more
easily

Causes and Effects of Urban Inequalities

4) Cause: INCREASE in House Prices

House prices vary for lots of reasons — e.g. an **influx** of people into an area **for work** can cause an **increase** in house prices, which results in **inequalities** and **polarisation** (see below).

EXAMPLE

CAUSE: Rapid increase in house prices in southern areas of the UK from the late 1990s until recently.

→ Only wealthy can afford houses (economic inequality) → Increase in buy-to-let → Wealthier get richer as house prices rise (economic inequality) — Rich get richer → Increased polarisation between the rich and the poor

→ Lack of affordable housing (social inequality) → Decrease in population → Decrease in services (social inequality) →

→ Increase in debt, e.g. loans to buy houses (economic inequality) — Poor get poorer →

Inequalities Can Cause Polarisation

Polarisation is when there are **extreme inequalities** between **geographical areas**.

For example, an **increase** in **house prices** can cause **other inequalities** between the **rich** and the **poor** in an **urban area**. The rich can **afford** high priced housing, which is often in areas with **better services** and **better schools**. This leads to **better education**, and **better jobs** and **incomes**, **adding to** economic inequality — **polarisation** between the rich and poor.

Polar-isation was becoming a problem in some urban areas.

People Can be Excluded from Society Due to Inequalities

Social exclusion is the **exclusion** of **individuals** or **groups** of people from society on the basis of **gender, age, race, religion, education, health** or **disability**. **Economic exclusion** is the exclusion of individuals or groups on the basis of their **wealth**. Social or economic exclusion can be **caused by inequalities**.

For example, in urban areas of the **UK** there's been an **increase** in **jobs** in the **service industries**, e.g. financial services. Many of these jobs require certain **qualifications** or **skills** (e.g. IT skills), which can **exclude** some people from applying. This effect leads to **more** economic inequality in urban areas, as those **with** the desired skills gain **more wealth**.

Exclusion Can Result in Marginalised Groups

Marginalised groups may occupy or use a particular area of a city — called a ghetto.

Marginalised groups are groups of people that are **relegated** to the **edge** of **society**, usually **due to** social or economic **exclusion**. Marginalised groups may find it **hard** to **integrate** into the rest of the community. This might make it harder for them to **find jobs** etc., **increasing** the inequalities within the area.

For example, **unemployment** among **males** from **ethnic minorities** in Leicester was **16.11%** in 1991 — **double** that of the **white male population**, which was **8.04%**. This **economic inequality** may contribute to the **marginalisation** of **ethnic minority groups** in Leicester, as they **can't afford** the **services** and **lifestyle** enjoyed by white males.

Practice Questions

Q1   Describe polarisation.
Q2   Explain what social exclusion means.
Q3   What is a marginalised group?

Exam Question

Q1   The table provides information about lone-parent families and two-parent families in the UK.
Discuss the possible causes and effects of the inequalities shown.

[10 marks]

Measure	Lone-parent families	Two-parent families
% employed (2006)	56	81
% of total number of part-time students (2004 - 05)	8	31
% receiving income related benefits (2004 - 05)	89	62
% living in a detached house (2005)	8	28

Star Trek® fans are definitely a marginalised group...

When you're learning these two pages (in between watching the telly) remember that I haven't been able to cover ALL the causes and effects of inequalities on these pages — that would take about a gazillion years, especially if I explained how they're all interlinked too. So make sure you <u>understand</u> the causes and effects on these pages and how they're all interlinked.

Strategies to Reduce Urban Inequalities

You should be a bit more comfortable with inequalities now, which, let's face it, aren't great. So, next you need to know what's being done about them — it's called 'delivering solutions' in exam-board speak. I know, it sounds thrilling.

Different Organisations Help to Reduce Urban Inequalities

Different groups work at **different scales** (e.g. local, regional, national and international) to **reduce** urban inequalities. The **key players** are shown in the diagram below — they're in **order** of **increasing scale** of **operation**, **impact** and **cost**.

Increasing scale of **operation**, **impact** and **cost**		
	Individuals	— An individual who **picks up litter** in their neighbourhood helps to **reduce local environmental inequality**.
	Small groups	— A small group of people **cleaning graffiti** off buildings helps to **reduce local environmental inequality**.
	Community action groups	— A community group **collecting and distributing food** for the elderly helps to **reduce local social inequality**.
	Local charities	— North London Action for the Homeless helps to **reduce social inequality** by providing **literacy classes** for the homeless in North London.
	Local authorities	— The South Lakeland District Council sets up designated **parking areas** (so people don't park on grass verges) to **reduce environmental inequality** between local areas.
	Regional charities	— Alzheimer Scotland runs **drop-in centres** so people with dementia and their carers can socialise, **reducing social inequality** in Scotland.
	Regional authorities	— Cumbria County Council runs **recycling schemes** to **reduce environmental inequality** between regions.
	National governments	— The **UK** government sets the **minimum wage** (the lowest hourly wage employers can legally pay workers in the UK) to help **reduce economic inequality** across the country.
	International organisations	— The **World Health Organisation** (WHO) carries out immunisation programmes to **reduce social** (health) **inequalities** between **countries**.

There are Many Strategies to Reduce Urban Inequalities

1 Self-help Schemes — to help people reduce inequalities in their local urban environment

1) **Shanty builds** — schemes created by **people living in shanty towns** to **build** their **own homes**, **services** and **amenities**. They aim to **improve** their own living conditions and **reduce social inequalities** by building **better housing**, and getting **clean water supplies** and **electricity**. Some **governments** support these schemes by providing **building materials** and **basic services** (e.g. clean water, sewage disposal).

2) **Residents' associations** — associations formed by **groups** of people **living** in a **particular area**. Members meet to discuss **local issues** (e.g. **planning** applications, levels of **crime**, management of **green space**) in order to work out how they can **reduce social** and **environmental** inequalities in their own neighbourhood.

3) **Neighbourhood watch** — **local organisations** that aim to **reduce crime** in **neighbourhoods** where they're set up. Members agree to **look out** for signs of **crime** and **report** it to the local authorities. This helps to **reduce social** and **environmental** inequalities (e.g. antisocial behaviour, vandalism, graffiti). The **success** of a neighbourhood watch group can be **monitored** by looking at **crime statistics** in the area **before** and **after** the group was set up.

2 Traffic and Public Transport Strategies — to reduce social and environmental inequalities caused by urban road traffic

1) **Park-and-ride schemes** — schemes that let people **park** their cars **near to** city centres, then use **public transport** to **reach** the centre. They help people **avoid** the **high cost** of **city centre parking** and aim to **reduce** problems caused by **city centre traffic** (e.g. **air pollution, noise, accidents**). The **success** of park-and-ride schemes can be **measured** by looking at **air quality** in the city centre **before** and **after** the scheme was introduced.

2) **Congestion charging** — a scheme where **motorists** are charged to take their vehicles **into** city centres. Many cities have these schemes (e.g. **Singapore, London, Stockholm**) to **reduce** city centre traffic and the problems described above.

3) **Oyster cards** — a system of **electronic tickets** that makes it **easier, faster** and **cheaper** to pay for **London public transport**. This aims to **encourage** people to use public transport in London to **reduce** city centre traffic.

3 Business Initiatives — local and government schemes to reduce economic inequalities in urban areas

1) **The minimum wage** — the **lowest** hourly **wage** employers can **legally** pay workers in the UK. It's set by the UK **government** and aims to **reduce** economic inequality by providing workers with a **decent wage**. The **success** of this policy can be **measured** by looking at **how many people** were living in **poverty before** and **after** its introduction.

2) **Furniture schemes** — unwanted furniture is collected for **free** and sold at **affordable prices** to people on **low incomes**, helping to reduce social inequalities (lack of furniture) **caused by** economic inequalities (low income).

Strategies to Reduce Urban Inequalities

4) Town Planning Initiatives — government-led programmes to help improve the urban environments of a country

1) **Sustainable urban communities** — communities that aim to **meet human needs** while **preserving** the natural and urban **environment**, by promoting efficient land use, less pollution etc. For example, the **Masdar Initiative** in **Abu Dhabi** aims to make **Masdar City** a '**zero-carbon, zero-waste, car-free city**'. This will **reduce environmental inequalities** (e.g. reduced air pollution) and **economic inequalities** (e.g. fewer people affected by rising fuel prices).

2) **The WHO Healthy Urban Planning Initiative** — this scheme encourages **local governments** to **improve urban health** through projects that address **social inequalities** (health) and **urban poverty**. Over **1200 cities** are involved in it.

Successful Strategies Must Address Causes of Inequality and be Sustainable

Strategies to reduce urban inequalities have a **greater chance** of being **successful** if they:

1) **Address** the **root causes** of urban inequalities — they need to promote **long-lasting solutions**.
For example, strategies to help **homeless people** are more likely to be successful if they **enable** homeless people to find **secure employment** so they can **support themselves**, rather than just giving them a **bed** for the night. Schemes to help **starving communities** are more likely to be successful if they enable the community to produce their **own** reliable **sources of food**, rather than just giving them **free food**. If strategies **don't** address the root causes of inequalities, they will only provide **short-term** solutions.

2) **Are sustainable** — they need to be **maintained** in the **long-term**.
For example, schemes that require **high levels** of **financial support** are **less likely** to be successful because they'll only continue for as long as financial support is **available**. **Cheaper** or **self-financing** schemes are likely to run **long-term**.

> **EXAMPLE — Urban-rural migration in Asia, Africa and South America**
>
> - In Asia, Africa and South America **urban inequalities** are often **caused** by **mass rural-urban migration**. This is because mass migration into cities causes **rapid population growth**, so there isn't enough affordable housing, resulting in **shanty towns**. Shanty towns have **many** social, economic and environmental **inequalities**.
>
> - In order to **reduce** and **prevent further** urban inequalities the **root causes** (**push factors**), as well as the **existing urban inequalities**, need to be addressed.
>
> - Push factors are the **reasons** why people **leave** the rural areas. They can include **famine, drought, natural disasters, poor living conditions, lack of education, lack of health care, agricultural change** (leading to job shortages) and **conflict**.
>
> - Some of the push factors can be **reduced** by **improving rural areas** (e.g. building water sources, building health care facilities, developing industry in the area) and encouraging their **sustainable economic development**.
>
> - **Schemes** can be **introduced** in urban areas to **reduce inequalities**, e.g. **shanty builds** (see previous page).

Melanie had a lack of push factors...

Practice Questions

Q1 Give an example of an organisation that works to reduce urban inequalities at a local scale.

Q2 What are sustainable urban communities?

Q3 What are push factors?

Measure	1995	2005
Average number of visitors to city centre per month (thousands)	1224	1315
Average number of vehicles passing through city centre per month	753 124	215 376
Number of bus services to/from city centre	15	25
Average nitrous oxide concentration in the air (µg/m³)	18.2	10.1

Exam Question

Q1 In the UK in 1998, City X introduced some schemes to reduce inequalities caused by city centre traffic. The table above shows data about City X before and after the schemes were introduced.

Using data from the table, describe two schemes that City X may have introduced and evaluate how successful the schemes have been.

[10 marks]

Revision — an exam self-help scheme...

Okay, I think I've got it... There are many different schemes to help reduce each type of urban inequality and they're carried out by people at different scales — from individuals up to international organisations. To be a success these schemes must address the causes of inequalities and be sustainable. And the success of a scheme can be measured in different ways. By Jove, I've got it!

Urban Inequalities — Case Study

You were bound to get a case study sooner or later. It's what geography's all about. (PS — try not to fall asleep.)

There are **Inequalities** Between **North** and **South Cardiff**

Cardiff is the **capital** of **Wales**. The **north** of the city is relatively **wealthy**, but the **south** of the city shows signs of **deprivation**.

EXAMPLE — Cathays and Butetown

The map on the right shows two different areas of Cardiff — **Cathays** and **Butetown**. Cathays is in the **north** and includes part of the **city centre**. Butetown is in the **south** and includes some of the **docklands**. **Data** on these areas (from the **2001 Census** and **Cardiff Community Profile 2002**) is summarised in the table below.

This data shows economic inequality.

Over twice as many people in Butetown have 'not good' health.

Measures	Butetown	Cathays
% 16 - 74 year olds unemployed	5.2	1.8
% owner occupied households that own house outright	12.5	20.9
% 16 - 74 year olds with no qualifications	33.6	9.73
% people with 'not good' general health	14.1	6.23
Reported incidents of crime per 1000 population (in 2000)	1121.4	1189.7

There are over 3 times as many 16 - 74 year olds with no qualifications in Butetown than Cathays (that's quite high).

Both areas have similar, high levels of crime (there's only a 6% difference).

The table shows that the **incidence of crime** per 1000 population is **high** for **both** areas. This may be because the areas include the **city centre** and **bay**, which both attract **large numbers** of **visitors**. However, the crime figures are worked out by **reported** incidents of crimes per 1000 of the **resident** population — it doesn't include visitors. This means the data is **distorted** — the crimes **could** involve **visitors**, but they're **only** divided by the **number of residents**, so it seems **high** for the number of people who live there.

The table shows that **Butetown** has a **higher percentage** of **unemployed** residents, which means the **average income** is likely to be **lower** in Butetown. **Housing** can be the **greatest expense** for a household, so it's not surprising that in the poorer area of Butetown **only 12.5%** **own** their own **home**, compared to **20.9%** in Cathays. **Over three times** as many **16 – 74 year olds** in **Butetown** have **no qualifications**, compared to Cathays. This all means that families in Butetown **live** in an area of **higher unemployment** and have **fewer qualifications**, which leads to **lower income jobs** and **poorer health** (e.g. **less money** for **food**, **prescriptions**). This causes a **cycle of decline** (see p. 91).

There are **Multiple Causes** of **Inequalities** in **Cardiff**

1) The **decline** of the **coal** and **steel industries** in the **late 20th century** (e.g. **coal exports** from Cardiff port **stopped** in **1964**, the **steelworks closed** in **1978**) caused **high unemployment** in Cardiff, especially in the south where workers from the docklands lived. This led to **dereliction** in the **docklands** and in residential areas as people **moved away** to **find work**. The **decrease** in **employment** caused **further inequalities**, leading to a **cycle of decline**.

2) The **south** of Cardiff has some of the **most densely populated** and **poor quality housing** estates. People on lower incomes are likely to **buy** poor quality housing because it's **cheaper**. This causes **polarisation** (see p. 93) between the north and the south of Cardiff because the poorer people are all **concentrated** in the south.

3) The **population** of Cardiff has **rapidly increased** during the last decade (by more than 1% a year). This population growth **hasn't** been even across the city and has caused **overcrowding** in the **south**, leading to **further** inequalities.

Inequalities Reduce Opportunities and Cause Social Exclusion

The **effects** of the **inequalities** between the north and south of Cardiff include:

1) **Reduced employment** in the **south** of the city — due to the **decline** of **industries** (see above) and an **increase** in the **population** (so there are **fewer jobs** to go round). This has led to **lower average wages** and **more** inequalities.

2) **Poorer education** in the south — e.g. because there are **larger** class sizes (due to **more children**) and good teachers are **less likely** to be attracted to the area (because of the inequalities).

3) **Poorer health** in the south — e.g. due to **less money** for **food**, **poor housing** that could be **damp** etc.

4) **Environmental issues** in the south — e.g. **poor quality housing** and **high crime rates** (e.g. **vandalism**).

5) **Social exclusion** (see p. 93) of some groups (e.g. **lone-parent families**, **ethnic minorities**) in the **south** — e.g. **lone parents** may find it **harder** to get work because they don't have **child-care facilities**.

The redevelopment of Cardiff Bay (see next page) has created more jobs in the south of the city, but unemployment there is still high.

Urban Inequalities — Case Study

Strategies Have Been Used to Address Inequalities in Cardiff

1990s Redevelopment of South Cardiff

Scheme: In the **1990s**, **£2.4 billion** was spent on regenerating Cardiff **docks** and **waterfront** (south Cardiff), including new **residential**, **business**, **retail** and **leisure** developments.

Success: **High unemployment rates** were addressed by the **17 000 new jobs** created. These new jobs have **decreased** unemployment in some areas, e.g. unemployment in **Butetown** fell from **8.6% 1991** to **5.2%** in **2001**. **Inadequate housing** has been addressed by **6000 new homes**. However, **wealthy** people have moved into the new homes and the **older housing estates** have just become '**boxed in**', which has led to **increased** feelings of **exclusion** in those areas. The scheme is **long-term** — there are plans for **further redevelopments** of the **south** of Cardiff (e.g. there's a new health centre, shopping parade and affordable housing planned in Butetown).

The success of a scheme depends on addressing the root causes (see p. 95).

Butetown Community Centre

The **Butetown Community Centre** aims to **improve** the **quality of life** for **local** people by providing **educational**, **recreational**, **health** and **leisure opportunities** (e.g. the community food co-op provides **cheap**, **good quality**, **fresh** fruit and vegetables to local people). The **success** of this scheme could be **measured** by looking at the **number of people using** the centre or the **perceived increases in local opportunities** (via **questionnaires**).

Ethnic Minority Communities Programme

The **Ethnic Minority Communities** programme aims to **support** ethnic minority groups across Cardiff and **reduce deprivation** within these communities. The success of this programme could be **measured** by examining **census data**, such as the **level** of **unemployment** in ethnic minority groups **before** and **after** it was set up.

You Can Investigate the Causes and Effects of Inequalities in an Urban Area

You can use a **range** of **fieldwork** and **research techniques** to **study** the causes and effects of **inequalities**. For example:

1) You could examine **census data** to look for **inequalities** in **house prices**, **education** or **health** and to **analyse changing patterns** in **employment** or **population**. Census data can be obtained from the **Office for National Statistics**, the **local authority** or **websites**.

2) You could examine **CVA scores** (**Contextual Value Added scores**) to find out **how well** schools are **performing** and enable you to **identify social** (educational) **inequalities** between areas.

3) You could use **questionnaires** to determine **mobility patterns** (how easy it is for people to **get around** in an area), perceived **quality of life** and **environmental quality**. These factors can **indicate** other inequalities, e.g. a person's mobility is affected by **personal transport** (e.g. car ownership). If a questionnaire shows that an urban area has **low car ownership**, it may indicate **economic inequality** (as people on low incomes **can't afford** a car). However, questionnaires are based on people's **opinions**, which can be **biased**, so they need to be backed up with **other forms** of **data**.

4) You could carry out **surveys** to **collect data**. For example, you could **count** the number of **bus services** in **two areas**. A **lack** of bus services could show **social inequality**, because people will have to rely on their **own cars** to get around. If they **can't afford** their own cars they will find it **harder** to **access other services** and **employment**.

5) You could also assess the **environmental quality** of two areas by visiting them and recording factors like how many houses have **chipped paint**, how many **gardens** are **unkempt** and how many buildings have **graffiti**. These are useful factors when trying to find **correlations** between **economic** and **environmental inequalities**.

The success of a strategy to reduce inequalities can be measured by looking at these things before and after the strategy was introduced.

Practice Questions

Q1 Describe one strategy used to tackle the inequalities between north and south Cardiff.
Q2 How could you measure the success of the Ethnic Minority Communities programme?
Q3 Suggest three ways to investigate inequalities in your area.

Exam Question

Q1 With reference to one named example, discuss the causes and effects of urban inequalities. [15 marks]

2001 Census data shows that 98% of students are bored with revision...

Did you know that 'census' comes from the Latin word meaning 'assess'? I guess it makes sense, because every 10 years a UK census is taken, which assesses the levels of health, education etc. across the country. One of the ways this data can be used is to find out how successful strategies to reduce urban inequalities have been. So the census is still useful today.

Causes and Effects of Rural Inequalities

I hope you saved some of your enthusiasm for these pages. After all, we're nearly at the end of the section — just need to learn the causes, effects, strategies and a case study for rural inequalities and we're done. Easy peasy, lemon squeezy. (Oh dear...)

There are **Multiple Causes** and **Effects** of **Rural Inequalities**

Just like urban inequalities, **rural inequalities** have **many causes** and **effects**. They include:

1 Cause: DECREASE in Rural Employment

Industry may be **lost** from a rural area due to **changes** in **technology**, or **cheaper** labour **elsewhere**, or because companies go **out of business**. This has **huge effects** on the local community and can lead to **inequality**.

EXAMPLE

There's a cycle of decline as services close, leading to more unemployment, which leads to more decline.

Be careful when making **generalisations** about inequalities — in the example above you could say that **reduced employment** in rural areas may lead to **poor health** because people have **less money** for food, prescriptions etc. However, **health** is **affected** by **many factors**. People in rural areas tend to suffer from **fewer** mental health problems and often have access to **fresher**, local **food**, which can have a **positive effect** on health.

Betsy couldn't understand why people thought living in rural areas was boring...

2 Cause: INCREASE in House Prices

House prices in **rural areas** are **higher** than those in **urban areas** — in 2007 house prices in rural areas were **14% higher** than in urban areas. However the **average income** in rural areas is **lower** than in urban areas. This **economic inequality** can lead to many **more** social and economic inequalities, as shown below.

EXAMPLE

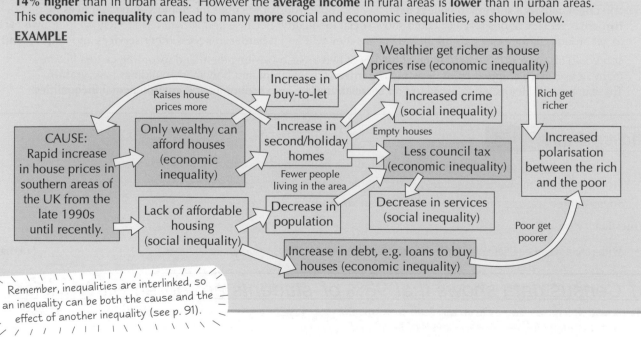

Remember, inequalities are interlinked, so an inequality can be both the cause and the effect of another inequality (see p. 91).

Causes and Effects of Rural Inequalities

You can find out more about cyclones on p. 5.

3 **Cause: Environmental Changes**

Environmental changes, such as droughts, floods and land degradation, have **massive effects** on **rural communities**, especially those that **rely** on **agriculture** to survive. They usually **worsen inequalities** already present in rural areas.

EXAMPLE

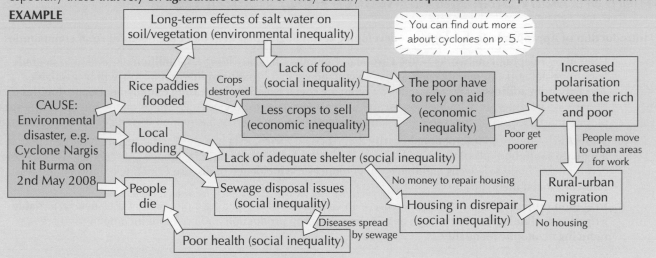

Inequalities are Barriers to Equality

Inequalities can **reduce opportunities** because they're **barriers** to equality. Barriers that occur in **rural areas** include:

Inequalities, opportunities and barriers are all interlinked — inequalities reduce opportunities, creating barriers.

1) Lack of **affordable housing** (economic inequality) — this **reduces** housing opportunities for people on **lower incomes** in rural areas and so is a barrier to **housing equality**.

2) Lack of **local employment** (social and economic inequality) — this reduces **employment opportunities**, so people have limited **job choice**, often associated with **low incomes**. It's a barrier to **economic** and **employment equality**.

3) Lack of **services** (social inequality) — e.g. a lack of **public transport** means people find it hard to travel to **work**, limiting the **jobs** they can do. This reduces **employment opportunity** and so is a **barrier** to **economic equality**.

Polarisation and Exclusion Occur in Rural Areas

Polarisation occurs when **inequalities** between two groups become **extreme** (see p. 93). Rural inequalities often lead to polarisation **between** the **rich** and the **poor**. E.g. an **increase** in **house prices** means **only** the **wealthy** can **afford** to buy homes. Wealthy people may visit **scenic** rural areas and buy **second homes** there to use as **holiday homes**. This **increases** the house prices **even more**. Less wealthy, local people are **priced out** of the **market** and wealthy homeowners become **more wealthy** as their properties **increase** in **value**.

Different groups of people can experience **exclusion** in **rural areas**. E.g. people who are **unemployed** in rural areas (e.g. due to a decrease in agricultural jobs) will have **lower family incomes** and may be on **benefits**. This means they are **less likely** to be able to **afford** a **home**, **car**, **good clothes**, **social activities** etc. Therefore they're **excluded** from some areas of **society** on the **basis of income** (economic exclusion).

Practice Questions

Q1 Describe how a decrease in employment can lead to one rural inequality.
Q2 Describe how environmental changes can lead to one rural inequality.

Exam Question

Q1 Explain how the causes and effects of inequalities in a rural area can lead to polarisation. [10 marks]

Cow poo — the worst inequality between rural and urban areas...

Yep, you're right, there are lots of similarities between the causes and effects of inequalities in rural and urban areas. E.g. a root cause of inequality in both areas is an increase in houses prices. One of the effects of this is a boom in the rental market in both areas. However, rural areas are also affected by people buying second homes. Gosh, it's all made my head go funny...

Strategies to Reduce Rural Inequalities

You've learnt about strategies that can help to decrease inequalities in urban areas and now you need to learn about them for rural areas too. So go grab some biccies and prepare yourself for some quality revision time...

There are **Many Strategies** to **Reduce Rural Inequalities**

1) Introduction of Appropriate Technologies — developing technologies that help meet the needs of rural communities

1) **Upgrading telephone networks** — the **European Commission** is providing **£3.4 million** of funding to **upgrade** telephone networks in **remote rural areas** of **Scotland**, so that **broadband internet** access will be **available**. This may help **address** rural inequalities by **reducing social isolation, increasing employment opportunities** (e.g. job hunting on the internet, web businesses) and **increasing access to services** (e.g. shops on the internet). The **success** of this strategy could be **measured** by **asking residents** how the internet has helped them (e.g. using **questionnaires**).

2) **WaterAid** — this is an **international charity** that works in **Africa, Asia** and the **Pacific region** to provide people with **adequate sanitation** (clean water and sewage disposal). For example, in rural **Ghana** (Africa) they work to help communities build **safe wells** and **toilets**. This **reduces** the **incidence** of **disease** from unclean water and waste, **reducing social inequality**.

3) **Irrigation projects** (crop watering systems) — in **Ghana** the **UN** is funding a project that uses **new, affordable irrigation technologies**. The project aims to **improve crop production** and therefore **income** in rural areas, **reducing economic inequality**.

2) Community Schemes — to help rural communities reduce inequalities in their own areas

1) **Village Action Plans** — these are being developed by many **rural communities** in the **UK** as part of the **'Vital Villages' scheme** run by the **Countryside Agency**. They help local communities **identify** rural inequalities and they work together to **organise** more specific **schemes** to **address** these inequalities.

2) **The Devon Social Inclusion Programme** — this programme works with **small rural communities** to tackle **social exclusion**. The programme **supports** many **community groups** (e.g. youth clubs) and **community events** (such as festivals and family fun days).

3) **The Village Enterprise Fund** — this is a scheme in **rural East Africa** that aims to address **economic inequalities** in the region by helping rural communities **create their own businesses**. The scheme provides **business training, financial grants** and **mentoring** to **give** people the **skills** and **means** to create and operate small businesses, e.g. small farms, carpenters', tailors', bicycle repair workshops and cafes. The **success** of such a scheme could be monitored by **counting** the **number** of **small businesses** in a part of rural East Africa **before** it's introduction and **six months after**.

3) Transport and Services Schemes — to help increase access to transport and services in rural areas

1) **Rural Wheels scheme** — a UK scheme, based in **Cumbria**, that provides **door-to-door transport** on **demand** and at a **reasonable cost**. The scheme involves **different transport providers** (e.g. taxis and patient transport services). People book a journey **48 hours in advance**, so that the **best use** of transport can be made. The scheme **reduces social inequality** as it helps tackle **social isolation, dependence on car ownership** and **lack of access to services**.

2) **Vital Villages scheme** — a UK scheme to help **villages** in **Warwickshire** and **Worcestershire** gain **access** to the **services** they need, reducing **social inequality**. The scheme provided **grants** to **improve village shops** and **support** for **new developments** (e.g. new community-run shops, internet cafes and delivery services). The **success** of such a scheme could be measured by asking residents how they **perceive** improvements in local village shops etc., via questionnaires.

3) **Peru Decentralised Rural Transport Project** — this project aims to **address rural poverty** (economic inequality) in **Peru** by **improving access** to **goods, social services** and **income-generating opportunities**. The project involves **improving transport infrastructure** and **reducing transport costs** in rural areas, to **help** people become **more mobile**.

4) Local Employment Schemes — to help create new jobs in rural areas

1) **Changes to EU agricultural policies** — these aim to **encourage farmers** to **move away** from **intensive farming techniques** and use more **environmentally friendly methods** (e.g. organic farming). This **increases** the **labour** needed, **creating** more **employment opportunities** in **farming** and decreasing social inequality. The **success** of these policies could be **measured** by **counting** the **number** of **workers** on farms **before** and **after** their introduction.

2) **Business Development Scheme** — this is run by **Lancaster Council** and **promotes job creation** in rural areas by providing **grants** to **existing** businesses and to businesses **relocating** into rural areas.

3) **National Rural Employment Guarantee Programme** — this is run by the **Indian** Government and provides the **legal right** of **100 days of employment per year** at a **minimum wage** to rural households. This means **job opportunities** are **provided** by the **government**, e.g. building irrigation systems, digging wells.

Strategies to Reduce Rural Inequalities

Local Development Frameworks (LDFs) Target Local Areas

Local Development Frameworks (**LDFs**) are **plans** for the **development** of **local areas** (e.g. for new roads, schools, housing etc.) in England and Wales. Before LDFs, development was **planned** at the **county** and **district level** — taking into account the **needs** of a county as a whole, **not** the specific needs of smaller areas within the county. In contrast, LDFs **aim** to meet the needs of **small, local** areas, which means they're more **flexible**. E.g. they may use **different planning strategies** for **adjacent**, local areas because they recognise that **even** adjacent rural locations can have **different issues** that require **different solutions**.

> For example, inequalities across rural **Cumbria** have **different causes** and require **different solutions**. In the heart of the **Lake District National Park** traffic **congestion** (environmental inequality), **second homes** and a **lack of affordable housing** (social inequality) are **key issues**. However, in more **remote west Cumbria, employment** and **inaccessibility** (social inequalities) are key issues. LDFs mean that any plans for development in these areas will aim to **solve** the **specific key issues** for the area, instead of **general, county-wide** issues.

Successful Strategies Address Root Causes and are Sustainable

Strategies to reduce rural inequalities have a **greater chance** of being **successful** if they:

Address the root causes of rural inequalities

If strategies **don't** address root causes, they will only provide **short-term** solutions. For example, the **UK government** has announced plans to provide **young people** in poor, isolated, rural areas with **free computers**. It hopes that **computer access** will **reduce** social and economic inequalities in rural areas by **increasing** young people's **employment opportunities** (e.g. people can gain **computer skills** or **look for jobs** advertised on the internet). However, this scheme doesn't address the **root cause** of the inequalities, which is a **lack** of **local employment** — it doesn't help having a computer to **search** for jobs if there **aren't** any in the first place. A more successful scheme would have been one that **created jobs** in rural areas **too**.

Are sustainable

Successful strategies need to be able to be **maintained** in the **long-term**. For example, **Africa Now** (an international development organisation) runs a **commercial bee-keeping project**. The project introduces **small-scale farmers** to commercial bee-keeping by providing **training** and access to **equipment**. To ensure the project is **sustainable**, a **private company** has agreed to buy the honey produced at a **fair price**, enabling the **reinvestment** of any money earned.

Rural Inequalities and Urban Inequalities are Linked

1) **Rural-urban migration** leads to **inequalities** in **both** the **rural** and **urban** areas.

2) In **poorer countries** (e.g. Brazil) rural-urban migration leads to a **decrease** in the **young, able population** in rural areas. The older, less able people left behind have **less help** with **daily activities** (**social inequality**) and there's **less chance** of **services** being **created** for a **smaller population** (**social inequality**).

3) In **richer countries** rural-urban migration also leads to a **decrease** in the **population** in rural areas, which can cause a **decrease** in **services** (**social inequality**) and **dereliction** (**environmental inequality**).

4) **Strategies** that **address rural inequalities** will **reduce push factors** (see p. 95), which will **decrease** rural-urban **migration** and also **reduce urban inequalities**.

Practice Questions

Q1   Describe one example of how appropriate technologies can help reduce rural inequalities.
Q2   What are LDFs?
Q3   Why do schemes to solve rural inequality need to be sustainable?

Exam Question

Q1   With reference to one or more named examples, describe strategies that are used to reduce rural inequalities.   [10 marks]

'STRATEGY' — I'm sure that was a song by Steps...

There are loads of strategies (carried out in loads of different communities) to reduce all types of rural inequalities — so make sure you know a good range of them for the exam. Also, it's important to think about how you'd monitor the success of these strategies — this could include using questionnaires, surveys and census data. Right, on to the next page we go. Whoop whoop.

Rural Inequalities — Case Study

If you've found the last few pages on rural inequalities a bit unexciting then never fear here's another case study...

There are **Inequalities** Between **Areas** in the **Brecon Beacons National Park**

The **Brecon Beacons National Park** is situated in **south-east Wales**. It's a large, **rural** area dominated by **agricultural land**. Many areas in **central** parts of the park have a thriving **tourist industry** and are relatively **wealthy**. However, there are some **deprived areas** situated on the **outskirts** of the park.

EXAMPLE — Llanelly Hill and Llangynidr

Llangynidr is a small area situated near the **centre** of Brecon Beacons National Park. **Llanelly Hill** is an area situated on the **outskirts** of the park.

This table shows some **statistics** for the two areas from the 2001 census: ⇨

More people own second homes or holiday homes in Llangynidr.

Llanelly Hill has a larger population

Measures	Llangynidr	Llanelly Hill
Population	1005	3810
% houses that are second or holiday homes	4	0.6
% aged 16-74 unemployed	1.7	3.0
% 'not good' health	8.9	13.3
% 16-74 year olds with no qualifications	19.7	28.1
% households with no vehicle	6.6	15.9

More than twice as many households in Llanelly Hill have no vehicle.

- Llanelly Hill has a **higher unemployment rate** of **3.0%**, compared to only **1.7%** in **Llangynidr**. This is probably because Llanelly Hill is situated on the **outskirts** of the Brecon Beacons National Park and so **doesn't** have as many **jobs** created by the **tourist industry** as areas in the centre of the park, like Llangynidr.

- **More houses** are used as **second homes** or **holiday homes** in **Llangynidr** — probably because it's situated **further into** the National Park. This can **drive house prices up**, causing **economic inequality**.

- A **higher percentage** of people in Llanelly Hill have **'not good' health**, possibly because they **don't** have **enough money** for **prescriptions** and **health care**.

- A higher **percentage of 16-74 year olds** in Llanelly Hill have **no qualifications** (**28.1%** compared to **19.7%** in Llangynidr). This can lead to **further unemployment** as people **don't** have the right **qualifications** to get jobs, leading to **further decline** in the area. This creates a **cycle of decline** (see p. 91).

- **Fewer people** have no vehicle in Llangynidr (**6.6%**) compared to Llanelly Hill (**15.9%**). This can also lead to **further unemployment** as people might have trouble **travelling** to work. Also, this can cause **social inequality** as people are **less mobile** and have to rely on public transport to get around.

There are **Multiple Causes** of **Inequalities** in the **National Park**

1) The **decline** of the **coal** and **iron industries** to the **south** and **south-east** of the National Park caused **high unemployment** in the **south** of the park, e.g. **Llanelly Hill** was badly affected when the nearby **Blaenavon coal mine closed in 1980**. Llangynidr, with its long-established **tourist industry, wasn't** so badly affected.

2) There's a **lack of affordable housing** in the **National Park**. This is because the houses are in a **desirable** area, which **pushes prices up**. Also people from outside the area are likely to buy **second homes** there, **increasing prices further**.

3) There's a **lack of access to transport services** in the National Park, due to a **low population**. This affects the people in Llanelly Hill more because **fewer** of them **own vehicles**.

Inequalities Reduce Opportunities and Cause Social Isolation

The **effects** of the **inequalities between areas** in the Brecon Beacons National Park include:

1) **Lack of affordable housing** (e.g. in both areas above) — first-time buyers **can't** get on the 'housing ladder'.

2) **Reduced employment** opportunities on the **outskirts** of the park (e.g. Llanelly Hill) — this leads to **lower family incomes** and a **reduced population** as people **move away** to **find work**.

3) **Social isolation** in the **poorer, southern** areas of the park — because of a **lack of car ownership** and **public transport**. This also leads to **reduced employment opportunities** as it's **difficult** to **commute** to work.

Rural Inequalities — Case Study

Strategies are Being Used to Address Inequalities in the National Park

1 A new **Unitary Development Plan** for the **Brecon Beacons National Park** was approved by the **National Park Authority** in March 2007. It includes **policies** and **proposals** that will **control development** in the National Park up to **2016** and beyond, so the park is **protected** and the **needs** of **local communities** are met. It includes **quarry planning permission** for an area to the north-east area of **Llanelly Hill**, which could **provide jobs** in the area. Also a **housing allocation** for an area to the south of **Llandgynidr** is included, which could provide more **affordable housing**.

2 The **Beacons Project** was started in **2000** and involves several organisations including the **Brecon Beacons National Park Authority**, the **Brecons Trust**, the **National Park Authority**, **Powys County Council**, **local tourism operators** and **local agricultural businesses**. It aims to **improve employment** and **training opportunities** for **young people**, **support** the **local economy**, **conserve** the **landscape** and help **keep local services open**. The project has run many schemes, including a **marketing campaign** to boost **tourism** across the **whole park**. This may help **provide more jobs** in **tourism** in **less wealthy areas**, such as Llanelly Hill, and generate **more trade** for **local businesses** there too. The success of a scheme like this could be measured by **examining data** on the **number of tourists** to the National Park **before** and **after** the marketing campaign was introduced.

3 The **National Park Authority** is developing its **agricultural policies** to encourage more **environmentally friendly farming methods** and **farm diversification**. This may **increase employment opportunities** in agriculture. The **success** of these policies could be measured by looking at **data** on **unemployment** in areas of the park **before** and **after** new policies are introduced.

4 **Blaenavon** (the **coal mine** — see previous page) has been designated a **World Heritage Site** and is investing in its **tourist industry**, which could **provide jobs** for people in **Llanelly Hill**.

5 The **Brecon and District Disabled Club** run a 'dial-a-ride service'. **Disabled** people can **ring up** and **book transport**, which **increases transport services** for the **disabled** across the park. It's been running for over 30 years and is funded by several organisations, e.g. the **National Lottery**. The **success** of this **scheme** can be measured by **monitoring** the **number of users** and **surveying** the users to see how it **affects** their lives.

6 A **community action group** in Llanelly Hill obtained **EU** and **council funding** to **renovate** the **village hall**. It's now used as a **venue** for **computer classes**, a **youth club**, bingo, a **food co-operative** and a **playschool**. The success of the village hall could be measured by **distributing** a **questionnaire** to **local people**, asking **how many** of them **use** the village hall and how they **perceive** its success.

You Can Investigate the Causes and Effects of Inequalities in a Rural Area

The **fieldwork** and **research techniques** that you can use to **study** the **causes** and **effects** of **rural inequalities** include the **same** ones that are used to **investigate urban inequalities** (see p. 97), such as **census data**, **CVA scores**, **questionnaires** and **surveys**. You could also map **zones of exclusion** — areas with **no bus service**, **shops** or **secondary schools** for **2 miles**. These maps can **indicate** the areas that are the **most deprived** and are most in **need** of **schemes** like the ones above.

Michael found a perfect example for his fieldwork on deprivation in rural areas.

Practice Questions

Q1 Describe two inequalities between Llanelly Hill and Llangynidr.
Q2 Give one cause of the inequalities between Llanelly Hill and Llangynidr.
Q3 Describe a strategy that has been used to address the inequalities in the Brecon Beacons National Park.

Exam Question

Q1 With reference to one named example, discuss the causes and effects of rural inequalities. [15 marks]

I didn't know that whales have inequalities — boom, boom...

Oh dear, it's the end of the section. I hope you've enjoyed all this juicy information. Remember that inequalities in rural and urban areas are pretty similar. And that all inequalities are interlinked. Also, make sure you learn the case studies because you'll probably have to answer a question that needs references to a 'named example'. Right, that's all from me now... ter-rah.

Introduction to Rebranding Places

Rebranding is all about improving a place's image so that people will want to go there, and take their wallets...

Rebranding Aims to Improve a Place and Its Image

1) **Rebranding** a place usually involves **regeneration** — making actual **improvements** to an area, e.g. new buildings and services.

2) It also involves **re-imaging** — using **marketing** to improve the **image** and **reputation** of a place.

3) Rebranding is aimed at **internal** users (e.g. residents and employees) and **external** 'customers' (e.g. visitors and potential investors).

4) It occurs at all **scales**, from rebranding individual **villages** to changing the image of an entire **country**, like **China**.

5) Its aims can include improving the **quality of life** for **residents** and **attracting new residents**, **tourists** and **businesses**.

6) Ideally a '**virtuous cycle**' will be created.

Regeneration is often followed by re-imaging — to make people aware of the improvements that have been made.

Rebranding is Needed When a Place is in Decline

A place can be in **decline** due to **social**, **economic** and **environmental** problems. Each of these problems causes **more problems**, creating a **spiral of decline**. In the UK, places that need rebranding fall into **three** groups:

Urban areas

1) Many **industrial** towns have lost their **factories** and so have seen a massive **decrease** in manufacturing **jobs**.

2) The **loss of industry** results in **high unemployment**, creating **economic problems** as people have to live on **low income** or **income support** (welfare).

3) The economic problems lead to a **spiral of decline** as people **move out** of the area to look for **work**, which leads to **services closing** (e.g. shops), leading to **fewer** job opportunities, resulting in further **economic** and **social decline**.

4) Rebranding is **needed** to **encourage new investment** that should bring **jobs** and **money** to the area. **Improvements** in **housing** and the **local environment** will **attract** people **back** to the area.

Rural areas

1) The **decline** of **agriculture** has led to **reduced employment** and **economic problems** in **rural** areas.

2) The lack of **job opportunities** leads to the **out-migration** of **young** people, resulting in an **ageing population**.

3) Services such as **shops**, **schools** and **post offices** close as people **move away** for **work**, leading to a **spiral of decline** as **economic problems** and **social isolation** become worse.

4) Attracting new **business** and **tourists** to the area through **rebranding** will increase **employment** and **services**. This will then encourage **young people** to **stay** in the area, and **new people** to **move** to the area.

Coastal Resorts

1) **Cheap flights** abroad mean **fewer British tourists** are visiting **UK** coastal resorts, so resorts are **losing money** and **businesses** are **closing**.

2) The **decline** of the **fishing industry** has also led to **fewer jobs** and further **economic problems**.

3) This leads to the **out-migration** of **young people** and a **spiral of decline** as **problems** get worse.

4) As with urban and rural areas, **rebranding** encourages new **investment**, bringing **jobs** and **money** to the area.

You Need to be Able to Investigate the Need for Rebranding

Here are some ideas for **fieldwork** and **research** you could carry out into the **need** for **rebranding**:

Fieldwork

- Design a **simple questionnaire**, asking **local** people whether they think there's a **need** for rebranding and **why**.

- Conduct an **environmental quality survey**, scoring areas for **greenery**, **litter**, **graffiti**, **vandalism**, **dereliction**, **pavement quality**, **pollution**, **noise levels** and **state of repair** of housing. This could show whether an area is in **decline** and so in **need of rebranding**.

Research

- Conduct an **internet image search** to find out what sort of pictures are **typical** for a specific place. If they're all **negative**, rebranding may be required.

- Look at **census** data for information on **unemployment**. If an area has **high** unemployment, it may be in **need** of a rebranding scheme that will **create** more **jobs**.

- Use **GIS** to overlay **census** data on **deprivation** with **environmental quality data**. You could use this data to identify the locations most in **need** of **rebranding**.

Introduction to Rebranding Places

Rebranding Can Use Many Different Strategies

1) There are lots of different ways to **rebrand** an area. Projects can **focus** on:
   - **Attracting tourists** — with **leisure** and **sports facilities**, **culture** and the **arts**.
   - **Improving conditions for residents** — with **better housing** and more **amenities**.
   - **Attracting investment** — with new **shops**, **commercial buildings** and **waterfront developments**.

2) Rebranding can be **achieved** through projects that help to **regenerate** or **re-image** a place:

Regeneration		**Re-imaging**	
Developing new...		**Promoting...**	
• Housing	• Technology	• National parks	• Food towns (see below)
• Shops	• Leisure and sports facilities	• Rural and historical heritage	• Links with the media
• Commercial buildings			• Leisure and sports
• Art and cultural centres		• Festivals	• Art and culture

3) There's a lot of **overlap** between **regeneration** and **re-imaging**, and **most** projects involve a bit of **both**.

4) Focusing on **one strategy** can **speed up** the rebranding process by acting as a **catalyst** for **further change**.

5) For example, **culture** has been used as a **catalyst** for rebranding **Liverpool**. Since being named **European Capital of Culture** for 2008, it's begun a major **redevelopment process**. This includes new **housing**, a **cruise-liner terminal**, and the £900 million **Paradise Street shopping** complex. It shows how **re-imaging** can lead to **regeneration**.

6) In **successful** rebranding projects the **strategies** will be **linked**. The aim is to create a **virtuous cycle**, where the **first** change leads to **further** improvements, and so on. For example, building a shopping centre creates **more jobs**, bringing **more money** and **visitors** to an area. This helps to improve a place's **image**, attracting **more visitors**, etc.

Rebranding Can Involve Flagship Projects...

Flagship projects are **large-scale**, **expensive** projects designed to make a **radical change** to a place's **image** and generate **media interest**. They're '**top-down**' initiatives, which means the **idea** and **funding** come from local or national **government** and **big business** (the 'top'). The **Guggenheim Museum** in **Bilbao**, **Spain** is an example of a flagship project:

CARLOS DOMINGUEZ / SCIENCE PHOTO LIBRARY

1) The **decline** of **industry** in **Bilbao** (an **industrial port**) in the 1970s and 1980s led to **high unemployment** and many **social problems** in the area.

2) The **Guggenheim Museum** was opened in 1997 as a **flagship project** designed to act as a **catalyst** for **regeneration** of the Bilbao area.

3) The **art museum** is housed in an **eye-catching building** that attracts around **1 million visitors** and an estimated extra **150-200 million euros** each year.

4) **Further regeneration** of the area has included new **tram** and **bus lines**, further **cultural centres** and **concert venues**, and **improved buildings** and **services**.

...or Community Projects

Community projects tend to be **smaller** than flagship projects. They're '**bottom-up**' initiatives, which means they're started by **local** people (the 'bottom'). The rebranding of **Ludlow** is an example of a community project:

Ludlow is a **market town** in Shropshire (**UK**). It started to be rebranded as the '**slow food town**' in 1995 when a few **local people** came up with the idea of holding a **food festival** there. The festival now more than **doubles** the town's population for **one weekend** each September. It attracts visitors with top-class **restaurants** and **independent shops** selling **local produce**.

Practice Questions

Q1 What is the difference between regeneration and re-imaging?

Q2 What is the difference between a flagship project and a community project?

Exam Question

Q1 Describe why urban, rural and coastal areas in the UK might require rebranding. [10 marks]

Re-e-brand, when the crowd say bo' selecta...

This stuff isn't too tricky really, but remember that rebranding doesn't have to be limited to towns and cities. Something as small as a school or as big as a country can benefit from a new image. Heck, you could even rebrand yourself. All it takes is some PVA glue, a couple of pillows, a pair of scissors and a bit of determination and hey presto! You've rebranded yourself as a chicken...

Urban Rebranding Strategies

Urban rebranding can be a bit of a complicated business — it takes a lot of people and a lot of money to get it right.

Urban Rebranding Involves Many Different Players

Rebranding an **urban** area **can't** be done by one **organisation** on its **own**. It needs many different **players** (people who have an **interest** in the rebranding). Each of these players will have **different roles** and **different reasons** for getting involved:

Player	Likely Role	Possible Reasons
Local government (e.g. district or city council)	Funding and planning permission.	To improve urban areas for social and economic benefit, to increase income from taxes, and to gain votes.
National government	Funding.	
Urban Regeneration Companies (URCs)	Coordinating government and private investment and deciding priorities for rebranding.	It's the job of these companies to support regeneration and rebranding.
Private companies	Project funding.	Publicity, association with vibrant modern projects.
	Moving into the rebranded area.	Profit — taking advantage of the likely increase in business as a result of rebranding.
Private investors (e.g. venture capitalists)	Funding local projects and companies.	Profit — taking advantage of the likely increase in business as a result of rebranding.
Not-for-profit organisations (e.g. Arts Council England)	Funding, support and advice.	Regeneration is often the aim of the organisation or it supports the aim (e.g. improving social problems).
Local tourist board	Marketing and promotion.	Leads to increased tourist numbers and improved visitor experience.
The local community	Backing the rebranding process and helping to decide priorities for rebranding.	Desire to live and work in a place with improved facilities, environment and reputation.

Urban Rebranding Can Involve Regeneration

One of the most obvious ways to regenerate an urban area is to **improve** its **buildings**. This can involve **smartening up existing** buildings or building eye-catching **new** ones. Building **improvements** tend to focus on **four** main areas:

1 Residential

Improving **existing** housing or building **new** estates, e.g. the 1700 new homes in **New Islington**, **Manchester** (see p. 108).

2 Shopping

Building **new shopping centres** or improving **existing** ones to attract **consumers** and **investors** to the area.

3 Commercial

New **business** buildings — e.g. the **Burj Al Arab hotel** in **Dubai**. This **flagship** building shows that Dubai wants to **promote** itself as a **tourist destination** for the **jet-set** — it's not just an oil industry city or a business location.

4 Waterfront developments

Regenerating former **industrial** areas like **docks**. This can be done with new **housing**, **shops** and **commercial buildings**. Waterfront projects also often focus on **culture** — e.g. the **Baltic Mill** in **Gateshead** (UK) has been turned into a **modern art gallery**, helping to **increase tourism**.

Urban Rebranding Can Involve Promoting an Existing Image...

1) Cities often **promote** themselves by **reinforcing** a **positive aspect** of their **identity** that people already know about, rather than actually **changing** anything about the place.

2) For example, **historic centres** can promote their existing links with history to combine **heritage** and **tourism**, e.g. **York** is marketed as '**England's first city of history**'.

3) Promoting an existing image can create a **virtuous cycle** — people are persuaded to **visit**, which encourages more **investment** (e.g. by encouraging businesses to relocate there), which encourages more **visitors** and so on.

4) For example, **Hay-on-Wye** (UK) set up a **literary festival** in 1988 on the back of its **reputation** for second-hand bookshops. The originally small festival **developed** into a big attraction, bringing over **80 000** visitors and an **extra £3 million** to the town **each year**.

5) However, promoting an image can sometimes be **risky**, as developers can be **accused** of '**spin**' if they just **remarket** the place **without** actually making any **improvements**.

Urban Rebranding Strategies

...or *Marketing a New Image*

Sometimes promoting a city's identity involves **changing existing** perceptions of the place. For example, **Amsterdam** has tried to **alter** its **reputation** for **prostitution** and **drugs** by promoting itself as a **historic** place filled with **art** and **culture**. **Declining coastal towns** can also benefit from a **new image**, e.g. **Eastbourne**:

1) **Eastbourne** is known for being a popular **tourist** and **retirement destination** for **older people**. When the **number** of elderly visitors started to **decline**, **Eastbourne Borough Council** launched the 'Change Your View' poster **campaign** in **2004**. It aimed to diversify the tourist economy by attracting **younger visitors** and **families** with children.

2) The campaign **promoted** Eastbourne as a place to enjoy **extreme sports**, **live bands** and **theme parks**.

3) The rebranding seems to have been **successful** — **visitor numbers** are **increasing** (they increased 66% from 2007 to 2008) and over **half** of the **4 million** people who **visited** Eastbourne in **2008** had **never** been **before**. This suggests that the campaign had **reached out** to a **different** 'types' of tourist.

Urban Rebranding *Can Use* Sport *as a* Catalyst *for* Change

1) **Sport** can act as a **catalyst** for **rebranding** — it **speeds up** urban rebranding by generating **publicity**, attracting **visitors** and **investors**, and creating **jobs** for residents.

2) **Hosting** a **major sporting event** can have a **huge** impact on an area. For example, the **Chinese government** was willing to spend over **$40 billion** on hosting the **Beijing 2008 Olympic Games** because the massive **global publicity** would raise China's **profile** around the world. The aim is that this will **increase tourism** and **international investment** in China.

3) On a smaller scale, building **new sports facilities** can help **rebrand** an area too:

> The development of **Arsenal Football Club's** £430 million **Emirates Stadium** in Ashburton Grove, **North London** has provided **2600 new jobs** for the area and **2500 new homes**. The project has also replaced the old **recycling facilities** and provided a **nursery** and a **health club** for the local community.

Urban Rebranding *Can Have* Disadvantages

Sometimes urban rebranding can have a **negative** impact. A particular problem is that **unrebranded** areas can become **isolated** as a result of rebranding **elsewhere**. For example:

1) Over the last 20 years, **Manchester** has been rebranded as a '**happening place**'. The **regeneration** included **improving** former **run-down suburbs** like **Hulme** and **derelict industrial areas** like **Eastlands** (where the **City of Manchester Stadium** was built for the **Commonwealth Games** in 2002).

2) But **research** by the **William Temple Foundation** has revealed that as a result, **crime** and **poverty** have become **more concentrated** in places that **haven't** been **regenerated** yet, like parts of **Moss Side**.

3) This **gap** between **regenerated areas** and **unregenerated areas** has led to:

- A **decline** in **local shops** in the **unregenerated** areas because there are **large-scale retail outlets** nearby.
- **Fear of crime**, particularly among **older people**, in the areas that **haven't** been **regenerated**.
- A **reduction** in **volunteer work**, **social interaction** and **local clubs** and **societies**. This has happened particularly in the **regenerated areas** as **young professionals** have moved **in** and **families** have moved **out**.

Practice Questions

Q1 Name two players that might be involved in urban rebranding.
Q2 Outline the four main areas that building improvement regeneration strategies can focus on.
Q3 Briefly describe how sport can act as a catalyst for rebranding.

Exam Question

Q1 With reference to named examples, explain how rebranding strategies might regenerate urban areas. [10 marks]

If you're using football as a catalyst — you'll need at least 11 players...

Once a town or city gets a bit grotty then you've got to make a choice about what to do to improve it. You could knock down all the buildings and redo all the houses and shops from scratch, smarten up the docks, build a new sports centre, or spend billions of pounds hosting the Olympics. Or you could just give it a lick of paint and get a new sign. Genius...

108

Urban Rebranding — Case Study

You might have to write about an urban rebranding case study in detail in your exam. Well, look what I have here...

The **Cardroom Estate** in **Ancoats** Needed **Rebranding**

1) The **Cardroom estate** was built in the **1970s** in the **Ancoats** area of **Manchester**, just **east** of the **city centre**.

2) The estate was built to **replace** the **old**, **cramped** Victorian housing in the area.

3) By the **mid 1990s** the estate had become **run-down** and had a **bad reputation**. **50%** of the **houses** were **empty** or being used as **squats**.

4) The area suffered from a **spiral of decline** caused by **economic** and **social problems** like **high unemployment**, **burglary**, **joyriding**, **drug problems**, **graffiti** and **vandalism**.

The **Cardroom Estate** Has been **Replaced** by the **New Islington** Development

1) **New Islington** is a **flagship housing development** that has **replaced** the **Cardroom estate**.

2) The estate was chosen as the location for the rebranding because it's a **brownfield** site that was an area of **deprivation** and **dereliction**. It's a good location because it's within **walking distance** of the **shops**, **offices** and **entertainment facilities** in the city centre.

A brownfield site is one that has been built on before. It's the opposite of a greenfield site — one that has never been built on before.

3) **New Islington** has **colourful**, **eye-catching buildings** and lots of **new facilities**:

Facilities in New Islington

1700 new homes	Restaurants and cafes	Angling club
Primary school	Orchard	Tram links
Health centre with 8 GPs	31 acre ecopark	50 moorings on the Ashton and Rochdale Canals
Village hall	Community football pitch	

4) The **total cost** of the redevelopment has been estimated at **£250 million**.

5) It's being managed by property developers **Urban Splash** and the urban regeneration company **New East Manchester** (NEM) Ltd — a partnership between **Manchester City Council**, **English Partnerships** (the government's regeneration agency) and the **Northwest Regional Development Agency** (NWDA).

6) It's hoped that the **regeneration** will **improve** the area's **image** and **encourage** more people to **move** there. It will also **attract** more **businesses** to the area, which in turn will **create jobs** and **increase wages** (a **virtuous cycle**).

The **Rebrand** Has **Involved** the **Local Community**

Despite being a multi-million pound **flagship development**, the **local community** has been **involved** in the **decision-making**. Everything that's happened at New Islington has followed **consultation** with **residents** of the **Cardroom estate**.

1) There have been regular **meetings** between the **developers** and the **locals** in the **Cob o'Coal pub**. The choice of design for the **new council houses** was a **result** of these **consultations**.

2) Each **Cardroom estate resident** was offered a **new house** in New Islington, or a **transfer** to **another Manchester estate**.

3) In one area of New Islington people can **design their own homes**. The idea is that **each house** on the terraced street will be **different** and the **residents** will take real **pride** in their home. This is called the **Tutti Frutti development**.

New Islington Will be More **Environmentally Sustainable**

The development includes a number of **environmentally friendly initiatives**:

- A 'Combined Heat and Power' (CHP) station to supply heat and electricity.
- Extensive new recycling facilities.
- Energy-efficient buildings and lots of green space.
- The water supply will come from the development's own borehole (which used to supply the Boddington's brewery).

The new borehole was an instant hit with the locals.

Unit 2: Topic 4 — Rebranding Places

Urban Rebranding — Case Study

The Rebrand Has Involved Modern Marketing Methods

The **internet** has played a vital role in **marketing** New Islington.

1) Internet searches for New Islington bring up some feel-good **video clips** set to **upbeat music**. They show happy **young professionals** living in **designer flats**.

2) The development has its own **website**, with colourful **photos** and artists' impressions of the project. The website helps to **communicate** the **brand message** that New Islington is **quirky**, **vibrant**, **community-focused** and **eco-friendly**.

The New Islington Development Has Good Points...

There's been a lot of **focus** in the **planning** on New Islington's **long-term impact**.

1) **Locals** have been **involved** in the **planning** and they've been **consulted** at **all stages** throughout the development. This means they're more likely to **support** the development and **stay** in the area, which in turn gives it a **better image**.

2) The regeneration has created **new businesses**, such as a **newsagents**, a **greengrocers** and a **gastro pub**. This creates lots of **new jobs**, helping to **decrease** the **high unemployment** in the area and leading to a **virtuous cycle**.

3) There's a focus on **improving infrastructure**. New Islington has a new **tram stop**, which gives the area better **public transport links**. This makes the area more **attractive** to **new residents**, and should stop it from becoming **isolated**.

4) **Conservation** is important in New Islington. It's built on a **brownfield site**, which is **better** for the **environment** than building on a **greenfield site**. The **buildings** have been designed to be as **energy-efficient** as possible, and the **CHP station** and new **recycling facilities** mean there should be much **less waste** than there was previously.

...and Bad Points

New Islington has been **criticised** by **different groups** for **various reasons**:

Residents

- Some **residents** of the old **Cardroom estate** have **complained** that they're considered to be **less important** than the **new residents**. This is because the **social housing** area of the development, where they've been **rehoused**, is at the **opposite end** of the site from the **public spaces** and **amenities**.

- All the houses have **locked gates** over the **doors**, which has led some residents to voice **concerns** about the emphasis on **personal security** in the development. They're worried that it might **damage** the **community spirit** that the developers are keen to **promote**, because it suggests that people can't **trust** their neighbours.

The media

New Islington is named after a **street** on the old **Cardroom estate**, and was **chosen** by **local residents**. However, some **newspapers** have **criticised** it because it suggests the area is trying to be like the trendy suburb of **Islington** in **London**.

Experts

Some **experts** on rebranding have **criticised** New Islington for **not** providing enough **council houses** for residents of the old Cardroom estate. The development has been described as "**a bit light on social housing**".

Practice Questions

Q1 Why was the Cardroom estate chosen as the location for a major rebranding project?
Q2 Name five new facilities in New Islington.
Q3 Name two environmentally friendly initiatives in New Islington.

Exam Question

Q1 With reference to a named example, outline and evaluate an urban rebranding scheme. [10 marks]

I want to be a part of it — New Islington, New Islington...

Who'd be an urban developer eh? You do the best you can but you'll never be able to please everyone. I had to get out of the rebranding game in the end, it was too much stress — endless meetings and rows and the hours were awful. Plus, I look terrible in a hard hat. So now I just spend my days doing sudoku and listening to country and western, and I've never been happier...

Rural Rebranding Strategies

It's not just towns and cities that need to be rebranded — rural areas can benefit from a bit of restyling too.

Rural Rebranding Involves Many Different Players

1) As with **urban areas**, rebranding a **rural** area **can't** be done by **one organisation** on its **own**.
2) Creating a **virtuous cycle** (see p. 104) needs the **involvement** of **many** different **players**.
3) These players are basically the **same** as those for **urban** areas (see the **table** on p. 106). The main **differences** are:

Less money is available

- **Rural** locations in need of **rebranding** are **unlikely** to generate as much **money** as **urban** areas, because not as many people live there.
- This means there's **less interest** from 'big business'.
- **Exceptions** to this include **energy developments** like **nuclear power stations** and **wind farms**.

Planning permission can be hard to get

- It's **harder** to get **planning permission** in **rural** areas than it is in **run-down urban** areas.
- It can be **especially difficult** to get planning permission in **National Parks**. National Parks Authorities might **not approve** new buildings because they want to **preserve** the **landscape**, even if the buildings would be **good** for **rebranding**.

Technology and the Media Can Help with Rural Regeneration

The internet

- With the advent of the **internet**, there's been an **increase** in the number of people able to **move** to **rural** areas and **work from home**.
- But there have been **problems** with this because **high-speed broadband connections** have been focused on more **densely populated** areas where there are **more customers**.
- To **tackle** this in the most **remote** parts of Scotland, the **Scottish Executive** (the government) and the **Highlands and Islands Enterprise** (**HIE**) have funded a **£70 million project** to **connect** every **community** to **high-speed broadband**.
- This has been used by the **HIE** to **market** the **Highlands and Islands** as a good place to **base small businesses** for people who want a **slower pace** of life.

Jo and Nancy couldn't wait to work from home — their boss wore horrific aftershave.

Community radio

- Community radio **reaches out** to **rural communities** by catering to their **specific needs**. For example, since 1994 a lot of community radio stations have been set up in **South Africa**. They **discuss** local **issues** in the local **dialect**, and play local **music**. They also often have an **educational** function, e.g. they broadcast plays on topics like **HIV/AIDS**.
- Many people in rural parts of South Africa **can't read or write**, so they can feel **isolated**. Community radio can help them to feel **part** of their community, e.g. people can **drop in** to the station and **get involved** in the **broadcasts**.
- This can help **rebrand** an area by making **residents** feel more **positive** about it. This gives it a **better image** and **encourages visitors** and **investors**. Stations can also **advertise** an area's **good points** and **support local businesses**.

Films

- **Rural areas** can be **rebranded** as good **locations** for **filming**. The **National Trust** promotes rural locations and **hires out** properties like **stately homes** to film-makers. This is particularly **popular** for **period dramas** like **Pride and Prejudice**.
- This brings **business** to the area and **generates interest** while the filming is taking place. The area can also be **promoted** as the **film location after** the film is **released**, attracting more **fans** and **tourists** (see below).

Rural Rebranding Can Involve Re-imaging

① Promoting Links with the Media

If a successful **film** or **TV series** is set in a particular rural area then it can attract more **visitors** to the area.
If the film or TV series portrays a particular **image** of the area, then this image can be used to help **rebrand** it. For example:

1) The children's TV programme **Balamory** is filmed in the village of **Tobermory** on the **Isle of Mull**, **Scotland**.
2) Since Balamory launched in **2003**, the island has attracted up to **160 000 extra visitors** each year.
3) Many of these visitors are families with **toddlers**, so the island has developed attractions specifically for them, e.g. **Tobermory Open Farm** and a business selling Balamory **souvenirs**.
4) The series has contributed an estimated **£5 million a year** to the **tourist economy** of Mull.

Rural Rebranding Strategies

② Promoting Heritage and the Arts

Rural rebranding can involve promoting the **art** and **heritage** that's **unique** to an area. Here are some examples:

Art

The **Angel of the North** is a huge steel **sculpture** on a hill by the side of a road near **Gateshead** (UK). It's **regenerated** the site of a **disused mine** and helped attract **visitors** and **investors** to the area.

Cultural Heritage

The **Lake District** is often called 'Wordsworth Country' because the poet **William Wordsworth** lived there and wrote many of his poems **about** the area.

Rural Heritage

The production of **whisky** in **Scotland** has become a way of **attracting tourists** to the region. People can go on **tours** of distilleries to see how whisky is produced. This brings **visitors** who also **spend money** on **accommodation** and **leisure activities**.

Historical Heritage

The **World Heritage Site** (and surrounding area) between **Newcastle** and **Carlisle** on the **border** of **England** and **Scotland** has been branded 'Hadrian's Wall Country', because of the **Roman wall** built by the **Emperor Hadrian**.

③ Giving an Area National Park Status

Large areas of **natural beauty** can be **re-imaged** as **National Parks**.

1) For example, the **New Forest** (an area of heathland and forest in **Southern England**) became the country's **newest National Park** in **2005**.
2) The **aim** is to attract **more visitors** and **protect** the area from **overdevelopment**.
3) This will hopefully create a **virtuous cycle**, where the **extra visitors** will bring more **money** to the area, which means **more** can be **spent** on **conservation**, which will then attract **more visitors** because they know the area is **unspoilt**, etc.

Integrated Projects are Good for Rural Rebranding

Integrated projects involve **more than one** rebranding **strategy**. They're more likely to be **successful** than other projects because they're **more sustainable** — if one strategy **fails** then there are **others** to **fall back** on. Integrated projects include:

1) Joining up **social**, **economic** and **environmental** strategies — to try to tackle **all** of these issues together.
2) Involving both **public sector activity** (EU, national or local government) and **private sector business development** in the rebranding project — e.g. linking government-funded **tourist boards** with new **tourist businesses**.
3) Having different **business sectors** working **together** — e.g. the rebranding of **Ludlow** as a **specialist food town** brings together **farming**, **food processing**, **restaurants** and **tourism** (see p. 105).

Integrating Projects Leads to Diversification

- The **decline** of **agriculture** in many places means that rural areas have to find **other ways** to generate income from the **post-production countryside**. This means lots of rural rebranding projects involve **diversification**.
- Many farms have **diversified** in order to make money in different ways, e.g. attracting visitors with **maize mazes**, **nature trails** and **farm shops**. **Diversification** can also create **new jobs**, which **encourages young people** to **stay** in the area.
- For example, **Lobbs Farm**, a small **farm** in **Cornwall**, has **branched out** and now has a **farm**, a **shop** and an **educational visitors' centre**. After only **three years** of opening it made over **£600 000** in additional sales.
- It's an **integrated project** that involves **farming**, **leisure** and **tourism**, with a focus on **sustainability** and **rural heritage**. It makes use of **farm buildings** that might otherwise become **derelict**. This **improves** the **image** of the area, which attracts even more **visitors**.

Practice Questions

Q1 Why can it be harder to get planning permission in rural areas compared to urban areas?
Q2 Outline three different strategies that can be used to re-image rural areas.

Exam Question

Q1 Using named examples, describe the rebranding strategies often used in rural areas. [10 marks]

Links with the media — Trainspotting didn't work so well for Edinburgh...

There's not too much to worry about with these pages because the examiners have done you a bit of a favour. Rural rebranding is really quite similar to urban rebranding — it's still about attracting visitors and investors and whatnot, just with more cows and mud.

Rural Rebranding — Case Studies

These pages cover some examples of rural rebranding in a bit more detail. Joy of untold joys...

The **Eden Project** is Helping to **Regenerate Cornwall**

Cornwall's economy used to **rely** on **farming**, **fishing**, **mining** and **quarrying**. These industries have been in **decline** since the **1970s**, which has **damaged** the **local economy** and the **landscape**, forcing people to **leave** the area to **find work**.

- The local economy relies on **tourism**, but most **jobs** in the **tourist industry** are **seasonal** and **low-paid** — Cornwall has the **lowest weekly wages** in Britain. This has led to the **out-migration** of **young people**.

- **Low wages** also leads to **young people leaving** because they **can't afford** to **buy property**. **House prices** have **risen** as people have bought **holiday homes** in the area. This means **rural areas** are **under-populated** for much of the year, so **small businesses** have to **close** because of a **lack** of **trade**. The **lack of services** makes the areas more **isolated**, which encourages more people to **leave**. All this leads to a **spiral of decline**.

Developers have aimed to regenerate the area with **flagship projects**:

> The **Eden Project** near St Austell in **Cornwall** opened in **2001**. It's an example of **rural diversification** and **rebranding**. It's **changed** the **rural landscape** and aims to **regenerate** the local area through **ecotourism** (tourism that focuses on the **appreciation** of **nature** and has **minimal negative impact** on the local **ecosystem**). It's a sort of **'eco theme park'** in a former **china-clay quarry**, made up of huge, futuristic **plastic domes**. There's a **tropical zone**, a **Mediterranean zone** and an **outdoor temperate zone**. They contain **plants** from each location and focus on **sustainable farming**.
>
> > The project has:
> >
> > 1) **Changed** the **image** of this part of Cornwall from a **summer-only**, **beach holiday** destination into a **year-round** destination for **ecotourists**.
> >
> > 2) Attracted over **1 million extra visitors** a year to the area, and attracted **visitors inland**, to the previously **run-down** former **mining** area.
> >
> > 3) Developed **scientific research** and **education resources**.
> >
> > 4) **Boosted** the **local farming** and **food processing industries** by using **local suppliers** wherever possible by working with **county** and **local councils** as part of an **Integrated Area Plan (IAP)**.
>
> The **Eden Project** is helping to create a **virtuous cycle** — the **extra business** creates **more jobs** and **higher salaries**, which encourages young people to stay in the area. It also means that **more money** is being **spent**, so **extra business** is **created** and rural services **stay open**, encouraging more people to **visit** and making **locals** more likely to **stay**.

The **Eden Project** Has **Attracted Tourists** But Created **Other Problems** Too

The **Eden Project** has been **very successful** in **rebranding** St Austell as a centre for **ecotourism**, but it's **not** all **good news**.

Positive effects

1) A **visitor survey** in **South Cornwall** showed that **36%** of people visited the area mainly **because** of the **Eden Project**.
2) The Eden Project buys over **£7 million** of **local food produce** every year.
3) It's generated an estimated **£150 million** each year in **extra revenue** to **local businesses**.
4) The Eden Project itself has **created over 500 jobs**, and an estimated **2500 jobs** have been created because of the effects of the **virtuous cycle**.
5) It's led to a **£75 million facelift** project for **St Austell town centre**.
6) In a **local business survey**, **22%** of responses specifically mentioned the **positive impact** of the area's **improved image** as a **result** of the **Eden Project**.

Negative effects

1) All the **extra visitors** have created serious **traffic problems** in the area, particularly in the **summer**. This **lowers** the **quality** of the **visitor experience** and **reduces** the chance that people will **visit again**.
2) The **extra cars** produce extra **greenhouse gas emissions** — a big **drawback** given the project's **focus** on **environmental sustainability**. The **Eden Project** and **Cornwall County Council** have addressed this with **reduced entry price** for **walkers** and **cyclists**, **cycle routes** from **local towns**, and the **Eden Branch Line** bus-rail link.
3) Another **criticism** of the project is that it keeps needing **more public money**. Despite a **£15 entry fee** and **high food prices**, the project has needed **£150 million** in donations from the **Millennium Lottery fund**, the **South West England Regional Development Agency (RDA)**, the **EU** and **Cornwall County Council**.

Rural Rebranding — Case Studies

The *Dorset* and *East Devon Coast* Has Become the *Jurassic Coast*

1) The **coast** of **Dorset** and **East Devon** was awarded **World Heritage Site** status by UNESCO in **2001**, because of the **prehistoric rocks, fossils** and **dinosaur remains** that are found there. It's since been **rebranded** as the **Jurassic Coast**.

2) The area was in **need** of **rebranding** because the local **economy** mostly relied on **tourists** visiting the beaches in the **summer**. This meant that it **couldn't** generate much **income** for the **rest** of the **year**.

3) The rebranding is mainly focused on **increasing visitors** to the area, especially at times **other than** the peak **summer season**. It aims to attract visitors to the area with **facilities** to **educate** them about the **coastal features, rocks** and **fossils**.

4) The rebranding was **also** designed to inspire **local communities** to **enjoy** the area, and **businesses** to **invest** in it.

The *Jurassic Coast Rebranding* Has Had *Positive* and *Negative* Effects

Positive effects

1) The number of **visitors** to the area has **increased**, especially **out-of-season**. Events like the **Lyme Regis Fossil Festival** attract **5000 extra visitors** to the town **one weekend** each April. The **best** time to **collect fossils** is after a **winter storm**, so this **attracts visitors** who might **not** otherwise visit until the **summer**.

2) **West Bay's** new **£16 million Jurassic Pier** has helped to **double** visitor numbers there since it was built in **2004**.

3) **New** or **renovated visitor centres** at **Beer, Exmouth, Swanage** and **Charmouth** have **increased** visitor numbers.

4) The **Bournemouth** to **Exeter X53 Jurassic Bus** service saw a **130%** rise in **passenger numbers** between **2002** and **2005**. This means that not all the extra visitors are coming by **car**, which **benefits locals** (as there's not as much traffic congestion) and it's **more environmentally friendly**.

5) Because the area is spread along **150 kilometres** of **coastline**, it's **avoided** a lot of the **traffic problems** faced by attractions like the **Eden Project**, which is in **one location**.

6) The **cliffs** of **Charmouth** and **Lyme Regis** are **well managed** in terms of **safety, litter** and **erosion**. In **2006** UNESCO reported that the coast is in as **good** a **condition** as it was when it gained **World Heritage Site** status in **2001**.

7) Changing the coast's **image** and building **visitor attractions** has **increased** the number of **visitors** to the area. This has generated more **income** for the **tourist economy**, and attracted more **investors**. This in turn will bring even more **visitors** and **create more jobs** for local people (another **virtuous cycle** — they get everywhere).

Negative effects

1) There's **concern** that the **rebranding** is **focused solely** on **tourism**, rather than **wider business** and **community benefits**. This is **risky** because it means that a **decline** in **tourism** could have a huge **negative impact** on the **local economy**.

2) Some **locals** feel that the rebranding has been **top-down** (the **decisions** have been made by local or national **government** and **big business** — the 'top'). Locals have complained that they **haven't** been **consulted** about the **changes**.

No rebranding project is perfect, so you need to include both positive and negative points if you're asked to evaluate them.

Practice Questions

Q1 How has the Eden Project tried to boost local farming?
Q2 Why is traffic a problem for the Eden Project?
Q3 What has been done to attract tourists to the coast of Dorset and East Devon?

Exam Question

Q1 Using named examples, compare the success of different rural rebranding schemes. [10 marks]

Jurassic Coast — I think I saw that at the cinema...

It's a scary place — I can't believe it's still open really. It's like a theme park — you go round in a jeep and look at dinosaurs they've cloned from a mosquito or something. I thought it must have been shut down after the T-Rex went on the rampage and someone got eaten on the toilet. Still, I reckon you can't argue with loads of extra visitors. I guess that's the beauty of rebranding...

Evaluating Rebranding Strategies

It's been written that only a lucky few will ever be told the secret of evaluating rebranding strategies. Read on, chosen ones...

The **Impact Rebranding** Will Have in the **Future** Has to be **Considered**

1) For a rebranding project to be **successful**, it needs to be **sustainable** — it needs to lead to **long-term benefits** and be possible to **maintain** in the **future**.

2) To achieve this, the project should involve **more than one strategy**. If it only focuses on one thing, like attracting tourists, a decline in that industry could be devastating.

3) It's also important for a rebranding project to be **self-sufficient**, which means creating a **virtuous cycle** (see p. 104). For example, in a **tourist destination** the rebranding needs to attract **more tourists**, which will bring in **more money**, which will lead to **more improvements**, which will lead to **more tourists**, and so on...

Sustainable Rebranding Can be Achieved in Different Ways

You need to look at whether a strategy is sustainable when you're **evaluating** how **successful** it's been. There are **four key ways** to make sure that a rebranding project will be **sustainable**, so make sure you look out for them:

① Involve local people in the planning
- Strategies are more likely to be **successful** if **local people** are **behind** it. They're more likely to **support** the scheme if they're able to make **suggestions** and **decisions**.
- Developers can involve local people by conducting **surveys** to find out what **residents** want.

② Improve infrastructure
- **Infrastructure** is the structures that **support a society**, e.g. **roads**, **public transport** and **power grids**.
- Improving things like the **public transport network** can attract more **residents** and **visitors** to an area. This can **improve** the area's **image** and bring in more **investment** — it helps create a **virtuous cycle**.

③ Build legacy facilities
- **Legacy facilities** are those that can **keep** being used once the **first stages** of rebranding are **over** — e.g. a **stadium** that the **public** can use **after** a sports event has finished.
- It's important for a rebranding strategy to leave a **legacy** if it's going to have a **long-term impact**.
- Legacy facilities often focus on **social improvement**, like **education** and **reducing crime**.

④ Include conservation measures
- It's important to consider the **environmental impact** of a strategy — if there's too much **waste**, it won't be **sustainable**.
- Showing concern about things like **energy efficiency** will also make the scheme more **popular**, so it's more likely to get **public support**.

An example of a rebranding strategy that has **planned** for the **future** is the **London 2012 Olympic Games**. The **site** chosen for the Olympic Park is **Stratford** in **East London** — an area in **need** of **rebranding**. The **strategies** involved in creating the Games and rebranding the area focus on **sustainability**:

1) **Planning** — the **Olympic Delivery Authority** has **written** to local residents to **inform** them of major planning decisions, and they've carried out **public consultations** to get **feedback** from local residents.

2) **Infrastructure** — £17 billion is being invested in **public transport**. By 2012 there will be **ten** railway lines into **Stratford**.

3) **Legacy** — sports facilities being built for the **athletes** will be available for **locals** to use **after** the Games.

4) **Conservation** — improved public transport should help **reduce traffic** in the area in the long term.

Evaluation Involves Looking at an Area Before and After Rebranding

1) To find out whether rebranding an area has been **successful**, you need to **compare** what the area's like **now** to what it was like **before** the rebranding.

2) This means that the **rebranding processes** should begin with a detailed **assessment**, measuring the **economic**, **environmental** and **social** state of the place before rebranding **starts**.

3) **Later evaluations** can then measure any **changes** by **comparing** the **data** — e.g. whether more **residents** are happy with the **facilities** after rebranding. They should also take into account the **impact** on **different groups** — e.g. **local businesses** and **visitors**.

4) **Comparing** the **data** can be a good way of measuring whether the rebranding has been **successful**, but it can **never** be completely **reliable** — e.g. residents might be **happier**, but that could be because the residents who **weren't** happy with the rebranding have **moved away**.

The rebranding of Whifftown sewer as a beach was a huge success.

Evaluating Rebranding Strategies

You Need to be Able to Do Fieldwork *into the* Success *of* Rebranding...

Your fieldwork should focus on the **economic**, **social** and **environmental** impact of rebranding:

Economic
- **Interview shoppers** and ask how far they've **travelled**, and if they would have come **before** the rebranding.
- You could then use this information to draw a rough **map** of the **spheres of influence** (the area the shoppers have come from) for **before** and **after** the **rebranding**.
- If **more** people **travel** from **far away** to shop there now, rebranding has been **successful**.

Social
- **Interview locals** to find out if there are people who have **moved away** or felt **marginalised** (left out) as a **result** of the rebranding. You can then see if the rebranding has had any **negative impact**.
- Where a city has had a rebranding campaign focusing on its **identity**, you could conduct a **survey** asking **local people** and **visitors** whether their **opinions** on the place's **image** have **changed**.
- If locals feel that the image has **improved**, they're more likely to want to **stay** in the area. This will lead to a **virtuous cycle**, attracting **more** people and investors to the area.

Environmental
- **Interview local people** and ask them if they think the **environment** has got **better** or **worse** since the rebranding.
- Ask **specific questions** about people's views on **litter**, **graffiti** and **access** to **green spaces since** the **rebranding**.
- If locals think the environment has **improved**, the scheme has been **successful**. **Residents** are more likely to **stay** in the area and other people are more likely to want to **visit**.

...and Research *to* Support *Your Fieldwork*

Economic
- Ask the **shop owners** for **data** about **shopper numbers**.
- **Compare** your findings with data from **similar nearby places** that **haven't** been **rebranded**.
- If the **rebranded** place gets **more** shoppers, then the scheme has been **successful**.
- Research **local trends** in **unemployment figures** for **before** and **after** rebranding.
- If the scheme has been **successful**, unemployment will have **decreased**.

Social
- Research **crime statistics** for **before** and **after** the **rebranding**. Be aware that a **drop** in **crime figures** in **one area** of a city could just mean that crime has **shifted** to a **different location**.
- Look on the **local newspaper's website** to find out **local opinion** of the scheme. **Public support** can help to **improve** a place's **image**, which can lead to more **benefits** like **more investment**.

Environmental
- Use the **internet** to research whether the scheme has **won** any **environmental awards**.
- Ask the **local council** for any **Environmental Impact Assessment** (EIA) they've done in the area. Compare the data from **before** and **after** the **rebranding** to find out the **environmental impact**.
- If a rebranding strategy includes providing more **recycling facilities**, you could look up **recycling rates** on the **local council website** and **compare** the **amount** of **recycling** done **before** and **after** the **rebranding**. This should tell you whether residents are using **new recycling facilities**.

Practice Questions

Q1 What are legacy facilities?

Q2 Suggest one piece of fieldwork you could do to analyse the economic success of a rebranding scheme.

Exam Question

Q1 Describe the results of your fieldwork and research into the success of a rural rebranding scheme. [15 marks]

Reinforced concrete toilets — just one example of legacy facilities...

To evaluate a rebranding strategy you need to look at whether it's improved the area, what problems it's caused, and whether it's sustainable. That's it really. Once you've got to grips with that then you can go and treat yourself to a nice cup of tea...

Exam Structure

And now onto the unpleasant topic of exams (sorry, I had to mention them sooner or later).
It's a pretty good idea to know what's in store for you so there are no nasty surprises on the day.

You Have to Sit **Two Exam Papers**

Unit 1 Exam — Global Challenges

1) It's **1 hr 30 mins** long and there are **90 marks** up for grabs (worth 60% of your AS grade).

2) It tests your knowledge of two topics — **World at Risk** and **Going Global**.

3) You get a fancy **resource booklet** with this paper (with things like **photos**, **maps**, **graphs** and **data** in).

4) There are **two sections** in the paper — **A** and **B**:

SECTION A

- You have to **answer ALL the questions**.
- The questions are worth up to **4 marks each**, so there are **no 'essay' answer questions**.
- There'll be questions where you have to use your **understanding** to **interpret** the **resources**, and questions that **test your knowledge** of the topics.

SECTION B

- You have to **answer ONE question** (which is in **two parts**) from a choice of four.
- **Part (a)** is worth 10 marks — this'll be based on **interpretation** of a resource from the **booklet**.
- **Part (b)** is worth 15 marks — this'll be an **'essay' question**, sometimes needing **case study** material (see page 118).

Unit 2 Exam — Geographical Investigations

1) It's **1 hr 15 mins** long and there are **70 marks** in total (worth 40% of your AS grade).

2) You also get a **resource booklet** with this paper.

3) It tests four topics, but you only have to answer questions on **TWO** of them:

> *Either* Extreme Weather ***OR*** Crowded Coasts
> **AND**
> *Either* Unequal Spaces ***OR*** Rebranding Places

For both of the exams you have roughly 1 minute per mark — so if a question's worth 10 marks you should spend about 10 minutes answering it.

4) For each topic there's **one question**, split into three parts:

> **Part (a)** is worth 10 marks — this'll be based on **interpretation** of a **resource** from the booklet.

Exams — who needs them, don't you know who my father is?

> **Part (b)** is worth 10 marks — this'll be an **'essay' question**, usually a **'case study' question'** (see page 118 for how to answer case study questions).

> **Part (c)** is worth 15 marks — this'll be an **'essay' question** where you have to write about **'fieldwork and research'** (see page 119 for how to answer these questions).

Answering Questions

No matter how much you revise you aren't going to do well in your exams if you don't answer the questions properly. This can be trickier than it sounds, but fear not, I've included a whole page on it, because I'm nice like that...

1) Make Sure You Read the Question Properly

It's dead easy to **misread** the question and spend 10 minutes writing about the **wrong thing**. **Five** simple tips can help you avoid this:

There are loads of hints about how to answer the questions in this book in the Answers section at the back.

1) Figure out if it's a **case study question** — if the question wording includes 'using **named examples**' or 'with reference to **one named area**' you **need** to include a case study.

2) <u>Underline</u> the **command words** in the question (the ones that tell you **what to do**):

Answers to questions with 'explain' in them often include the word '**because**' (or '**due to**').

E.g. for the question 'Explain where earthquakes occur', your answer would include '...earthquakes occur at plate boundaries because of a build up of pressure...'.

'Assess', 'Evaluate' and 'Discuss' all mean pretty much the **same thing**. They're all about **weighing something up**, e.g. the **success** of a coastal management scheme, or the **role** of human activities in causing climate change.

Command word	Means write about...
Describe	what it's **like**
Explain	**why** it's like that (i.e. give reasons)
Compare	the **similarities AND differences**
Contrast	the **differences**
Distinguish	the **differences**
Assess	the **advantages** and **disadvantages OR** the **arguments for** and **against**
Evaluate	
Discuss	
Examine	describe **AND** explain
Outline	describe **AND** explain
Define	the **meaning** of the word

If a question asks you to describe a **pattern** (e.g. from a map or graph), make sure you identify the **general pattern**, then refer to any **anomalies** (things that **don't** fit the general pattern).

E.g. for the question 'Describe the global distribution of volcanoes', you first need to say that they're mostly on plate margins, *then* mention that a few aren't (e.g. Kilauea in Hawaii).

When writing about differences, '**whereas**' is a good word to use in your answers, e.g. 'Employment in north-east England in 2007 was 6.1% whereas it was 4.1% in the south-west'.

'Examine' and 'Outline' are pretty similar. The main difference is that you do **more explaining** for '**Examine**' and **more describing** for '**Outline**'.

3) <u>Underline</u> the **key words** (the ones that tell you **what it's about**), e.g. rivers, population, social impacts etc.

4) For **essay** questions, **re-read the question** a couple of times **whilst you're answering it**, just to make sure you're still **sticking** to what the question is asking you to do.

5) For **all** questions, **re-read** the question and your answer **when you've finished**, just to check that your answer really does address **all parts** of the question being asked. A **common mistake** is to **miss a bit out** — like when questions say 'use data from the graph in your answer' or 'use evidence from the map'.

2) Figure Out Your Structure Before You Start

For any **longer answers**, you need to think carefully about how to **structure** your answer. Jot down the **order** you're going to cover things in under the question. **Label** your **plan** and **answer** clearly so the examiner knows which is which.

Q1 <u>Describe</u> the <u>physical</u> and <u>human</u> factors that can affect the <u>impacts</u> of <u>flooding</u>.
PLAN
1. Intro — say that the impacts of flooding are affected by physical and human factors.
2. Physical — prolonged and heavy rainfall, drainage basin, vegetation.
3. Human — impermeable surfaces, drainage systems, deforestation.
ANSWER
The impacts of flooding are affected...

3) Include Relevant Geographical Terms

Use the **proper geography words** for things, e.g. say 'tributary' rather than 'little river', and 'migration' instead of 'the movement of people'.

Don't Forget all the Usual Rules

1) Your answer should be **legible** (you won't get many marks if the examiner can't read it), use **correct grammar**, and **everything** should be **spelt correctly** (double-check jazzy geography words).

2) **Use diagrams** where they're appropriate — drawing a diagram can be way **quicker** than describing the same thing in words.

3) If you're **running out of time** at the end of the exam, **don't panic** — just write what you can as **bullet points**. You'll still get some marks for doing this.

Answering Case Study Questions

Geography examiners are even keener on case study questions than they are on tweed jackets with fetching elbow patches...

Don't Forget the **Three Tips** When Answering **Case Study Questions**

1) For **every question** you need to do the following three things:

> ① **Read** the **question properly**.
> ② **Figure out** your **structure before** you **start**.
> ③ **Include** relevant **geographical terms**.

2) But for case study questions you also **need to**:

Include **PLENTY** of **RELEVANT DETAILS**

3) This includes things like **place names**, **dates**, **statistics**, **names** of **organisations** or **companies**.

4) Don't forget that they need to be **relevant** though — it's no good including the exact number of people killed in a flood when the question is about the causes of a flood.

5) For many case study questions, a great way to show your specific knowledge is to learn an **annotated map** and re-draw it in the exam (e.g. the California disaster hotspot map on page 6) — but take care to only include labels relevant to the specific question being asked.

Jeremy's case study revealed very few relevant details... black, handle, smells a bit funny...

Here's an **Example Answer** to a Case Study Question

*'With reference to one named area' means you **have to include** a **case study**.*

*Whenever you write about **causes** it's a really good idea to split them up into **physical** and **human**.*

*Include **relevant details**, e.g. if the coast is made from an easily eroded rock type, say exactly **what rock type** it is.*

*Use relevant **geographical terms**, e.g. **corrasion** and **slumping**.*

Q1   With reference to one named area <u>describe</u> and <u>explain</u> the <u>causes</u> of <u>coastal erosion</u>.   [10 marks]

<u>PLAN</u>
1. Introduce Holderness
2. Describe the physical causes of erosion — rock type, narrow beaches, powerful waves
3. Describe the human causes of erosion — sea defences

<u>ANSWER</u>
Holderness is a 61 km long stretch of coastline in East Yorkshire. It's eroding at an average rate of 1.8 m/year, and in some places, e.g. at Great Cowden, the rate of erosion is over 10 m/year.

There are many physical causes of the high rate of erosion. There is a long fetch (from the Arctic Ocean), which means that waves that hit the coastline have a lot of energy and so a lot of erosive power. The coastline also faces the dominant wind and wave direction (from the north-east). This also increases the energy of the waves (and so increases their erosive power). Another important physical factor is that the coastline is made from till, which is an easily eroded rock type. As well as being susceptible to corrasion it is prone to slumping when wet. The presence of Flamborough Head also increases erosion along holderness. The longshore drift runs from north to south along the coastline, so Flamborough Head traps sediment from the north. This means that the beach material eroded along Holderness is not replenished. Flamborough head is also made from chalk, which does not produce beach material when eroded (the chalk dissolves rather than forms sand). This means that the beaches along Holderness are quite narrow. Beaches slow the waves, reducing their erosive power. Narrower beaches protect the coast from erosion less than wider beaches.

Humans are contributing to the high rate of erosion. This is mainly through the building of sea defences, e.g. at Mappleton. Sea defences trap sediment and starve down-drift beaches of sediment. The thinner beaches don't protect the cliffs as well as wider beaches do.

*Don't think 'Ah, this is about the bit of coast I've studied' and then write everything you know about a particular coastline.
The key words are 'causes' and 'coastal erosion' and the command words are 'describe' and 'explain', so you need to write about the causes of erosion along a specific coastline (but not about the impacts of erosion).*

CHALK

Flamborough Head traps sediment from the north, reducing beach width. Erosion of the chalk produces little beach material.

Sea defences at Mappleton trap sediment, making beaches down drift narrower.

Mappleton

longshore drift

BOULDER CLAY

Humber Estuary

*You can't always include an **annotated map** in case study answers, but for this question including one **helps you illustrate** how Flamborough Head and sea defences at Mappleton increase erosion at Holderness.*

Answering Fieldwork & Research Questions

In the Unit 2 exam you'll have to answer 'Fieldwork and Research' questions. Unlucky.

You Need to **Write About What You Did**

1) The questions are really easy to spot — you only get them in the **Unit 2 exam paper** and they'll include the phrase '**fieldwork and research**'.

2) When answering fieldwork and research questions you need to write about **your own** fieldwork and research.

3) You also need to do the following:

This time relevant details are things like **where** you carried out your fieldwork, what **websites** you used to research a place, what the exact **results** were, what **method** you used to investigate something etc.

① **Read** the **question properly**.
② **Figure out** your **structure before** you **start**.
③ **Include** relevant **geographical terms**.
④ **Include** plenty of **relevant details**.

- If the question asks you to **describe a programme** of fieldwork and research, you need to talk about the **methodology** for your **fieldwork** (what you did) and talk about your **research sources**.
- If you're asked to **describe the results** of your fieldwork and research, don't forget to briefly say **what you did** first.
- If you're asked to use your results to **judge the success** of something, say whether your results showed **if it worked** (and if there were any problems).

Here's an **Example Answer** to a Fieldwork and Research Question

Q1 Describe the results of your fieldwork and research into the success of a rural rebranding scheme. [15 marks]

When you have to cover fieldwork **and** research it makes sense to split them up in your answer.

PLAN:
1. Introduce the Eden Project
2. Describe what fieldwork I did and what the results were
3. Describe what research I did and what the results were
4. Conclude whether it was a success or not

ANSWER:
I investigated the success of the Eden Project, near St.Austell in Cornwall. The Eden Project is a tourist attraction that opened in 2001.

I went to St Austell, a town 5 kilometres from the Eden Project, to conduct a questionnaire-based survey asking businesses and people in the street about the impacts of the project. 75% of businesses said that trade had increased since the Eden Project opened. One business owner reported a 100% increase in profits since 2001. 25% of businesses said that trade had remained unchanged or had decreased. These results could be slightly biased though, as the majority of the businesses I surveyed were shops and cafés on the high street and so are more likely to be affected by an increase in tourist numbers. Ideally I would have surveyed a wider range of business types. Of people in the street surveyed, 22% said that they had come to the area specifically to go to the Eden Project. 51% of people questioned said that traffic congestion had become more of a problem since the project opened.

The research I did mainly focused on using the internet to search for positive and negative impacts of the project. Cornwall County Council's website (www.cornwall.gov.uk) states that the Eden Project attracts more than 1 million visitors to the area every year and has contributed more than £100 million per year to the Cornish economy. The Eden Project website (www.edenproject.com) states that an economic impact study estimated that the project had added £800 million to the regional economy in the last 5 years. It also states that 85% of the approximately 500 staff are from the local area. The Eden Project Business Survey conducted in 2003 found that the number of customers had increased for 38% of local businesses questioned. This is much lower than what I found in my fieldwork, but this could be because the number of tourists between 2003 and now has increased. An article in The Independent in 2002 mentioned the traffic congestion problems. The business survey conducted in 2003 stated that 5% of businesses thought traffic had worsened, though this was down from 13% in a 2001 survey.

I think my fieldwork and research shows that the Eden Project has been successful because it has had a huge positive economic impact on the surrounding area. Jobs have been created and trade has increased for most businesses since it opened. Although there have been traffic problems since it opened the Eden Project are trying to minimise these, according to their website, by reducing admission prices for those arriving by bus, bicycle or on foot.

If there was something you could have done better then say so.

Name the websites that you used to research the place.

Include relevant details —don't just say that trade increased for most businesses, give the specific result (e.g. 75%).

If there's any reason why your results might be biased then mention it.

If there are any inconsistencies between your fieldwork and research suggest reasons why.

Answering Resource Interpretation Questions

In both Unit 1 and Unit 2, you're going to get some questions where you have to interpret a resource — the following pages show you the kind of thing that might crop up. Knock yourself out...

You Might Get a Question Based on an OS Map...

Q1   Below is a map showing Cockermouth. <u>Describe</u> what the <u>social</u> and <u>economic impacts</u> of <u>flooding</u> in Cockermouth might be.   [10 marks]

See page 126 for how to read OS® maps and give grid references.

The question only mentions **social** and **economic** impacts, so you **shouldn't** write about any possible **environmental** impacts. This makes your structure pretty simple.

When you're talking about somewhere specific on the map always **give the grid reference**.

Include **relevant details**, e.g. if there's a road that might flood, say what **road number** it is.

<u>PLAN</u>
1. Describe the possible social impacts — hospital, houses, roads
2. Describe the possible economic impacts — brewery, roads, campsite, farms
<u>ANSWER</u>

Possible social impacts of a flood in Cockermouth include loss of life, inconvenience and disruption to people's lives. The hospital at grid reference 125 321 is very close to the river so could be flooded. The lives of patients could be at risk if it floods.

There are lots of homes close to the river which would be affected if the river flooded (e.g. grid reference 1231). This could put lives at risk. It could also lead to the damage or loss of household goods and personal possessions. This is also an economic impact as they cost money to repair or replace.

Some roads run very close to the river at some points (e.g. the A5086 at grid reference 116 318). If these flood it would disrupt local traffic, which could cause congestion. It may also prevent people from reaching businesses, which would decrease trade.

The brewery at grid reference 125 317 is also close to the river so could flood. This would have economic consequences, as production could be stopped, reducing revenue. Equipment could be damaged and have to be replaced, which would also be expensive.

The campsite at grid reference 129 304 could be flooded. As well as disrupting holidays this would cause economic problems. The campsite owners would lose income whilst the ground was unusable for camping, and any facilities damaged by flooding would need repairing or replacing.

There is farmland near to the river, e.g. Green Bank Farm land (grid reference 125 297). If this farmland was flooded it could damage crops or kill livestock. This would be expensive for the farmer to replace.

Answering Resource Interpretation Questions

...or a Photo

The best thing to do first is to write a rough plan of what you need to cover in your answer (just so you don't miss out anything when you're busy scribbling).

The command words in the question are 'describe' and 'explain' so you need to say what the coastal defences are and give reasons for their impacts, both good and bad.

Q1 Describe and explain the impacts of the hard engineering coastal defences shown in the photo on the right.   [10 marks]

©iStockphoto.com/Linda Steward

You need to look carefully at the photo to make sure that you've got everything — it'd be really easy to miss the sea wall if you hadn't looked properly.

PLAN
1. Describe what groynes are and explain how they protect the coastline.
2. Mention the impacts of groynes further along the coastline.
3. Explain how sea walls protect the coastline.

ANSWER
The photo shows groynes, which are fences built at right angles to the coast. Groynes trap beach material transported by longshore drift (as shown in the diagram). The trapped material creates wider beaches, which slow down waves and reduce their energy. This reduces erosion in the area and protects the coastline from flooding.

However, the groynes prevent down-drift beaches from receiving sand by longshore drift. These beaches become thinner and don't protect the coast as well, leading to increased erosion and flooding in the area.

The photo also shows a sea wall at the head of the beach. Sea walls reflect waves back out to sea, preventing erosion of the coast. They also act as a barrier to prevent flooding.

Groynes viewed from above

trapped beach sediment
groynes
longshore drift

Include diagrams where they help illustrate your answer.

...or a Graph

The command word is 'examine' so you need to describe the trends on the graph and give reasons for them.

Q1 Examine the graph of global disaster frequency on the right.   [10 marks]

Number of disasters — Year
hydro-meteorological
geophysical
400 300 200 100
1950 1960 1970 1980 1990 2000

PLAN
1. Define hydro-meteorological and geophysical disasters.
2. Describe the trend shown for geophysical disasters, then describe the trend for hydro-meteorological disasters.
3. Explain the reasons for the trends.

ANSWER
Hydro-meteorological disasters are those caused by climatic processes, e.g. droughts, floods or tropical cyclones. Geophysical disasters are those caused by land processes, e.g. volcanic eruptions, earthquakes and landslides.

The frequency of geophysical disasters has increased in the last 50 years, e.g. there were 10 disasters in 1950, rising to about 40 in 2000. The frequency of hydro-meteorological disasters has also increased over the last 50 years, and has increased very rapidly in the last 10 years (from approximately 150 in 1990 to 390 in 2000).

The frequency of geophysical hazards has remained roughly the same for the last 50 years. The reason for the increase in geophysical disasters could be the increasing vulnerability of populations in hazard prone areas. A hazard is more likely to cause a disaster if the people it affects are more vulnerable.

There are many reasons for the increase in hydro-meteorological disasters. The most likely reason is the increase in the frequency of hydro-meteorological hazards, which may be due to the effects of global warming. El Niño events make hydro-meteorological hazards more difficult to predict and so they are more likely to result in a disaster. Human factors such as rapid population growth, urbanisation and increasing world poverty may also have contributed to the increase by increasing the vulnerability of people affected. Also, the exploitation of resources (e.g. deforestation) can increase the risk of some hydro-meteorological hazards, e.g. flooding and landslides.

However, if the data shown in the graph is based on media information the trend could just be caused by increased media coverage of disasters over the last 50 years.

As well as describing general trends, describe specific details, e.g. hydro-meteorological disasters have increased, but you also need to say that they've increased very rapidly in the last 10 years.

Use evidence from the graph to back up your points (to get accurate figures from the graph it often helps to draw working lines on with a ruler).

Answering Resource Interpretation Questions

Q1　Outline how well the information in the table shows the inequalities between Bradford and Harrogate.　[10 marks]

*This question is asking about how well the **information** in the table shows inequality, **not** about the causes and effects of these inequalities.*

Measure	Bradford	Harrogate
Total population (2001)	467 665	151 336
Average detached property selling price (Aug 2001)	£112 723	£191 024
% unemployed (2001)	4.4	1.8
% people of working age claiming a key benefit (Aug 2001)	17	8
% people with 'not good' general health (2001)	10.2	7.21
Police recorded offences of theft from a motor vehicle (Apr 01 - Mar 02)	9961	698
% 15 year old pupils achieving 5 or more A* - C GCSE grades from schools within the area	37.3	68.6
Total number of students aged 16-17 (2001)	10 256	3041
Area of green space (km^2) (Jan 2005)	0.27	1.25

PLAN
1. Define inequality and describe the three types of inequalities.
2. Describe and explain data that shows an inequality.
3. Describe and explain data that doesn't show an inequality.

ANSWER

Inequalities are differences in wealth, social opportunity and environmental quality between different areas. There are three main types of inequality — economic, social and environmental. Economic inequalities include differences between income or assets. Social inequalities include differences between types of employment, as well as education or crime levels. Environmental inequalities include differences between pollution, quality of housing or quality of surroundings.

The data in the table shows economic inequalities between Bradford and Harrogate. For example, the percentage of people unemployed is higher in Bradford than in Harrogate (4.4% compared to 1.8%). The average selling price of a detached property is higher in Harrogate (£191 024) than Bradford (£112 723). The percentage of people claiming key benefits is lower in Harrogate, at 8%, than in Bradford, where it's 17%. This information tells you that Harrogate is a wealthier area than Bradford.

The table shows social inequalities between the two areas. For example, in Harrogate there were 46 reported thefts from a motor vehicle per 10 000 residents (Apr 01 to Mar 02), compared to 213 per 10 000 residents for Bradford. Bradford also has a higher percentage of people with 'not good' general health (10.2% compared to 7.21%). In addition, the percentage of 15 year olds achieving 5 A* to C grades is over 30% higher in Harrogate than it is in Bradford. Together, this data tells us that there is more social opportunity in Harrogate than in Bradford.

The area of green space is higher in Harrogate, where there's 1.25 km^2, compared to Bradford, where there's only 0.27 km^2. This is an environmental inequality.

However, not all the data in the table shows inequality. The data on total population tells you that Bradford has a larger population, but it doesn't show any inequality. This is because it doesn't tell you anything about the population's wealth or social opportunity, or the area's environmental quality. The table also shows that there are 7000 more students aged 16-17 in Bradford than Harrogate, but both areas have a similar proportion of students (2% of the total population). So, this data doesn't show any inequalities either, because it doesn't tell you anything about the student's education or lifestyle.

*The command word is 'outline' so you need to **describe** the information in the table **and explain** how the information does or doesn't show an inequality.*

*Always **quote data** from the table to back up your points.*

*Try to **manipulate data** from the table where appropriate, e.g. instead of giving the percentage of 15 year olds getting A* to C for each place, give the difference between them.*

You can't directly compare the number of thefts from a motor vehicle because the total populations are different. You need to work out thefts per 10 000 of the population.

*The data's been manipulated to show there's **no difference** in the percentage of students.*

Investigative Skills

Whether you consider yourself a modern-day Poirot or not, you need to know this basic stuff about investigating things through fieldwork and research.

You Need to Have an *Aim* and a *Hypothesis*

1) When you're doing fieldwork and research you won't get very far without an **aim**, and a **hypothesis** to **test**.

2) An aim is **what you want to find out**, e.g. 'To see if coastal defences at Holderness affect the rate of erosion of the coastline'.

3) A hypothesis is a **specific testable statement**, e.g. 'Coastal defences at Holderness increase the rate of erosion downdrift of the defences'.

4) Both your aim and hypothesis should be '**developed**' — this just means that they have to be **really specific**. E.g. the above aim is better than 'To see if coastal defences affect erosion', and the hypothesis above is better than 'Coastal defences do affect erosion'.

Herman's hypothesis that large brown bears could drive German police cars was very specific (and seemed to be correct).

You Need to *Select* Your *Sites Carefully*

1) When you're investigating an urban area, river or coast you **can't study** the **whole thing**, so you have to **select sites** to investigate instead.

2) Selecting sites can be **tricky** though — you need places that are **easy to get to** (e.g. places with **footpath access**) and **not too far** from a **parking place** (if you've got **heavy equipment** to carry you don't want to be walking for miles). But you also need sites that are a **good representation** of all the things you want to study, e.g. if you're studying how **channel characteristics** change along the **course** of a **river** it's no good selecting three sites at the **top** of the river (sites near the **source only**) — this would be a **biased sample**. You need to select sites at **different stages** along the course of the river, **from source to mouth**.

3) **Systematic sampling** is often used to select sites in geography fieldwork — this involves selecting sites in a **regular**, **structured way**, e.g. **every 2 km** along a coastline, or **every third shop** on the high street. Doing it this way means you should be able to **cover** the **whole area** in an unbiased way.

4) You can also use **random sampling** — e.g. using a **random number table** to find the distance of a site from the source of a river. As long as you're using a big enough sample this should **remove** any **bias**.

You Need to *Collect Data*

1) You'll **collect data** when you're doing your **fieldwork** and when doing your **research**.

2) There are two types of data — **primary** and **secondary**:

- **Primary** data is data you **collect yourself** (i.e. the data you get from your **fieldwork**).
- **Secondary** data is data **someone else** has **collected** (i.e. the data you get from your **research**).

3) You might have to **describe** how you collected your data **in detail** in the **exam**. This includes mentioning things like what type of **equipment** you used (e.g. a velocity meter), **how you did it** (e.g. you conducted a questionnaire containing 10 questions) or **what source** it came from (e.g. 2001 census data from www.statistics.gov.uk).

4) Also, point out any **limitations** of the **data**, e.g. whether it could be **biased** due to the collection method.

You Need to Know About *Risk Assessment*

1) When you're out and about doing your **fieldwork** you need to be **pretty careful**.

2) You need to **identify** any **risks** there might be and **take action** to reduce the risks.

3) Risks basically include any way you could **get hurt**.

4) Here are a few examples:

Area	Risk	Action
City	Being run over	Cross roads using pedestrian crossings where possible.
	Abuse (verbal and physical)	Be polite.
		If you're asking people questions make sure you introduce what you're doing and give them an opportunity to refuse to answer.
River	Drowning	Don't go into deep water (e.g. past knee height) or water that's fast flowing.
		Don't tread on slippy rocks (e.g. ones with moss on them).
Coast	Rock falls from cliffs	Where possible, keep away from cliff faces.
	Drowning	See above. Also, make sure you're aware of when the tide's coming in.

Graph and Map Skills

As sure as death and taxes, there'll be graphs and maps in your exam. So make sure you know all the different types...

There are Loads of **Different Types** of **Graphs** and **Maps**

1) There are some types of graphs and maps that you'll have come across lots of times before. These include **line graphs**, **bar charts**, **pie charts**, **scatter graphs**, **atlas maps** and **sketch maps**.

2) Some graphs and maps are trickier than others, so the next three pages are full of tips to help you interpret the tougher ones.

3) When you're **interpreting** graphs and maps you need to remember to **read** the **scale** or **key really carefully**.

4) If you have to read from a graph **draw working lines on** to help you get an accurate figure.

Triangular Graphs Show **Percentages** Split into **Three Categories**

1) To read a triangular graph start by **finding the point** you want on the graph.

2) **Follow** the **line** that goes **down** from the **point** to the **lowest end** of the **scale** and record the percentage.

3) Then **turn the graph around** so that the next axis is at **the bottom**, **follow** the **line** down to the lower end of the scale and record that percentage.

4) Do the same for the **third axis**.

5) The three readings should **add up** to **100%**.

6) The graph on the right shows the age distribution of three populations. There are **three age groups** so a triangular graph can be used. **Each point** represents **one population**.

Population A
Under 30 — 50%
30 – 60 — 30%
Over 60 — 20%

Population B
Under 30 — 30%
30 – 60 — 50%
Over 60 — 20%

Population C
Under 30 — 15%
30 – 60 — 45%
Over 60 — 40%

On this scale the lowest end is on the **left**, so to find the percentage you follow the line down and towards the left of the scale.

Dispersion Diagrams Show the **Frequency** of Data

There are **31 dots** altogether so the graph shows data for **31 houses**.

The **most common** percentage of energy supplied by wood is 60 to 69% (8 houses).

Only **one house** uses wood for **between 10 and 19%** of its energy needs.

1) Dispersion diagrams are a bit like a cross between a **tally chart** and a **bar chart**.

2) The **range** of **data that's measured** goes on one axis. **Frequency** goes on the other axis.

3) **Each dot** represents **one piece** of **information** — the **more dots** there are in a particular category, the **more frequently** that event has happened.

4) The dispersion diagram on the left shows the **percentage** of **household energy** that comes from **wood** for **houses** in a **particular village**.

Logarithmic Scales are Used When the **Data Range is Large**

1) The **intervals** on logarithmic scales are **not fixed amounts** (e.g. they don't go up by 5 every time).

2) Instead, the **intervals** get **increasingly larger** at the top end of the scale (e.g. 10, 20, 40, 80).

3) This lets you fit a **very wide range** of **data** onto one **axis** without having to draw an enormous graph.

4) The graph on the right uses a **logarithmic scale** on the **vertical axis** to show how the world's population changed between 1950 and 2000.

This interval represents **1.28 billion** people.

This interval represents **20 million** people.

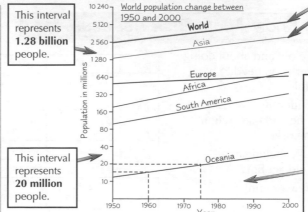

Be careful, it looks like the world's population isn't much bigger than Asia's but that's only because there are **big jumps** at this end of the scale.

Graphs with log scales are **really tricky** to read. It's OK if your working line hits a label on the log axis (e.g. there were 20 million people in Oceania in 1975), but if it doesn't it's easiest to **give a range** (e.g. it was between 10 and 20 million in 1960).

Graph and Map Skills

Choropleth Maps Show Information Using Colours and Patterns

1) Choropleth maps show how something **varies** between **different areas** using **colours** or **patterns**.
2) The maps in exams often use **cross-hatched lines** and **dots**.
3) They're straightforward to read but it's **easy to make mistakes** with them as the patterns can be very similar.
4) If you're asked to talk about all the parts of the map with a **certain type of hatching**, look at the map carefully and put a **big tick** on each part with that hatching, to make them all **stand out**.

Life Expectancy in Southern Africa

Life expectancy in this country is **51 to 55 years**.

Life expectancy in years
□ No Data
■ 51-55
■ 46-50
■ 41-45
■ 36-40
□ <35

Dot Maps Show Distribution and Quantity Using Identical Symbols...

1) Dot maps use **identical dots** to show how something is **distributed** across an **area**.
2) Use the **key** to find out what **quantity** each dot represents.

Incidence of Mumps in Byrnshire

● = 10 cases of mumps

Most dots, and therefore **most cases**, are in the **north**.

Individual dots show **10 cases**.

A cluster of **four dots** shows **40 cases** of mumps.

...Proportional Symbol Maps Use Symbols of Different Sizes

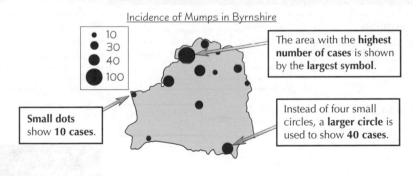

Incidence of Mumps in Byrnshire

● 10
● 30
● 40
● 100

The area with the **highest number of cases** is shown by the **largest symbol**.

Small dots show **10 cases**.

Instead of four small circles, a **larger circle** is used to show **40 cases**.

1) **Proportional symbol maps** use symbols of **different sizes** to represent **different quantities**.
2) A **key** shows the quantity each symbol represents. The **bigger** the symbol, the **larger** the **amount**.
3) The symbols might be **circles**, **squares**, **semi-circles** or **bars**, but they're always read the **same way**.

Flow Line Maps Show Movement

1) Flow line maps have **arrows** on, showing how things **move** (or are moved) from **one place to another**.
2) The map on the right shows the movement of people **to the UK from** the **USA**, the **rest of the Americas** and the **Middle East**. It also shows the movement of people **from the UK** to those areas.
3) It's also a **proportional symbol map** as the size of the arrows show **how many** people are moving.

The **largest flows** of people are **to** and **from** the **USA**, as these are the **largest arrows**.

For all three areas **immigration** to the UK is roughly the **same** as **emigration** from the UK. This is shown by incoming and outgoing arrows of the **same size**.

Some of the flows of people to and from the UK

USA

Middle East

Rest of the Americas

Emigration

Immigration

The **smallest flows** of people are **to** and **from** the **rest of the Americas**, as these are the **smallest arrows**.

EXAM SKILLS

Graph and Map Skills

Isoline Maps Show Where Conditions are the Same

1) **Isolines** are lines on a map **linking** up all the **places** where something's the **same**, e.g. on **weather maps** isolines show places that are the **same air pressure**.

2) If the place you're being asked about lies **on** an isoline you can just **read** the value off the line.

3) If the place is **between** isolines you have to **estimate** the value.

Map of low pressure system

Helsinki and Lecce both lie **on** this line so both have a pressure of **996 mb**.

Madrid lies **between** the lines for **988** and **992**. It's pretty much in the middle of the lines, so has a pressure of roughly **990 mb**.

Town Centre Plans Show Detailed Information of Urban Areas

Roads

Park (obviously)

School and college (also obvious)

Railway track

Rows of **houses** — the little plots of land are **gardens**

Fields and woods

© Crown copyright all rights reserved, License no. 100034841

1) When you get a plan, start by looking at the **types of buildings** and what's **around** them.

2) **Small buildings** are probably **houses** or **shops**. **Bigger buildings** are probably **factories** or **schools**.

3) Work out what kind of **area** it is — lots of **car parks** and **shops** mean it's a **Central Business District** (CBD), **houses with gardens** mean a **residential area**.

4) The plan to the left shows a **residential area**.

Ordnance Survey Maps Show Detailed Information of All Areas

1) Ordnance Survey® (OS®) maps use lots of **symbols**. It's a good idea to **learn** the most common ones.

2) You can find places on OS maps using **grid references**.

3) **Four-figure grid references** direct you to a 1 km × 1 km **square** on the map, e.g. for **1534** go **across** to the number **15** (the **eastings** value) and then **up** to the number **34** (the **northings** value). This grid reference refers to the **square above** and to the **right** of the point 1534.

4) **Six-figure grid references** are more precise and can direct you to a more **exact spot** (a 100 m × 100 m square). E.g. for 155341 the eastings value is 155, so go across to 15 again and then a further **5 "tenths"** across the square. For the northings value of 341 go up to 34 and a further **1 "tenth"** of that square. The spot you're looking for is where the easting and northing values **cross**.

5) Every map has a **scale** so that you can work out the **distance between points**. If the scale is **1:25 000**, it means that every **1 cm** on the map represents **25 000 cm** (250 m) in real life.

6) **Altitude** (height above sea level) is shown on OS maps using a type of isoline called **contour lines**. The **closer together** the contour lines are, the **steeper the gradient** is.

Common OS Map Symbols

— Railway
▫ Building
+ Place of worship
⚲ Place of worship, with a tower
♦ Church with a spire, minaret or dome

Motorway
Main (A) road
Secondary (B) road

◖● Bus station
PO Post office
PH Pub
–·–·– County boundary
▭▭▭ National Park boundary
–––––– Footpath

Grid reference: 1534

Grid reference: 155341

The contour lines did look very close together on the map, but nothing would stop Chaz and Dave getting to the Public House at grid reference 613 574.

Altitude rises from **200 m** to **250 m**.

Altitude rises from **200 m** to **300 m**.

The contour lines on the right are closer together and show a **steeper slope** (there's a **greater increase in height** over the **same distance**).

Statistical Skills

As if knowing about loads of weird graphs and maps wasn't enough, you also need to be familiar with statistics. These next two pages cover the ones you're most likely to stumble across.

There are **Different Ways** of Finding the **Average** Value of a Set of Data

1) The **mean**, **median** and **mode** are different ways of finding the **average** value of a set of data.

2) You find the **mean** by **adding up** all the numbers in a set of data, then **dividing** by the number of **sample points**, **n**.

Take a look at the data in this table:

Location	1	2	3	4	5	6	7	8	9	10	11
Temperature in °C	3	7	4	3	7	9	9	5	5	7	6

n = 11, so the mean temperature is: $\dfrac{3+7+4+3+7+9+9+5+5+7+6}{11} = $ **5.9 °C**.

3) The **median** is the **middle value** in an ordered set of data. So you need to **sort the numbers into order**, then work out which one is in the middle. So for the data above the median is **6 °C**.

3 3 4 5 5 (6) 7 7 7 9 9

If there are an even number of sample points the median is the mean of the middle two numbers.

4) The **mode** is the **most common value** in a set of data. So for the data above the mode is **7 °C**.

3 3 4 5 5 6 (7 7 7) 9 9

Sometimes there isn't a mode, and sometimes there's more than one.

The **Interquartile Range** is a **Measure of Dispersion**...

1) The **interquartile range** (**IQR**) is the range of values covered by the **middle 50%** of a set of data.

2) To find the interquartile range you first need to find the median of the values **to the left** of the median. This is called the **lower quartile** (**LQ**). Next find the median of the values **to the right** of the median. This is the **upper quartile** (**UQ**). Then you just **subtract** the **UQ from the LQ** to give you the **IQR**.

3) So, for the data above, the **LQ** is **4** and the **UQ** is **7**, and the interquartile range is UQ – LQ = 7 – 4 = **3 °C**.

LQ   Median   UQ
3 3 (4) 5 5 (6) 7 7 (7) 9 9
IQR

4) The interquartile range tells you about the **spread** of data **around** the **median**. If it's a **big** number, it shows that the numbers are pretty **spread out**. And yep, you've guessed it — a **small** number means that a lot of the data is pretty **close** to the **median**.

...and so is **Standard Deviation**

1) The **standard deviation** is a bit trickier to calculate than the IQR, but it's often a **more reliable** measure of dispersion (spread). The symbol for it is **σ**.

The formula is $\sigma = \sqrt{\dfrac{\sum(x - \bar{x})^2}{n}}$

Σ just means 'sum of', and $\bar{x}$ is just a way of writing 'mean'.

2) To calculate it, it's easiest to **work out** the **individual bits** in the formula **first**, e.g. the mean. It's a good idea to **draw** a **table** to help you. Below is a simple example for the set: 5, 9, 10, 11, 14.

- For these numbers, the **mean** is (5 + 9 + 10 + 11 + 14) ÷ 5 = **9.8**. This is shown in the 2nd column in the table.
- For each number, **calculate** $x - \bar{x}$ (3rd column in the table).
- Then **square** each of those values (4th column) — remember that the square of a **negative number** is always **positive**.
- Then **add up** all the squared numbers you've just worked out — this will give you $\sum(x - \bar{x})^2$.
- Now just **divide** your total by **n**, then take the **square root**.
- In this example, n = 5, so $\sigma = \sqrt{\dfrac{42.8}{5}} = $ **2.93** (2 d.p.)

x	$\bar{x}$	$x - \bar{x}$	$(x - \bar{x})^2$
5	9.8	−4.8	23.04
9	9.8	−0.8	0.64
10	9.8	0.2	0.04
11	9.8	1.2	1.44
14	9.8	4.2	17.64
		Σ	42.8

Standard deviation can be represented by σ or s.

3) If the standard deviation is **large**, the numbers in the set of data are **spread out** around the **mean**. If it's **small**, the numbers are **bunched** closely around the mean.

Statistical Skills

Make Sure You Know How to Find Spearman's Rank Correlation Coefficient

The Spearman's Rank correlation coefficient is a handy way to find out whether two sets of numbers are **correlated** (there's a **relationship** between them). The example below uses the test to see if **river discharge** (m³/s) and **rainfall** (mm) are correlated.

1) The bad news is that it's a bit of a pain to calculate. The first step is to give a **rank** to each number in both sets of data. The **highest** number is given rank **1**, the second highest is given rank 2... you get the idea. ➡

2) Then you **calculate 'd'**, the **difference** between the ranks for each item, e.g. if the ranks for River F are 4 and 6, the difference is –2. ➡

3) Next you **square 'd'** and **add up** the **d² values**.

4) Finally you need to work out the **Spearman's Rank Correlation Coefficient** (known as r_s).

The formula is: $r_s = 1 - \dfrac{6\sum d^2}{n^3 - n}$

River	Discharge	Discharge rank	Rainfall	Rainfall rank	d	d²
A	14	5	28	5	0	0
B	19	4	27	6	2	4
C	9	9	15	8	–1	1
D	6	11	9	11	0	0
E	21	3	35	3	0	0
F	13	6	30	4	–2	4
G	22	2	36	2	0	0
H	35	1	38	1	0	0
I	5	12	6	12	0	0
J	7	10	14	9	–1	1
K	11	8	10	10	2	4
L	12	7	20	7	0	0

$\sum d^2$ = 14

5) So for the example above, $\sum d^2 = 14$ and n = 12. So $r_s = 1 - \dfrac{6 \times 14}{12^3 - 12} = 1 - \dfrac{84}{1716} = 1 - 0.05 = \mathbf{0.95}$.

6) The number you get is always **between –1** and **+1**.

7) A **positive number** means the variables are **positively correlated** — as one variable **increases** so does the **other**. The **closer** the number is to 1 the **stronger** the correlation. ➡

8) A **negative number** means that the two sets of variables are **negatively correlated** — as one variable **increases** the other **decreases**. The **closer** the number is to –1 the **stronger** the correlation. ➡

9) If the coefficient is **0**, or near 0, there probably isn't much of a relationship between the figures.

10) The value of r_s in the example above was **0.95**, which is **close to 1**, so there's a **strong positive correlation** between the **data** for river discharge and rainfall.

Strong positive correlation · Weak positive correlation

Strong negative correlation · Weak negative correlation

You Have To Check the Correlation Is Significant Though

1) A **Spearman's Rank correlation coefficient** might tell you that **two sets of numbers** are **correlated**. But you need to check whether this is evidence for a **genuine link** between the two quantities you're looking at. (You sometimes get correlations between sets of data **by chance**, even if there's no underlying relationship. For example, there **is** a correlation between river discharge and rainfall **for the data shown above**, but this might have been a fluke and there might be **no real relationship** between the two things.)

2) You can check whether it's evidence for a genuine link by looking at the **probability** that a correlation would happen by chance. If there's a 5% (or higher) probability that a correlation is because of chance then it's **not significant** evidence for a link. If there's a **0.1% or less** chance, then it's **very significant** evidence for a link. (This is what's meant by the **significance level** of a statistical test — it's a kind of 'cut-off' probability.)

3) To test whether the value of r_s is evidence for a relationship between discharge and rainfall, you'll need a **graph** like the one on the right. You'll also need to know the **degrees of freedom** (this is just n – 2, so in the example above degrees of freedom = 12 – 2 = **10**). Since r_s = **0.95**, you can use the graph to find that this correlation has a **less than 0.1%** ➡ probability of being due to chance. This means you have **very significant** evidence for a **relationship** between river discharge and rainfall.

Probabilities of Spearman's Rank correlation coefficients (assuming no relationship between variables

Answers

Unit 1: Topic 1 — World at Risk

Page 3 — Global Hazards

1 Maximum of 15 marks available. This question is level marked.
HINTS:
- You need to <u>structure</u> your answer into clearly separate parts, e.g. write a short <u>introduction</u>, then divide the main answer into two main sections talking about the <u>number of deaths</u>, and then the <u>economic losses</u>. At the end write a short <u>conclusion</u>.
- In your <u>introduction</u> define what 'disaster' means, e.g. 'A disaster occurs when a hazard (something that's a potential threat to human life or property) actually seriously affects humans'.
- In each of the two sections (number of deaths and economic losses), start by <u>describing in detail</u> how they are <u>changing</u>, e.g. 'On a global scale, the number of deaths caused by disasters has been decreasing, but the trend has recently levelled off'. The question's worth 15 marks so make sure you give plenty of detail.
- Then you should <u>explain</u> why this is happening, e.g. 'Deaths are decreasing because of improvements in risk management strategies. But the trend is levelling off because there are an increasing number of vulnerable people, meaning more people are affected by disasters, and so more are likely to be killed'.

Page 5 — Hazard Distribution

1 Maximum of 3 marks available.
Earthquakes occur because tectonic plates don't move in a uniform way **[1 mark]**. Some parts move faster than others, which causes pressure to build up **[1 mark]**. When the pressure becomes too much the plates crack or jerk past each other, causing an earthquake **[1 mark]**.

2 Maximum of 10 marks available. This question is level marked.
HINTS:
- Make sure you have a clear structure — write an <u>introduction</u>, then describe <u>where</u> they occur, followed by a section <u>explaining</u> why volcanoes occur there.
- In the introduction, define 'volcano', e.g. 'A volcano is a point where magma has risen from below the Earth's surface and been ejected above ground'.
- Next <u>describe</u> the <u>global distribution</u> of volcanoes, e.g. 'Volcanoes can be found all along the mid-Atlantic ridge. They are also found around the edges of the Pacific Ocean, particularly around Japan and Indonesia, and along the west coast of America. They're also found in the centre of the Pacific Ocean in Hawaii'.
- Now <u>explain</u> why volcanoes happen at each of the locations you've described. Make sure you use <u>appropriate language</u>, e.g. 'The mid-Atlantic ridge is a constructive boundary. Here the mantle is under pressure from the overlying plates, and when they move apart pressure is released and the mantle melts, forming magma. This is less dense than the plates so it rises and can erupt to form a volcano'.

Page 7 — Disaster Hotspot Case Study — California

1 Maximum of 15 marks available. This question is level marked.
HINTS:
- Start by introducing the <u>key terms</u> in the question — <u>define</u> the term 'disaster hotspot', e.g. 'A disaster hotspot is a vulnerable place at risk from two or more hazards'.
- Next <u>describe</u> and <u>explain</u> each of the hazards that threaten California, e.g. 'California is at risk from earthquakes because the San Andreas fault runs the length of the state. This forms part of a conservative plate boundary — where two plates are moving past each other. Earthquakes occur here because pressure builds up as the plates move past each other. Eventually the plates crack or jerk past each other, releasing energy as an earthquake'.
- Include specific examples for each hazard, e.g. 'Two or three large earthquakes occur every year, and there have been disastrous earthquakes before, e.g. the San Francisco earthquake (1906), which destroyed much of the city'.
- Include a section explaining why the population is vulnerable e.g. 'California is a wealthy state, but some people are very poor, so they have a lower capacity to cope when affected by a disaster'.

Page 9 — Disaster Hotspot Case Study — The Philippines

1a) Maximum of 4 marks available.

Mount Pinatubo (1991)

Luzon earthquake (1990)

Fault lines

Plate boundary

1 mark for each of the following: a volcano disaster, an earthquake disaster, and the approximate positions of the plate boundary and fault lines.

b) Maximum of 15 marks available. This question is level marked.
HINTS:
- '<u>Compare</u>' and '<u>contrast</u>' means you need to talk about the <u>similarities</u> and the <u>differences</u> between the two disaster hotspots.
- You can structure this in different ways, but make sure you <u>compare</u> the two places — don't just write about them separately, e.g. 'Both California and the Philippines are at risk from volcanoes, earthquakes, landslides, tsunamis and droughts, but the Philippines is also at risk from typhoons'.
- <u>Define</u> the term 'disaster hotspot' e.g. 'A disaster hotspot is a vulnerable place at risk from two or more hazards'.
- Write a paragraph for each hazard. Make sure you include which place is vulnerable to each hazard — California, the Philippines or both.
- Write a paragraph about the populations of both places, e.g. 'Both the Philippines and California have many settlements built in hazardous areas, e.g. the Aeta tribe in the Philippines live on the slopes of Mount Pinatubo, a volcano, and over 70% of California's population live within 30 miles of a fault line. However, the population of California is more wealthy and there's a better infrastructure to cope with hazards, so it's likely that fewer lives would be lost in a disaster in California than in the Philippines'.

Answers

Page 11 — Evidence for Climate Change

1   Maximum of 10 marks available. This question is level marked.
    HINTS:
    - To get full marks you need to _outline_ (_describe_ and _explain_) a number of sources of evidence for _long-term_ climate change, e.g. ice cores, pollen analysis and indicators of sea-level change.
    - Structure the answer to have an _introduction_, then separate sections outlining _each_ of the sources of evidence and finish with a _conclusion_.
    - In your introduction, define the _key terms_ of the question such as 'climate change' and 'long-term', e.g. 'Climate change is any significant change in the weather of a region over a period of at least several decades'.
    - For each source of evidence _describe_ it and then explain how it's used to determine past climate, e.g. 'Scientists can drill deep into ice sheets (huge masses of ice) to extract cores of ice. When the ice was formed, gases were trapped inside it. Scientists can analyse these gases to tell what the temperature was when the ice formed'.

Page 13 — Causes of Climate Change

1   Maximum of 15 marks available. This question is level marked.
    HINTS:
    - Start by stating that humans are causing global warming, e.g. 'There's a scientific consensus that the rise in average global temperature, especially over the last century (called global warming) is being caused by human activity'.
    - Then split the rest of the answer into _two parts_ covering the two main human activities that cause climate change — enhanced greenhouse gas emissions and destruction of natural CO_2 sinks.
    - _Describe_ and _explain_ how each activity contributes to global warming, e.g. 'Human activity, e.g. burning fossil fuels, means more greenhouse gases are released into the atmosphere. More greenhouse gases increase the greenhouse effect, which warms the planet more'.
    - Where possible _quote facts_, e.g. 'In the last 150 years atmospheric levels of CO_2 have increased from 280 ppm (parts per million) to 380 ppm. This is thought to be mostly due to human activity'.

Page 15 — Impacts of Climate Change

1   Maximum of 15 marks available. This question is level marked.
    HINTS:
    - Start by describing global warming and some of its impacts, e.g. 'Global warming is the rise in average global temperature over the last century. Impacts include... '.
    - Then you need to explain that people are trying to _predict_ what changes will occur, using the _example_ in the question, e.g. 'The Intergovernmental Panel on Climate Change (IPCC) has developed a number of different emissions scenarios. They range from predictions where emissions won't increase any more, to scenarios where they increase a lot'.
    - Then write a paragraph on each of the reasons why these predictions are _difficult_ to make, e.g. 'Scientists don't know how much of the emissions will be absorbed by natural CO_2 sinks like oceans and plants'.
    - To get full marks you should explain at least _four_ reasons why predictions are difficult to make.

Page 17 — Climate Change — Case Studies

1   Maximum of 10 marks available. This question is level marked.
    HINTS:
    - The question is asking about the specific impacts in a _named area_ — this means using a _case study_, e.g. the Arctic or Africa.
    - Write an introduction _defining_ what global warming is, then name the place you're going to talk about and describe where it is, e.g. 'Global warming is having significant impacts on the Arctic — the area around the North Pole'.
    - Then split your answer into two sections — _ecological_ impacts and _environmental_ impacts. Remember to _quote facts_ when you're describing the impacts, e.g. 'Increasing temperatures are causing the area of sea ice (frozen sea water) in the Arctic to shrink at an increasing rate — some scientists think there won't be any in the summer by 2030. Polar bears need sea ice to hunt for food, so loss of sea ice may mean they become an endangered species'.

Page 19 — Coping with Climate Change

1   Maximum of 15 marks available. This question is level marked.
    HINTS:
    - It would be a good idea to explain why global agreements are _complex_ before you go into your named example. It'll have more impact this way.
    - Write an _introduction_ explaining that climate change is a _global hazard_, there are lots of strategies to cope with it (at many levels) and global agreements involve lots of different groups (key players).
    - Briefly explain _who_ all the key players are and how they _influence_ agreements on how to cope with climate change. You can then go on to say that agreements are _difficult_ because there are different views and levels of influence between and within all the groups.
    - Write a _detailed_ section on a _named example_, e.g. Kyoto Protocol.
    - It's important you quote as many _relevant facts_ as you can, e.g. 'The Kyoto protocol was an international agreement between more than 180 countries to cut greenhouse gas emissions'.

Page 21 — Global Hazards — The Future

1   Maximum of 10 marks available. This question is level marked.
    HINTS:
    - You'll need to use material from p. 20 for this answer.
    - Don't forget to _structure_ your answer. First _link_ global warming to famine and water shortages, e.g. 'Changes in temperature and precipitation brought about by global warming can result in drier conditions in some areas, leading to water shortages, and a decreased ability to grow food'.
    - Then write a section _linking_ water shortages to conflict, e.g. 'Conflict can occur where there isn't enough of a resource for different groups, e.g. increasing water shortages due to global warming could lead to conflict over the diminishing water resource'.
    - Use examples, e.g. 'The Nile river's two main tributaries flow through Sudan and Ethiopia. These join together and the river then flows through Egypt. If Ethiopia and Sudan need to use more water from the tributaries because of global warming, Egypt's supply will be reduced, and conflict may occur'.

Answers

Unit 1: Topic 2 — Going Global

Page 23 — Introduction to Globalisation

1 Maximum of 15 marks available. This question is level marked.
   HINTS:
   • First write a short <u>introduction</u>, then divide the answer into <u>four sections</u> explaining why TNCs, new markets, improved communications and international organisations have accelerated globalisation.
   • In your <u>introduction</u> give a short definition of what globalisation is, e.g. 'Globalisation is the process of all the world's systems and cultures becoming more integrated'.
   • In each of the four sections you need to <u>describe</u> what the factor is and <u>explain</u> how it's accelerating globalisation. For example, 'Improved communications are improvements to transport mechanisms, e.g. aeroplanes or high-speed rail, as well as to information exchanges, e.g. the internet and e-mail. Individuals and businesses have easier access to places that are further away (and to more products brought from far away) and they can communicate instantly with any part of the world. The world seems smaller as distance becomes less important'.

Page 25 — Global Groupings

1 Maximum of 4 marks available.
   LDCs are countries defined by very low incomes, poor health, low education and economic instability [1 mark]. LDCs have economies based on agriculture [1 mark]. In comparison, NICs aren't fully developed countries, but they're more wealthy than LDCs and their economies are growing quickly [1 mark]. NICs have economies that have recently moved from agriculture to manufacturing and exporting [1 mark].

2 Maximum of 2 marks available.
   Being in a trade bloc means it's easier to trade for all the different goods and services a country needs, because trade is less restricted. So countries can specialise in producing the things they're good at making and trade for the things they're not good at making [1 mark]. Member countries of the trade bloc benefit from comparative advantage because production increases for each country as they're concentrating on what they do best [1 mark].

Page 27 — Trans-National Corporations

1 Maximum of 4 marks available.
   Mergers [1 mark], acquisitions [1 mark], sub-contracting [1 mark] and Foreign Direct Investment (FDI) [1 mark].

2 Maximum of 10 marks available. This question is level marked.
   HINTS:
   • You need to make sure you write your answer about one <u>named example</u>.
   • <u>Structure</u> your answer by writing a short <u>introduction</u>, then write two sections on how the TNC has <u>grown</u>, and how the <u>labour force is divided</u>.
   • Use the <u>introduction</u> to define TNCs and name the example you're using, e.g. 'TNCs are large companies that produce, sell or are located in two or more countries. The largest retail TNC is Wal-Mart®'.

• In the first section introduce your example and <u>describe</u> how it has grown, e.g. 'Wal-Mart® is a chain of department stores started by Sam Walton in Arkansas, USA. It first grew by opening new stores across Arkansas, then across the USA. It has grown more recently across the globe by buying retail companies in other countries, e.g. ASDA in the UK and Seiyu in Japan. Wal-Mart® is currently trying to expand into NICs, e.g. in India it's working with a company called Bharti Enterprises'.
• In the second section talk about the <u>spatial division of labour</u>, e.g. 'Wal-Mart® sub-contracts the production of a lot of its goods to NICs like China and Malaysia. Some Wal-Mart® production has been moved back to more developed countries because they were criticised for exploiting cheap labour in poorer countries, e.g. George clothing have switched a lot of their production to the UK'.

Page 29 — Global Winners and Losers

1 Maximum of 4 marks available.
   Switched-on countries are countries that are well connected to global networks [1 mark]. Trade, money, people and information easily flow between them — they're global hubs [1 mark]. People in switched-on countries are significant consumers and producers of goods and services [1 mark]. Energy usage and the ecological footprint are large because of the high levels of production and consumption [1 mark].

Page 31 — Consequences of Globalisation

1 Maximum of 15 marks available. This question is level marked.
   HINTS:
   • For this answer you should start with a short <u>introduction</u>. The main part of your answer could then be divided into <u>three sections</u> where you <u>evaluate</u> strategies at different levels: governments, businesses and individuals.
   • Remember, <u>evaluate</u> means talk about <u>both</u> the advantages and disadvantages of something.
   • The <u>introduction</u> should briefly cover what the problems caused by globalisation are, e.g. 'Increased global trade means people have access to more products at low prices, so they can afford to be more wasteful. Lots of waste ends up as landfill'.
   • Then you should write three sections <u>evaluating</u> the strategies to solve the problems, e.g. 'Businesses can use more recycled materials to make their products, e.g. recycling old drinks cans to make new ones. This reduces the amount of waste going into landfill sites, but could increase carbon emissions and oil pollution if the recycled material is shipped long distances'.

Page 32 — Migration and Globalisation

1 Maximum of 4 marks available.
   Push factors are the things that make people want to move out of the place they're in [1 mark]. They're negative factors about the place they're leaving, e.g. lack of jobs or poor living conditions and services, fear of political persecution [1 mark]. Pull factors attract people to a new place [1 mark]. They're positive factors about the place they're moving to, e.g. better jobs and more job opportunities, better living conditions and services [1 mark].

Answers

Page 35 — Population Basics

1 Maximum of 10 marks available. This question is level marked.
HINTS:
- Write an introduction briefly explaining what the DTM is,
e.g. 'The Demographic Transition Model (DTM) shows how the
population of a country changes over time through five stages.
The model shows birth rate, death rate and total population'.
- The question asks you to refer to the DTM, so you can use this to
structure your answer — start by explaining what stage of the
DTM the country was in in 1600. E.g. 'In 1600 the birth rate and
death rate were very high (38 and 37 respectively) and the
population was low (2 million). The country was in Stage 1 of the
DTM. Birth rate was high because there was no birth control or
family planning, and education was poor. Also, infant mortality was
high, so people had more children to replace those who'd died.
The death rate was high because of poor health care, sanitation
and diet, which led to disease and starvation'.
- Next, describe how the data changes and relate the changes to the
stages of the DTM, e.g. 'Between 1600 and 1800, the death rate
decreased (from 37 to 18 per 1000 per year) and the population
had more than tripled, from 2 million to 7 million. The birth rate had
dropped very slightly from 38 to 35 per 1000 per year. The country
had reached Stage 2 of the DTM'. Don't forget to give reasons for
the changes.
- Make sure you use data from the table in your answer.

Page 37 — Changes in the UK Population Since 1900

1 Maximum of 10 marks available. This question is level marked.
HINTS:
- Write an introduction explaining what is meant by 'internal factors',
e.g. 'Populations can change in lots of ways, e.g. changes in the
average family size. These changes can be caused by internal
factors — things that are happening within the country or area'.
- For each factor state what it changed, then explain how it caused
the change, e.g. 'Life expectancy in the UK has changed since the
introduction of the NHS in 1948. Free health care for everyone has
led to increased life expectancy — from around 50 in 1900 to 77
for men and 81 for women today'.

Page 39 — Impacts of an Ageing Population

1 Maximum of 10 marks available. This question is level marked.
HINTS:
- First, briefly explain what an ageing population is, e.g. 'An ageing
population is a population where the proportion of older people
(over 65) is increasing'.
- Then write a section describing and explaining each social effect.
E.g. 'An ageing population means there's increased pressure on
public services such as hospitals and hospices. More people are
needed to care for the elderly, so more carers and nurses will
need training'.
- Next write about the economic effects, e.g. 'There could be
increased taxes for the working population. Pensions and services
are paid for by taxes, so if there's a greater proportion of older
people claiming pensions and support, there'll be higher taxes for
the working population'.

Page 41 — Migration into Europe

1 Maximum of 10 marks available. This question is level marked.
HINTS:
- In the introduction say that the consequences of migration can be in
Europe (the destination), and in the countries that migrants are
leaving (the source). Introduce the main headings the consequences
can fall under — demographic, economic, social, cultural, political
and environmental.
- Then write a paragraph for each of the headings, discussing the
consequences for both the source and destination countries,
e.g. 'Migration into Europe results in demographic changes
(e.g. changes in population structure and characteristics).
Most migrants are of working and reproductive age, so the
population structure of European destination countries will have
an increased proportion of people of these ages. The population
structure of source countries will have a reduced proportion of
people of these ages'.

Page 43 — Intra-EU Migration

1 Maximum of 10 marks available. This question is level marked.
HINTS:
- Start by defining intra-EU migration and introducing the named
example you'll be using, e.g. 'Intra-EU migration is migration between
two countries within the European Union. Many people have
migrated to the UK from Poland since it joined the EU in 2004'.
- Next write a section on the reasons for this migration. Divide the
reasons into push and pull factors and write a paragraph on each,
e.g. 'Push factors show why people left Poland. For example,
unemployment was high in Poland (around 19% in 2004) so people
left Poland to find work in the UK — they were economic migrants'.
- Then write two sections on the consequences — one for each country
in your example, e.g. 'Poland's population has shrunk because so many
people have migrated to other countries, e.g. it fell 0.3% between
2003 and 2007'.

Page 45 — Rural-Urban Migration

1 Maximum of 10 marks available. This question is level marked.
HINTS:
- First of all define rural-urban migration, and introduce the named
example, e.g. 'Rural-urban migration is the movement of people from
areas with low population density (rural) to areas with high
population density (urban). Massive rural-urban migration has been
going on in China, where 300 million people are now thought to live
in cities'.
- Then write a section describing the push factors, e.g. 'One of the push
factors from rural areas in China is poverty. In 2004, 26.1 million
people were living in absolute poverty in rural areas (too poor to
afford enough food or clothing). So people are migrating to urban
areas to escape poverty'.
- Finish by writing a section describing the pull factors,
e.g. 'One of the pull factors to urban areas in China is higher wages.
Average income is three times higher in urban areas than rural
areas and the difference is getting bigger. So people migrate to
increase their income and escape poverty'.

Answers

Page 47 — Megacities

1 Maximum of 10 marks available. This question is level marked.
HINTS:
- _Define_ megacity and _introduce_ the two that you're going to talk about, e.g. 'Megacities are metropolitan areas with a population of over 10 million people. London is a megacity in the south-east of the UK with a population of around 13 million, and Mumbai is a megacity on the west coast of India with a population of more than 20 million people'.
- The question is asking you to _compare_, so you need to talk about the _similarities_ and _differences_.
- Write a paragraph comparing the two cities for each of the following things — the urban cycle, economy and housing patterns. E.g. 'The population of Greater London is increasing. It's grown by 1 million since 1981. This is partly because there's a large number of international migrants, e.g. in 2006 there was a net gain of almost 70 000 international migrants. The population of Greater Mumbai is also growing, but much more rapidly. It's grown by more than 6 million since 1971. Unlike London, it's because so many people are moving into Mumbai from the rest of India, rather than from international migration'.

Page 49 — Urban Sustainability

1 Maximum of 10 marks available. This question is level marked.
HINTS:
- You should write a good _definition_ of sustainable development in your _introduction_, e.g. 'Sustainable development means growth in a way that lets the people living now have the things they need, but without reducing the ability of people in the future to get what they need. It means developing in a way that doesn't irreversibly damage the environment or use up resources faster than they can be replaced'.
- Next you should write a few sections _describing_ the things an urban area could do to become more sustainable, and _explaining_ how these things help. E.g. 'An urban area could become more sustainable by building more carbon-neutral homes. These are houses that generate as much energy as they use by having things like solar panels to produce energy. Carbon-neutral homes increase the amount of housing without increasing the ecological footprint of the area, so the environment isn't damaged as much for future generations'.

Unit 2: Topic 1 — Extreme Weather

Page 51 — Extreme Weather Events

1 Maximum of 10 marks available. This question is level marked.
HINTS:
- Start off by _stating_ what tropical cyclones are.
- Then _describe_ the conditions needed for tropical cyclones to form, e.g. 'Tropical cyclones form over warm water (26.5 °C or higher at the surface)'.
- Next, explain _where_ tropical cyclones are found, linking the _distribution_ to the _conditions_ needed for cyclones to form. E.g. 'Tropical cyclones are found in the tropics because the sea water temperature in this region is high enough for cyclones to form. They're not found below 5° latitude because the Coriolis effect isn't strong enough to make the winds spin'.
- If you can, add in a _relevant_ example, e.g. if you're writing about distribution mention that Hurricane Katrina developed in the south-eastern Bahamas in August 2005.

Page 53 — Extreme Weather Events

1 Maximum of 10 marks available. This question is level marked.
HINTS:
- Start off by _stating_ what an anticyclone is and the extreme weather conditions that it can cause, i.e. droughts and heatwaves.
- Then _describe_ how anticyclones _can lead to drought conditions_. E.g. 'Anticyclones are areas of high pressure caused by sinking air. No air can rise, which means there's no condensation and no precipitation. If the anticyclone remains stationary for a long period of time (because it's cut off from a jet stream) it can cause drought conditions'.
- Next _describe_ how anticyclones _can lead to heatwaves_. E.g. 'Anticyclones that remain stationary for a long period of time (blocking anticyclones) can lead to reduced cloud cover and higher temperatures as more solar radiation is absorbed by the land. If the blocking anticyclone lasts for a long time it can cause a heatwave'.

Page 55 — Extreme Weather — Fieldwork and Research

1 Maximum of 15 marks available. This question is level marked.
HINTS:
- This question asks you to _describe and explain_ how you would investigate the link between weather conditions and a depression, so it's not enough to say _what_ you did, you've got to explain _why_ as well.
- Describe what _fieldwork_ you did. E.g. 'I made a weather diary and recorded how pressure, wind speed, precipitation and temperature changed over time. This allowed me to see the correlation between extremely low pressure (depressions) and wind speeds and rainfall'.
- Include _details_ of exactly _how_ you carried out your fieldwork, giving _reasons_ for your choices. E.g. 'I took readings from the same place each day (to make sure that nothing else affected the readings) and I did this for ten days. This period of time was long enough to allow me to see any patterns that emerged'.
- Then describe what _research_ you did to further investigate the links and why you did this. E.g. 'I used the internet to look up reliable sources of data (e.g. from the Met Office) to see if this secondary data agreed with the primary data that I collected from my weather diary'.

Page 57 — The Impact of Extreme Weather

1 Maximum of 10 marks available. This question is level marked.
HINTS:
- The question asks you to explain the _factors_ that _influence_ the impact of extreme weather events — it's _not_ asking you to explain the impacts themselves.
- Start with an introduction saying what the three key factors are — severity of the event, economic development of the area affected and vulnerability of the people affected.
- Then _explain_ each of the three factors in detail, e.g. 'The bigger and more intense a weather event is the more severe it is. The greater the severity of the event the bigger the impact will be'.
- The best way to show how the impact of an event can differ due to each factor is to _compare_ two separate, specific weather events. E.g. compare the impact of two tornadoes that differ in severity or compare the impact of two hurricanes that hit economically different areas.
- When using examples _include relevant details_, e.g. don't just say one tornado was more severe than another, state what category each tornado was.

Answers

Page 61 — The Impact of Extreme Weather — Case Studies

1 Maximum of 10 marks available. This question is level marked.
HINTS:
- This question asks you for one or more named examples, which means you'll need to use at least one case study — e.g. you could use the Murray-Darling Basin drought in Australia, Hurricane Katrina or the Carlisle flood.
- First, you need to describe the social, environmental and economic impacts of your chosen weather event. E.g. 'One of the environmental impacts of the Murray-Darling Basin drought is that there's less vegetation and more soil erosion in the area, as well as increased wildfires and dust storms'.
- Use specific data in your descriptions. For example, instead of saying 'Unemployment has increased', say 'Unemployment has increased to 7% above the national average for Australia'.
- Then, you need to explain the impacts of the weather event. So you need to talk about how the severity of the weather event, the economic development of the area and the vulnerability of the population influenced the impact of the drought. E.g. 'Australia is a more economically developed country, so it's able to lessen some of the impacts of the drought. For example, 1500 small businesses have received income support from the government to help them survive'.

Page 63 — Increasing Risk from Extreme Weather

1 Maximum of 10 marks available. This question is level marked.
HINTS:
- Start with an introduction explaining that there are two main factors that have contributed to the increased risk of flooding occurring — climate change and poor land management (population growth increases the risk from floods).
- Then write about each of the factors in separate paragraphs. Make sure you explain how each factor is believed to cause an increased risk of flooding. E.g. 'Many scientists believe global warming has contributed to the increased frequency and severity of flooding in the UK. This is because higher temperatures (due to global warming) result in changes in global air circulation and ocean currents, which means some places in the UK will receive more rainfall due to more storms. Greater rainfall increases the risk of flooding'.

Page 66 — Increasing Flood Risk — Fieldwork and Research

1 Maximum of 15 marks available. This question is level marked.
HINTS:
- This question asks you to describe and explain how you have investigated physical factors that affect flooding, so it's not enough to say what you did — you've got to explain why you did it as well.
- Start your answer by writing the name and location of the river you studied.
- Then describe the fieldwork you carried out to explore the link between physical factors (e.g. precipitation, surface runoff, infiltration rates) and flooding. E.g. 'I measured the amount of rainfall in the area by using a rain gauge. I left the rain gauge in the same place beside the river and measured the amount of rainfall it had collected, at the same time each day for seven days'.
- Then describe the research you carried out into the link between physical factors and flooding. This could include rainfall data you looked up on the Met Office website or reports from the National Water Archive.

- Remember to only include fieldwork and research into physical factors, as the question requires — not human factors.
- Try to use lots of geographical terms in your answer, e.g. precipitation, discharge, hydrograph, infiltration, flood return intervals. But be careful, make sure you know exactly what they mean before you use them.

Page 69 — Managing Extreme Weather

1 Maximum of 10 marks available. This question is level marked.
HINTS:
- The question says 'outline' so it's asking you to describe and explain.
- Make sure you describe a range of ways in which new and more powerful technology has improved the management of extreme weather events, e.g. more accurate weather forecasts, drought-resistant crops, hurricane-proof and flood-proof buildings.
- Give appropriate examples to back up your answer. E.g. 'The Met Office uses supercomputers, which are more powerful and have faster processing speeds than previous models. This means scientists can run more complex weather models, making the forecasts more accurate. Forecasting accuracy rose from 79% in 1980 to 86% in 1996, because of computer upgrades'.
- Remember to explain how each of these things has improved the management of an extreme weather event. E.g. 'More accurate weather forecasts mean that earlier warnings can be given. This gives people more time to protect their houses or evacuate, which reduces damage and loss of life'.

Page 71 — Drought and Water Management

1 Maximum of 10 marks available. This question is level marked.
HINTS:
- The question asks you to refer to at least two named examples, so you should use at least two case studies you've learnt about, e.g. drought management in Australia and south-east England.
- Describe a range of drought management strategies used in each of your examples and include as much detail as you can. E.g. 'Perth, in Australia, has a desalination plant that supplies the city with 17% of its water by filtering, treating and desalinating seawater and mixing it with the public water supply'.
- The question asks you to 'discuss the sustainability', so for each strategy you describe you need to say if it's sustainable and why. E.g. 'Perth's desalination plant is powered by renewable energy (from wind farms) and permanently reduces water use, so it is sustainable'.

Unit 2: Topic 2 — Crowded Coasts

Page 73 — Coastal Population Growth

1 Maximum of 10 marks available. This question is level marked.
HINTS:
- You need to write about two locations and they need to be contrasting (i.e. very different). So you could cover either the development of a wealthy and poor location, or the development of an industrial port and a tourist resort.
- The question is asking you to explain (i.e. give reasons) why the population of the two locations has grown rapidly, so you need to write about the causes of the growth, e.g. 'Tourism grew in Brighton in the 18th century as people believed that bathing in seawater was good for their health. Brighton's population grew as people migrated to the area attracted by the jobs tourism provided'.

Answers

- Make sure you include plenty of _relevant facts_ about the two locations, e.g. 'Following the discovery of oil in the region, the population of Dubai City quadrupled between 1968 and 1975, as foreign workers flooded into the city to work in construction and oil production'.

Page 75 — Coastal Development and Conflict

1   Maximum of 10 marks available. This question is level marked.
HINTS:
- This question is asking you to _examine_ so you need to _describe_ the impact of the development, and _explain_ why this leads to conflict, e.g. 'Road building and construction of tourist amenities can destroy ecologically important land, such as sand dunes. This creates conflict between tourists, who demand improved infrastructure, and conservationists, who want to preserve these valuable coastal areas'.
- You're only asked to examine the _environmental_ impact, so don't start talking about conflict between tourists and locals because of traffic congestion. Stick to things that affect the environment.
- There are four main activities linked with development that have an impact on coastal environments: tourism, overfishing, aquaculture and industrialisation. Structure your answer so you describe the impact of each of these in turn. You can even find links between some of them, e.g. 'Demand from tourists for fresh, local fish can lead to overfishing'.

Page 77 — Coastal Development and Conflict

1   Maximum of 10 marks available. This question is level marked.
HINTS:
- This is similar to the question on page 75, but this time you need to focus on _specific case study details_, not just the theory.
- Again, there'll be a few main activities having an impact on the environment which you can use to structure your answer. _Be careful_ though because they might not be _exactly_ the same for your chosen areas as they are in the general case, e.g. for Dubai, it's 'oil production', not just 'industrialisation'.
- It might be tempting to write a whole load of stuff about conflict, but the question _doesn't actually ask for it_. You won't get top marks for answering what you THINK the question is asking you. You're only asked about how development has threatened the coastal environment.
- As ever with questions like this, you need to get in lots and lots of _place-specific details_ to back up your points. It's no good just saying 'more tourists in Dubai are damaging the coast' — you need to give details, e.g. 'The number of tourists visiting Dubai is forecast to increase from about 7 million in 2007 to 14 million by 2015. This increased tourism will lead to more sewage, litter and erosion of the coastline'.

2   Maximum of 15 marks available. This question is level marked.
HINTS:
- Structure your answer to explain your fieldwork plans, how you carried out those plans and how you used research sources.
- Make sure you say what you aimed to find out with your fieldwork and research, e.g. 'To assess the impact of tourism on the area and the potential conflict, I looked for articles in the local newspaper that described tourist development, and I interviewed different stakeholders'.
- Include details of where you studied, where you looked for information and what fieldwork you carried out.

Page 79 — Coastal Processes

1   Maximum of 4 marks available.
2 marks available for characteristics of constructive waves, from any of the following points: Constructive waves are flat and gentle **[1 mark]**. They have a low frequency **[1 mark]** of about 6-8 waves per minute **[1 mark]**. Their swash is greater than their backwash **[1 mark]** which carries material up the beach and deposits it **[1 mark]**. 2 marks available for characteristics of destructive waves, from any of the following points: Destructive waves are tall and steep **[1 mark]**. They have a high frequency **[1 mark]** of about 10-14 waves per minute **[1 mark]**. Their backwash is greater than their swash **[1 mark]** and removes beach material **[1 mark]**.

2   Maximum of 6 marks available. This question is level marked.
HINTS:
- 'Outline' means _describe_ and _explain_, so first you need to list the erosion processes that affect cliffs — these include abrasion/corrasion, hydraulic action, quarrying and corrosion/solution.
- Don't write about attrition — it's not a type of erosion that affects cliffs (it's the erosion of rocks in the water by smashing together).
- Then for each type of erosion you need to _explain how_ it erodes cliffs, e.g. 'Hydraulic action is where air in cracks in cliffs is compressed by waves. The pressure exerted by the compressed air breaks bits of rock off the cliff'.
- For top marks you also need to explain how _sub-aerial weathering_ makes cliffs more vulnerable to erosion, e.g. 'Freeze-thaw weathering weakens cliffs and so makes them more vulnerable to erosion'.

Page 81 — Coasts Under Threat — Erosion and Flooding

1   Maximum of 10 marks available. This question is level marked.
HINTS:
- The question asks for _possible_ impacts, so you need to write about what the impacts might be in the _future_.
- Make sure you include all the main impacts — more frequent and more severe flooding, submergence of low-lying islands and changes in the coastline.
- For each impact describe what could happen and _give an example_ to back up your point if possible, e.g. 'Low-lying coastal islands may be submerged if sea level rises, e.g. if it rises 0.5 m, most of the Maldives would be submerged'.
- Don't forget to include that the main impacts have _further impacts_, e.g. decrease in tourism, damage to infrastructure etc.

Page 83 — Coastal Flooding — Case Study

1   Maximum of 15 marks available. This question is level marked.
HINTS:
- The question says a _named coastal area_. It might sound obvious, but remember to write about a _case study_, not just the general causes and effects of flooding.
- Talk about both the _physical_ and _human_ causes of the flooding, e.g. 'Coastal areas in south-east Asia were flooded by a tsunami that was caused by a submarine earthquake measuring about 9.0 on the Richter scale off the coast of Indonesia. However, human activity, such as destruction of mangrove forests in Thailand to make way for fish farms, and coral mining in the Indian Ocean, meant that a lot of the coasts' natural protection was missing. This made the effects of flooding worse'.
- Make sure you know whether each effect is _social_, _economic_ or _environmental_ because you _might not always_ get asked for _all three_.

Answers

- Include plenty of <u>facts</u> and <u>figures</u> and make plenty of <u>place-specific statements</u> to show that you really know the case study, e.g. 'A quarter of hotels in southern Thailand were forced to close for at least 6 months because of damage from the flooding'.

Page 85 — Coastal Erosion — Case Study

1   Maximum of 10 marks available. This question is level marked. See page 118 for a full worked answer to this question.

Page 87 — Coastal Management

1   Maximum of 10 marks available. This question is level marked. HINTS:
- First you need to <u>describe</u> what hard engineering defences and soft engineering defences are and give a couple of <u>examples</u>. E.g. 'Hard engineering defences are built structures, e.g. revetments, groynes and sea walls'.
- Then go on to explain <u>why</u> soft engineering defences are <u>more sustainable</u>, e.g. 'Soft engineering defences usually require much less time and money to maintain than hard engineering defences. They also create habitats like dunes and marshland, e.g. coastal realignment leads to the formation of marshland. Hard engineering defences often disrupt natural processes'.
- Finish up with a <u>conclusion</u>, e.g. 'Soft engineering schemes have a lower environmental impact and a lower economic cost than hard engineering schemes, so are more sustainable'.

Page 89 — Coastal Management — Case Studies

1   Maximum of 15 marks available. This question is level marked. HINTS:
- The command word in this question is <u>evaluate</u>, so you need to talk about the costs <u>and</u> benefits of your chosen scheme.
- The question doesn't specify whether you need to write about a <u>hard</u> or <u>soft</u> engineering scheme, so the choice is yours. Make sure you pick one that you <u>know loads about</u>, so you can get plenty of <u>detail</u> in your answer.
- Whatever scheme you choose, the <u>benefits</u> are likely to be things like saving land, housing, transport routes, and industry, and preserving natural habitats. The <u>costs</u> will include things like the price of setting up and maintaining the defences, the appearance of the defences and the possible effects on adjacent areas of the coast.
- Examiners love '<u>specific and detailed reference</u>' to the case study, so it's always good to have some <u>numbers</u> to back up your points, e.g. '£2 million was spent on two rock groynes and 500 m of revetment at Mappleton in 1991'.
- But don't just scribble down all facts — you need to explain <u>why</u> these measures were used and the <u>effect</u> that they've had, e.g. 'They were built to protect the village and the B1242 road. The scheme has successfully protected these areas, but the groynes have starved down-drift beaches of sediment, which has caused increased erosion of the cliffs south of Mappleton'.

Unit 2: Topic 3 — Unequal Spaces

Page 91 — Introduction to Inequalities

1   Maximum of 10 marks available. This question is level marked. See page 122 for a full worked answer.

Page 93 — Causes and Effects of Urban Inequalities

1   Maximum of 10 marks available. This question is level marked. HINTS:
- Look at each row of data in the table and think about whether it shows any inequality — economic, social or environmental. E.g. the third row shows economic inequality because 62% of parents in two-parent families received income-related benefits, compared to 89% of lone parents. Write down the type of inequality next to each row of data.
- Next, note down any causes and effects you can think of next to each inequality. Try to find links between the inequalities too.
- Structure your answer — for each type of inequality, write down the data that supports it from the table, then discuss the possible causes and effects of that inequality. E.g. 'Only 56% of lone parents were in employment compared to 81% of parents from two-parent families, which is a social inequality. This could've been caused by a lack of child-care facilities in the area, which meant lone parents had to stay at home to look after their children rather than work. It could also be due to a lack of education — if the lone parent couldn't get a good enough job to pay for child-care facilities. An effect of this inequality is that lone parents have lower incomes, so fewer can afford to rent or live in detached housing (only 8% of lone-parent families lived in detached housing, compared to 28% of two-parent families)'. Repeat this with all three inequalities — economic, social and environmental.
- Write a short summary at the end that explains how causes and effects can be linked, which may lead to a cycle of decline, e.g. 'A lower percentage of lone parents are employed, so they're more likely to have lower incomes and receive income-related benefits. This means they're less likely to be able to afford to go back into education and less likely to get a better paid job, which could pay for child-care facilities. In turn, this worsens the economic and social inequalities between lone parents and two-parent families, causing a cycle of decline'.

Page 95 — Strategies to Reduce Urban Inequalities

1   Maximum of 10 marks available. This question is level marked. HINTS:
- First, think of two schemes that could have been introduced into a city to tackle city centre traffic, e.g. a park-and-ride scheme, congestion charging, public transport passes (e.g. Oyster card in London).
- Then for each scheme, state what it is and describe how it would decrease city centre traffic. Try to include the key players involved and the scale on which it would be carried out. E.g. 'A park-and-ride scheme could have been introduced into City X, which allows people to park their cars outside the centre and travel in by public transport. They're carried out on a local scale by the local authority'.
- Next you need to evaluate the success of each scheme. Look at the table and decide what pieces of data show that there's been an effect on city centre traffic. You need to look for data that shows a decrease in the number of cars in the city, a decrease in air pollution or an increase in public transport.
- Include the data in your answer and explain how it shows that the schemes have/haven't been successful. E.g. 'In 1995, there were 753 124 vehicles passing through the city centre on average each month, which decreased to 215 376 vehicles by 2005. So there was less traffic in the city centre after the schemes were introduced, suggesting they've been successful'.

Answers

Page 97 — Urban Inequalities — Case Study

1   Maximum of 15 marks available. This question is level marked.
    HINTS:
    • 'One named example' means a case study in an urban area,
      e.g. Cardiff.
    • First, plan your answer. Jot down the main inequalities in that
      area, then write a cause and effect next to each inequality.
      There may be multiple causes and effects of each inequality.
    • Begin your answer by describing the inequalities of your chosen
      urban area, e.g. 'There's economic inequality between the north
      and south of Cardiff, with the less wealthy generally living in
      the south'.
    • Next, discuss the key causes of the inequalities, e.g. 'The decline
      of industry in the 20th century (e.g. coal exports stopped in
      1964), caused high unemployment in Cardiff, especially in the
      south of the city where workers from the docklands lived. This led
      to lower incomes and economic inequality between the north and
      south of Cardiff'.
    • Then describe the effects of the inequalities and explain how they
      resulted from the inequality. To gain higher marks, describe how
      inequalities are linked. E.g. 'Lower wages (economic inequality)
      in the south of Cardiff have led to poorer health, because people
      have less money for food, prescriptions etc. People with poor
      health and a lack of money for smart clothes are less likely to
      gain employment, which leads to further economic inequality in
      the south of Cardiff'.
    • Make sure you learn the details of your case studies so you can
      quote data where possible, e.g. 'Lower wages in the south of Cardiff
      mean that fewer people are able to buy their own homes.
      For example, the 2001 census shows that only 12.5% of residents
      in Butetown (south Cardiff) owned their own house, compared to
      20.9% in Cathays (north Cardiff)'.

Page 99 — Causes and Effects of Rural Inequalities

1   Maximum of 10 marks available. This question is level marked.
    HINTS:
    • First, define polarisation, which is when the inequalities between
      two groups of people become extreme, e.g. the rich are very rich
      and the poor are very poor.
    • Then describe the causes and effects of inequalities in rural
      areas. Explain how an inequality leads to polarisation.
      Repeat this for two or three different inequalities. E.g. 'A lack of
      access to affordable housing in rural areas has caused social
      inequality between wealthy people who can afford to buy a house
      and local people on lower incomes who can't. Wealthy people have
      also bought second homes in rural areas, driving up property
      prices. In turn, they become wealthier as property prices increase,
      but people on lower incomes are less able to get on the property
      ladder. This increases polarisation between the rich and poor in
      rural areas'.
    • Include how inequalities are interlinked and that they can lead to
      a cycle of decline, which can cause polarisation as inequalities
      become worse.

Page 101 — Strategies to Reduce Rural Inequalities

1   Maximum of 10 marks available. This question is level marked.
    HINTS:
    • Describe specific examples of strategies from each of the four
      groups on p. 100 — introducing appropriate technologies,
      community schemes, transport and services schemes,
      and employment schemes.

• The question asks you to 'describe' the strategies, so make sure
  you include as many details as you can about each one,
  e.g. the name of the strategy, where the strategies are carried out
  and how they operate. E.g. 'The Village Enterprise Fund in East
  Africa gives people skills to set up and run their own businesses,
  e.g. small farms, bicycle repair workshops and tailors'. It provides
  local people with business training, financial grants and mentoring'.
• Make sure you address the question and say what inequality each
  strategy is trying to reduce and how it does this. E.g. 'The Village
  Enterprise Fund aims to reduce social inequality in rural areas by
  giving people new skills, and to reduce economic inequality by helping
  people to set up their own businesses in rural areas'.

Page 103 — Rural Inequalities — Case Study

1   Maximum of 15 marks available. This question is level marked.
    HINTS:
    • First, think of a case study you know that covers inequalities in a
      rural area, e.g. Llangynidr and Llanelly Hill in the Brecon Beacons
      National Park.
    • Then, jot down the main inequalities of the area and a few causes
      and effects of the inequalities. Look for any ways in which the
      inequalities are linked.
    • Structure your answer — begin by describing the inequalities of
      your chosen rural area and their causes. E.g. 'There's economic
      inequality between places situated in the centre of the Brecon
      Beacons National Park, such as Llangynidr, and those on the
      outskirts of the park, like Llanelly Hill. The more wealthy areas are
      in the centre of the park. These inequalities are partially caused
      by the decline of coal and iron industries to the south of the
      National Park, which caused high unemployment in areas like
      Llanelly Hill. This led to lower family incomes and
      economic inequality'.
    • Describe the effects of the inequalities and explain how they
      resulted from the inequality. To gain higher marks, describe how
      inequalities are linked — the effect of one inequality may be the
      cause of another inequality, leading to a cycle of decline.
      E.g. 'High unemployment in Llanelly Hill means people have lower
      average family incomes. This means residents of Llanelly Hill are
      less likely to be able to get on the property ladder, because they
      don't have enough money to buy their own house. There's a lack
      of affordable housing in the area, so this causes polarisation
      between residents of the National Park who can afford their
      own house and those who can't'.
    • Use data to support your points where possible, e.g. '13.3% of
      people in Llanelly Hill have 'not good' health, compared to 8.9%
      in Llangynidr'.

Unit 2: Topic 4 — Rebranding Places

Page 105 — Introduction to Rebranding Places

1   Maximum of 10 marks available. This question is level marked.
    HINTS:
    • To get full marks you need to give reasons why urban, rural and
      coastal areas might require rebranding.
    • Write a paragraph for each kind of area, covering why it might go
      into decline and need rebranding. For example, 'Rural areas can go
      into decline because of the decline of agriculture and its effect on
      the economy. The lack of job opportunities leads to the out-
      migration of young people, resulting in an ageing population.
      Services such as shops, schools and post offices close as people
      move away to find work, leading to a spiral of decline as economic
      problems and social isolation become worse'.

Answers

- *Quote facts* and *mini case studies* where possible, e.g. 'An example of an urban area that was in need of rebranding is Bilbao in Northern Spain. It was a successful industrial port until the decline of industry in the 1970s and 1980s. This led to high unemployment and many social problems'.

Page 107 — Urban Rebranding Strategies

1   Maximum of 10 marks available. This question is level marked.
    HINTS:
    - You need to include a *range* of urban rebranding strategies — so cover regeneration (changing the built environment), re-imaging and using sport as a catalyst.
    - The question says 'with reference to named examples' so you need to include relevant *mini case studies* for each strategy.
    - Make sure you *explain how* the rebranding strategy has led to *regeneration*. For example, 'Urban rebranding can involve marketing a place with a new image. Some coastal towns have been re-imaged, e.g. Eastbourne Borough Council used the slogan 'Change Your View' to try and change Eastbourne's reputation as a tourist and retirement destination for older people. The campaign has promoted attractions like extreme sports and theme parks, to try and attract younger visitors. It's helped bring new tourists to the area, which in turn brings in more money and investment, helping to regenerate the area'.
    - Quote *facts* and *relevant data* where possible, e.g. 'The development of the Emirates Stadium, Arsenal FC's £430 million new ground in North London, has provided 2500 new homes and 2600 new jobs for the area'.

Page 109 — Urban Rebranding — Case Study

1   Maximum of 10 marks available. This question is level marked.
    HINTS:
    - You need to write about *one case study* for this question. You can use any case study you know well, e.g. New Islington.
    - The question says '*evaluate*' so you need to comment on *how successful* the scheme has been.
    - Start by describing why the area needed to be rebranded (don't forget to include relevant facts). For example, 'New Islington is a replacement for the Cardroom estate, which had experienced a spiral of decline. By the mid 1990s the area had social problems like high unemployment and crime, and 50% of the houses were empty'.
    - Then describe the details of the scheme, e.g. 'New Islington is a flagship development. New facilities in the development include 1700 new homes, a primary school and a community football pitch. The estimated cost is £250 million'.
    - Next, discuss the *strengths* and *weaknesses* of the development. For example, 'One of New Islington's strengths is that the development has improved the area's infrastructure by improving public transport, e.g. New Islington has a new tram stop. This makes the area more attractive to new residents, and should stop it from becoming isolated'. You could also include points on how the development is environmentally friendly and has involved local people in the planning. A weakness of New Islington could be that experts have criticised it for not having much social housing. You could also mention that some residents are unhappy with the development, e.g. 'Some residents have complained that the new social housing has been built far away from the public spaces and other amenities in the development. This has led them to feel less important than new residents'.

Page 111 — Rural Rebranding Strategies

1   Maximum of 10 marks available. This question is level marked.
    HINTS:
    - To get full marks you need to discuss a *range* of named examples. Structure your answer to cover named examples of regeneration, re-imaging and integrated projects. Write a paragraph for each.
    - You can use any relevant case studies you know, but make sure you cover *how* the place has been rebranded. For example, 'Rural regeneration can involve introducing new technology to a rural area. In the remote Highlands and Islands area in Scotland, a £70 million project was set up to connect communities to high-speed broadband. It meant that the Highlands and Islands Enterprise (HIE) could then market the area as a good place to base small businesses, encouraging new residents who could work from home and bringing extra income to the area'.
    - Quote *facts* and *relevant data* where possible, e.g. 'The children's TV programme Balamory was filmed in the village of Tobermory on the Isle of Mull. The village has had up to 160 000 extra visitors every year since the show launched in 2003, and the tourist economy has been boosted by around £5 million a year'.

Page 113 — Rural Rebranding — Case Studies

1   Maximum of 10 marks available. This question is level marked.
    HINTS:
    - '*Compare*' means talk about the *similarities* and *differences*. So you need to write about how the effects of at least two rural rebranding schemes are similar or different.
    - You can use any rural rebranding case studies that you know about, e.g. the Eden Project and the Jurassic Coast. Include the *positive effects* and *negative effects* of the different schemes. This could include things like the creation of jobs, the amount of traffic, and how residents feel about the rebranding.
    - Write a paragraph for each comparative point you make. For example, 'The Eden Project has had a positive economic impact on the surrounding area, e.g. it's led to a £75 million facelift project for St Austell town centre. The Jurassic Coast rebranding has also had a positive impact on the local economy, e.g. West Bay's new £16 million Jurassic Pier has doubled visitor numbers to the area since 2004'.
    - Make sure you compare any *negative effects* too. For example, 'The Eden Project has created serious traffic problems in the area. This makes it less environmentally sustainable, as well as irritating visitors and local residents. On the other hand, the Jurassic Coast area doesn't have as big a problem with traffic and pollution because tourists aren't just attracted to one location'.
    - Quote facts and relevant data where possible, e.g. 'The Eden Project has had a positive impact on the surrounding area — it's influence has helped local businesses make around an extra £150 million every year'.

Page 115 — Evaluating Rebranding Strategies

1   Maximum of 15 marks available. This question is level marked. See page 119 for a full worked exam answer.

Acknowledgements

Page 3 and 121 — Graph reproduced with kind permission from EM-DAT: The OFDA/CRED International Disaster Database: www.emdat.net, Universite catholiqué de Louvain, Brussels, Belgium.

Page 10 — Short-term climate change graph adapted from Crown Copyright data supplied by the Met Office.

Page 10 — Medium-term climate change graph reproduced with thanks to the NOAA for the graphic and to the Alley (2000) paper for the underlying data.

Page 10 — Data used to construct the graph of modelled temperature change over the last 1000 years from IPCC 2013: In: *Climate Change 2013: The Physical Science Basis. Contribution of Working Group I to the Fifth Assessment Report of the Intergovernmental Panel on Climate Change*, Box TS.5, Figure 1(b) [Stocker, T.F., D. Qin, G.-K. Plattner, M. Tignor, S.K. Allen, J. Boschung, A. Nauels, Y. Xia, V. Bex and P.M. Midgley (eds.)]. Cambridge University Press, Cambridge, United Kingdom and New York, NY, USA.

Page 15 — Graph of emissions scenarios modified and based on Special Report of Working Group III of the Intergovernmental Panel on Climate Change on Emissions Scenarios (IPCC 2000).

Page 15 — Data used to compile table of sea level rise modified and based on Climate Change 2007: The Physical Scientific Basis. Working Group I Contribution to the Fourth Assessment Report of the Intergovernmental Panel on Climate Change. Cambridge University Press.

Page 17 — Map reproduced with kind permission from the World Resources Institute, http://www.wri.org.

Page 36 and 38 — Data used to construct the UK population pyramids reproduced with kind permission from National Statistics online. Reproduced under the terms of the Click-Use license.

Page 44 — World population graph reproduced with kind permission from Jean-Paul Rodrigue (underlying data from the United Nations).

Page 52 — Map of drought risk © UCL Global Drought Monitor.

Page 59 — Photo of New Orleans © iStockphoto.com

Page 60 — With thanks to Science Photo Library for permission to reproduce the Carlisle flooding photo.

Page 62 — Natural disasters graph reproduced from Centre for Research on the Epidemiology of Disasters (CRED), Emmanuelle Bournay, Environment and Poverty Times #3: Disaster issue, 2005, United Nations Environment Programme.

Page 74 — Seaside resort land use model reproduced by permission of HarperCollins Publishers Ltd © Prosser, Bishop & Raw, 2000.

Page 80 — Graph adapted from Climate Change 2001: The Scientific Basis. Contribution of Working Group I to the Third Assessment Report of the Intergovernmental Panel on Climate Change. Figure 5. Cambridge University Press.

Page 82 — Photo of fishing boat © iStockphoto.com

Page 83 — Photos of mangrove trees and Indonesian village © iStockphoto.com

Page 91 and 122 — Data used to compile the table comparing Bradford and Harrogate, source: National Statistics website: www.statistics.gov.uk. Crown copyright material is reproduced with the permission of the Controller Office of Public Sector Information (OPSI). Reproduced under the terms of the Click-Use license.

Page 93 — Data used to compile the table comparing lone parents to two parent families Copyright © 2001 One Parent Families Scotland.

Page 96 — Data used to compile the table comparing Cathays and Butetown is taken from the following sources: National Statistics website: www.statistics.gov.uk, © Cardiff Community Safety Partnership 2001 & Crown copyright material is reproduced with the permission of the Controller Office of Public Sector Information (OPSI).

Page 102 — Data used to compile the table comparing Llangynidr and Llanelly Hill source: National Statistics website: www.statistics.gov.uk. Crown copyright material is reproduced with the permission of the Controller Office of Public Sector Information (OPSI). Reproduced under the terms of the Click-Use license.

Page 105 — With thanks to Science Photo Library for permission to reproduce the Guggenheim museum photo.

Page 106 — Photo of Burj-al-Arab hotel © iStockphoto.com

Page 112 — Photo of the Eden Project © iStockphoto.com

Page 120 and 126 — Mapping data reproduced by permission of Ordnance Survey® on behalf of HMSO © Crown copyright (2009). All rights reserved. Ordnance Survey® Licence No. 100034841.

Page 121 — Photo of coastal defences © iStockphoto.com

Page 124 — World populations graph, data from *World Population Prospects: 2008 Population Database* © United Nations, 2009. Reproduced with permission.

Page 125 — Movement map source: International Passenger Survey, Office for National Statistics © Crown copyright reproduced under the terms of the Click-Use License.

Every effort has been made to locate copyright holders and obtain permission to reproduce sources. For those sources where it has been difficult to trace the originator of the work, we would be grateful for information. If any copyright holder would like us to make an amendment to the acknowledgements, please notify us and we will gladly up date the book at the next reprint. Thank you.

Index

A

abrasion 79
adaptation strategies 18
Africa 17
age-sex pyramids 34
ageing populations 38, 39
Agenda 21 21
aims (of investigations) 123
answering exam questions 117-122
anticyclones 52
Arctic 16
asylum seekers 40
attrition 79
Australia 58, 70
averages 127

B

backwash (not the soapy kind) 78
bankfull discharge 65
beach nourishment 87
beach stabilisation 87
birth rates 33
Blackwater Estuary 89
blizzards 53
breakwaters 86
Brecon Beacons 102, 103
Brighton 72
Burgess land use model 74
business development schemes 100

C

California 6, 7
carbon credits 31
carbon footprints 19
carbon offsetting 18
carbon taxes 18
carbon-neutral homes 48
Cardiff 96, 97
Cardroom estate 108, 109
Carlisle flood 60, 61
case study questions 118
CBA (Cost-Benefit Analysis) 21, 77
China
    rural-urban migration 45
    urban sustainability 49
choropleth maps 125
climate change 2, 10-21
    causes of 12, 13
    evidence for 10, 11
    impacts of 14-17
CO_2 (carbon dioxide) sinks 13

coasts 72-89
    coastal development
        and conflict 72, 74-77
    coastal environments 72
    coastal erosion 79, 80, 84, 85
    coastal flooding 80-83
    coastal management 86-89
    coastal population growth 72, 73
    coastal realignment 87
command words 117
community projects 100, 105
community radio 110
comparative advantage 25
conflict
    due to coastal development 74-77
    due to impacts of climate change 20
conflict matrices 76
congestion charging 94
conservative plate boundaries 5
constructive plate boundaries 4
constructive waves 78
Coriolis effect 5, 51
corrasion 79
correlations 128
corrosion 79
Cost-Benefit Analysis (CBA) 21, 77
counter-urbanisation 46
cycle of decline 91
cycle of inequality 91
cycle of urbanisation 46

D

dams 67
data collection 123
data questions 122
death rate 33
degrees of freedom 128
deindustrialisation 30
dependency ratio 38
dependent places 28
depressions 50
deprivation 91
desertification 17
destination countries 41
destructive plate boundaries 4
destructive waves 78
Devon Social Inclusion Programme
    100
disasters 2
disaster hotspots 6-9
disaster risk equation 2
discharge 64
dispersion diagrams 124
Dongtan 49
dot maps 125

droughts 6, 9, 52, 68, 70, 71
    management of 70, 71
drought-resistant crops 69
DTM (demographic
    transition model) 33-35
Dubai 73, 76
dune regeneration 87

E

earth banks 86
earthquakes 4, 5
Earth's orbit 12
ecological footprints 48
economic exclusion 93, 99
economic migrants 40
economies of scale 25
ecotourism 112
Eden Project 112
EIA (Environmental Impact
    Assessment) 76
El Niño 3
emigration 32
emissions scenarios 15
eustatic sea level changes 14, 81
evapotranspiration 64
ex-Soviet states 24
exam structure 116
extreme weather 50-71
    impacts of 56-61
    management of 67-71

F

fair trade 31
fault lines 4
FEMA (Federal Emergency
    Management Agency) 68
fertility rate 33
fetch 78
fieldwork
    on coastal development
        and conflict 77
    on coastal erosion 85
    on coastal management schemes 89
    on coastal population growth 73
    on extreme weather events 54, 57
    on flood risk 65
    on rebranding 104, 115
    on rural inequalities 103
    on urban inequalities 97
fieldwork & research questions 119
flagship projects 105
flooding 51, 64, 67
    management of 67
flow line maps 125
food miles 31

Index

fronts (weather) 50
Fujita scale 56
furniture schemes 94

G

G8 24
gabions 86
GDP (Gross Domestic Product) 23
gentrification 46
geophysical hazards 2, 3, 5
GIS (Geographic Information Systems) 68
global groupings 24, 25
global warming 2, 10-21, 62
global winners and losers 28, 29
globalisation 22-32
graph skills 124-126
greenhouse effect 13
grid references 126
groynes 86
Guggenheim museum 105

H

hard engineering 67, 86
Harris and Ullman land use model 74
hazards 2-5, 20
    geophysical hazards 2, 3, 5
    hydro-meteorological hazards 2-5
HDI (Human Development Index) 90
heat waves 52
Holderness 84, 88
Hoyt's land use model 74
hurricanes 5, 51, 68
Hurricane Katrina 59
hydraulic action 79
hydrographs 65
hydro-meteorological hazards 2-5
hypotheses 123

I

ice cores 11
ice storms 53
ICZM (Integrated Coastal Zone Management) 87
illegal immigrants 40
IMF (International Monetary Fund) 23
immigration 32
industrialisation 30
inequalities 25, 90-103
    urban 92-97
    rural 98-103
infant mortality rate 33
infiltration 64

interception 64
interconnected places 28
internal migration 35
interquartile range (IQR) 127
investigative skills 123
involuntary migrants 40
IPPC (Intergovernmental Panel on Climate Change) 14, 15
irrigation projects 100
isobars 55
isoline maps 126
isostatic sea level changes 81
ITCZ (Intertropical Convergence Zone) 52

J

Jurassic Coast 113

K

Kyoto Protocol 19

L

lag time 64
land use management 63, 87
land use models 74
landslides 6, 8
LDCs (Least Developed Countries) 24
LDFs (Local Development Frameworks) 101
LEDCs (Less Economically Developed Countries) 24
legacy facilities 114
levees 67
life expectancy 33
littoral cells 78
local employment schemes 100
logarithmic scales 124
London 46
longevity 33
longshore drift 79
lower quartile 127

M

managed retreat 87
map skills 125, 126
marginalised groups 93
mass movement 78
mean 127
MEDCs (More Economically Developed Countries) 24
median 127

megacities 44, 46, 47
Met Office 69
meteor impacts 12
middle-income countries 24
migrants 40
migration 32, 35, 40-45
    from Poland to the UK 42
    from the UK to Spain 43
    into Europe 40, 41
migration rate 33
million cities 44
minimum wage 94
mitigation strategies 18
mode 127
multiplier effect 28
Mumbai 47
Murray-Darling River Basin 58, 70

N

NAFTA (North American Free Trade Agreement) 25
National Parks 111
National Rural Employment Guarantee Programme 100
natural change (in population) 33
neighbourhood watch schemes 94
New Islington 108, 109
NICs (Newly Industrialised Countries) 24, 30
NOAA (National Oceanic and Atmospheric Administration) 69

O

occluded fronts 50, 55
OECD (Organisation for Economic Cooperation and Development) 24, 30
OPEC (Organisation of Petroleum Exporting Countries) 24
OS® (Ordnance Survey®) maps 120, 126
Oyster cards 94

P

park-and-ride schemes 94
permafrost 14
Perth 70
Peru Decentralised Rural Transport Project 100
Philippines 8, 9
photo questions 121
Poland 42

Index

polarisation 93, 99
pollen analysis 11
population 33-39
    population density 33
    population pyramids 34, 35
    population structure 34, 35
positive feedback loops 15
post-accession flow 42
post-colonial flow 40
precipitation 64
primary data 123
proportional symbol maps 125
pull factors 32
push factors 32

Q

quarrying erosion 79

R

re-imaging 104, 105, 110
re-urbanisation 46
reafforestation 21
rebranding 104-115
    rural 110-113
    urban 106-109
recycling 48
refugees 40
regeneration 104, 105
research
    into changes in population 37
    into coastal development
      and conflict 77
    into coastal erosion 84, 85
    into coastal management schemes 89
    into coastal population growth 73
    into extreme weather events 54, 57
    into flood risk 66
    into hazard risk 7
    into rebranding 104, 115
    into rural inequalities 103
    into urban inequalities 97
residents' associations 94
resource interpretation
      questions 120-122
revetments 86
Richter scale 6
riprap 86
risk 2
risk assessments 123
River Eden 60, 61
runoff 64, 78
rural inequalities 98-103
rural rebranding 110-113
Rural Wheels scheme 100
rural-urban migration 44, 45

S

sea level change 15, 80, 81
sea walls 86
secondary data 123
sediment cells 78
self-help schemes 94
shanty builds 94
shanty towns 46-48
share trading 23
sinks (for CO_2) 13
SMPs (Shoreline Management Plans) 87
social exclusion 93
soft engineering 67, 87
solar output 12
solution erosion 79
source countries 41
South-East England drought 71
South-Eastern Australia drought 58, 71
Southern Asia tsunami 82, 83
Spain 43
spatial inequalities 90
Spearman's Rank
      correlation coefficient 128
SSSIs (Sites of Special
      Scientific Interest) 77
stakeholders 75
standard deviation 127
statistical skills 127, 128
Stern Review 21
storm surges 80
sub-aerial weathering 78
suburbanisation 46
surface runoff 64
sustainability of urban areas 48
sustainable development 48
sustainable rebranding 114
sustainable urban communities 95
swash 78
sweatshops 30
switched-off places 28
switched-on places 28
synoptic maps 55

T

TBD (Tourist Business District) 74
temperate storms 50
tidal barrages 86
tidal barriers 86
tides 78
tipping points 15
TNCs (Trans-National
      Corporations) 23, 26, 27
tornadoes 50
town centre plans 126
trade blocs 25, 26
tree rings 11

triangular graphs 124
tropical cyclones 5, 51
tsunamis 6, 8, 80, 82, 83
typhoons 5, 8, 51

U

UK
    aging population 38, 39
    population change 36, 37
unequal spaces 90
urban inequalities 92-97
urban rebranding 106-109
urban regeneration 106
urban sustainability 48, 49
urbanisation 44, 46

V

values analysis 77
Village Action Plans 100
Village Enterprise Fund 100
vicious cycles 91
virtuous cycles 104
Vital Villages scheme 100
volcanoes 4, 5
voluntary migrants 40
vulnerability 2

W

Wal-Mart® 26, 27
WaterAid 100
waves 78
weather diaries 54
weather forecasts 69
WHO Healthy Urban
      Planning Initiative 95
wildfires 53
winners and losers 29
winter weather 53
World Bank 23
WTO (World Trade Organisation) 23

Z

zero growth rate 33